D0152956

The Caregiver's Guide

The Caregiver's Guide

For Caregivers and the Elderly

Jerrold S. Greenberg
University of Maryland

Marlyn Duncan Boyd
University of South Carolina

Janet Fraser Hale
George Mason University

Nelson-Hall Publishers/Chicago

Project Editor: Sheila Whalen
Illustrator: Corasue Nicholas
Cover painting: *Sitting Figure* by Jeff LeGro

Library of Congress Cataloging-in-Publication Data

Greenberg, Jerrold S.
   The caregiver's guide : for caregivers and the elderly / Jerrold
S. Greenberg. Marlyn Duncan Boyd, Janet Fraser Hale.
     p.   cm.
   Includes bibliographical references (p.   ) and index.
   ISBN 0-8304-1253-0.———ISBN 0-8304-1328-6 (pbk.)
   1. Aged—Care—United States—Handbooks, manuals, etc.
2. Caregivers—United States—Handbooks, manuals, etc. I. Boyd,
Marlyn Duncan. II. Hale, Janet. III. Title.
HV1461.G74   1992
362.6—dc20   91-39775
                                         CIP

Manufactured in the United States of America

10 9 8 7 6 5 4 3 2 1

Contents

Preface   vii

Contents

Contents

Preface

The well-being of the frail elderly is directly
dependent on the well-being of the caregiver.

Each of us—Jerry, Marlyn, and Janet—has been called on to care
for an elderly relative. And each of us was at a loss along the way.
It would have been much easier if we had had a guide accompanying us to point the way. Well, a human guide is not available, but a
written one now is. The need for a handbook specific to the needs
and concerns of informal caregivers for the elderly is glaring! Not
only do our own experiences demonstrate this need, but data from
a number of published and unpublished surveys of caregivers, discussions with other caregivers, and what experts have said and
written also lead us to this conclusion. It would be negligent to
ignore the needs of these unsung caregiving heroes. With this
awareness, we wrote this book—for people just like you.

We chose to address those needs and concerns that have the
most bearing on the largest number of caregivers and care-
receivers. A study conducted at the University of Maryland served
as our guide in this respect. That survey found that caregivers
needed information identifying local, state, and national services
available to assist them. They wanted to learn how to manage their
time and finances better, how to communicate more effectively
with the care-receiver and the rest of the family, how to manage
the stress associated with caregiving and maintain their own
health, and how to handle both the daily needs of the care-receiver
and any emergencies that might arise. Beyond these basics, they
also wanted to know what changes they needed to make in their
homes to receive their elderly loved ones, to prevent falls and other
injuries, to help the care-receiver be more self-reliant, and to accommodate particular disabilities.

We made sure to discuss all these topics. We also included charts and tables, listings and appendices, and self-questionnaires and scales designed to make this book more organized and more entertaining. In addition, because we know caregivers sometimes feel guilty, angry, depressed, overburdened, hopeless, helpless, and frustrated, and because we know they desire an outlet for these feelings, we discuss support groups and actually provide a list of some (see Appendix 1a). Because we know caregivers are concerned with maintaining their family cohesiveness in the face of the immense pressure caregiving responsibilities can create, we discuss ways to assure that your family life remains satisfying and healthy. We present suggestions to help manage the financial strain that often accompanies caregiving, and the intimacy needs of both caregivers and care-receivers. We have also tried not to neglect seemingly little problems. For example, recognizing that getting enough sleep is difficult when caregiving responsibilities and responsibilities outside the home are overwhelming, we present suggestions from sleep researchers.

Our intent is to reflect on caregiving and care-receivers as other books have, but to expend as much concern on you, the caregiver, as on these other topics. We know that if you do not maintain your health—physical, emotional, financial, and spiritual—your care-receiver's health will suffer. We do our best to prevent that.

Some caregivers report that caregiving is the most rewarding experience they've ever had. We *insist* that it can be that way for you! So, let's begin.

1

The Growing Need

It was a dim nightclub seating approximately one hundred people. On the stage was a man wearing a turban and a long gown. His eyes were blindfolded, and he was obviously concentrating intently. In the audience was his partner—a grim-faced middle-aged gentleman wearing a business suit and looking as honest as anyone could. "Swami, we have a person in the audience," said the man in the suit, "with a copy of *The Caregiver's Guide: For Caregivers and the Elderly.* Concentrate hard and tell us what you can about this person." The swami's head rose, his eyes closed more tightly, and his forehead wrinkled as he seemingly pictured the owner of the book. Then he said:

> This person is a woman about fifty-seven years old. She is married and probably the wife or daughter of an elderly person for whom she provides care. She has probably been providing care for this person for at least one year (probably up to four years), spends some fifty-nine hours per week providing this care, and is extremely tired, tense, and anxious from her caregiving responsibilities. She may be working outside the home, but is most likely unemployed, and is probably middle-class.

How did the swami do it? Is he really psychic? Well, most swamis work on probabilities. That is, they learn one trait of a person and use that to generalize about other aspects of that person. The generalization is based upon what people with that trait are usually like. Having learned that the person in the audience was reading a book on caregiving, the swami used what is known about the characteristics of caregivers to describe that person. Perhaps the person the swami described is like you!

1

Characteristics of Caregivers

People like you, who provide care for others, generally have several characteristics in common. First of all, they usually feel a strong family commitment and perform their caregiving duties out of a sense of love or responsibility. You probably have these feelings, too. They motivated you to become a caregiver and, in fact, to read this book.

The federal government wanted to learn about caregiving and caregivers to identify what governmental planning and assistance was needed. The result of their inquiry is the report of the Subcommittee on Human Services of the Select Committee on Aging of the U.S. House of Representatives. In the pages that follow, the subcommittee's findings are presented. As you read about the characteristics of caregivers, see if you recognize yourself. As you read about caregiving, see if you recognize situations you have experienced or can anticipate experiencing. Subsequent chapters will provide you with what you'll need to know and the skills you'll need to develop to become a more effective caregiver while maintaining your and your family's health and financial well-being.

Gender

As depicted in figure 1.1, caregiving is a responsibility undertaken primarily by females. Approximately 72 percent of caregivers to functionally impaired elders are female. Daughters constitute 29 percent of this population, and wives make up another 23 percent.

Figure 1.1: Percent of Caregivers by Relationship

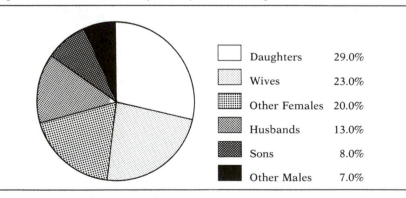

Daughters	29.0%
Wives	23.0%
Other Females	20.0%
Husbands	13.0%
Sons	8.0%
Other Males	7.0%

Figure 1.2: Ages of Caregivers

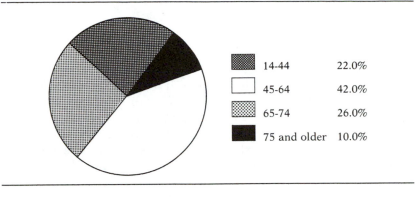

14-44	22.0%
45-64	42.0%
65-74	26.0%
75 and older	10.0%

Sons make up only 9 percent of caregivers, and husbands account for 13 percent. The remainder is composed of daughters-in-law, sons-in-law, grandchildren, siblings, other relatives, friends, and other unpaid helpers.

Age

As shown in figure 1.2, the average age of the caregivers is 57 years. However, one-quarter are between 65 and 74 years of age, and another 10 percent are 75 or older. Husbands are by far the oldest caregivers—42 percent of them are 75 or older. These figures suggest that caregiving is, in large part, a matter of the "young-old" caring for the "old-old."

Marital Status

Seventy percent of all caregivers are married. However, there are variations in marital status among different categories of caregivers. For example, male caregivers are almost twice as likely as females to have *never* been married. In addition, caregivers 45 to 54 years old are less likely to be married than noncaregivers of the same age. Furthermore, male caregivers in this age group are four times more likely to have never been married than are their contemporaries in the general population. In contrast, among the older caregivers, particularly those aged 65 and older, both males and females are more likely to be married than noncaregivers of

3

the same age—that is, they are often married and caring for their spouses.

Employment

Employment status is particularly relevant to caregiving, not only as a source of income but also because it presents a major demand for the caregiver's time and attention. One-third of caregivers are employed. Two out of five daughter caregivers and a little over one-half of son caregivers are in the labor force; one-third of the other female caregivers (e.g., sisters, other nonspousal relatives, and friends) and 46 percent of their male counterparts are also working (see figure 1.3).

Compared to the total U.S. population, caregivers were less likely to be employed (see figure 1.4). While 62 percent of females aged 45 to 54 are employed, only one-half of female caregivers in this age group are in the labor force. Similarly, while 42 percent of women aged 55 to 64 are working, only one-third of caregivers the same age are employed.

The disparity is even greater among male caregivers. While 90 percent of males aged 45 to 54 are employed, only two-thirds of caregivers the same age are in the labor force. For the 55- to 64-year-olds, 70 percent of the general male population is employed compared to only 46 percent of male caregivers the same age. Finally, among those 65 years and older, 18 percent of males in the general population were employed, but only 8 percent of male caregivers.

Figure 1.3: Percent of Caregivers Who Are Employed

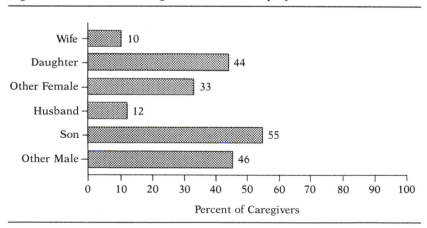

Figure 1.4: Percent of People in the Total U.S. Population and Caregiver Population Who Are Employed (By Age and Gender)

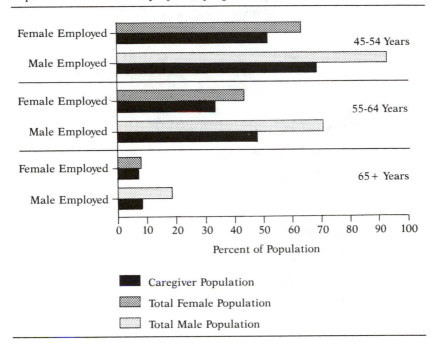

Economic Status

The majority of caregivers have family incomes that place them in the middle income bracket. However, just under one-third are classified as poor or near poor. Caregiving wives and other females (for example, sisters, other relatives, or friends) make up the largest portion of this economically disadvantaged subgroup. Relative to the general population, caregivers are more likely to have incomes below the poverty line.

Health Status

One-quarter of caregivers report they are in excellent health. However, one-third report being in fair or poor health. When a spouse is providing the care, the health status of the caregiver is even worse: 44 percent of wives and over half of husbands providing care report they are in fair or poor health. As shown in figure 1.5, caregivers are in poorer health than others their age. Although the exact causes of the poor health of caregivers are not known, it seems reasonable to suspect that the stress of caregiving is at least a contributing factor. For this reason we devote a whole chapter of this book to stress management.

Figure 1.5: Self-Assessed Health Status of Total U.S. Population and Caregiver Population (By Age and Gender)

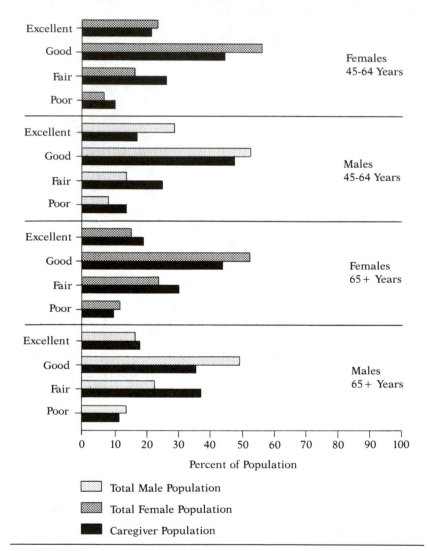

The Growing Number of Elderly

There are ever-increasing numbers of caregivers in the United States—an estimated 7 million at last count. This is the direct result of an increase in our elderly population. In 1986 there were 29.2 million people 65 years of age or older. The government estimates that that number will increase to 34.9 million by the year 2000. By 2030, the elderly population in the U.S. is projected to reach 64.6 million. In 1900 the elderly (65 and older) represented 4 percent of the American population. By 1980 they represented 11 percent of the population. Projections are that by the year 2000 they will represent 13 percent of our population and by the year 2050, 20 percent.

Furthermore, this "graying" of America is most prominent among the very oldest (those over 85) and the most frail. Between 1960 and 1980, the number of persons 85 and older increased by 165 percent, and this group is expected to be *seven times* as large in 2050 as in 1980. These "older elders" are more likely to need health and social services and the assistance of a caregiver (see table 1.1).

The older population, which is living longer because of improved health services and the like, is also becoming more and more female, because males die at a younger average age. This has implications for caregiving since elderly women are likely to live alone, to be economically disadvantaged, and to experience multiple chronic health problems.

Nowhere is the need for caregiving made more dramatic than in the statistics relating to the age at which most of us still have surviving parents. In 1980 40 percent of people in their late fifties had at least one surviving parent, as did 20 percent in their early sixties, 10 percent in their late sixties, and 3 percent in their seventies. Due to declining fertility rates (people having fewer and fewer children) in the 1980s, for the first time in American history *the average married couple has more parents than children.* Furthermore, women can expect to spend *more years caring for an aging parent than for a dependent child* (on average, 17 years for a child and 18 years for a parent).

The high divorce rate makes matters even worse. It means that women are often required to provide care for a parent without the support—emotional or financial—of a spouse. That can be extremely stressful and financially debilitating.

The Costs of Caregiving

The costs of caregiving involve many aspects of the caregiver's life. There are the financial burdens, the emotional strain, the effect on the family and relationships among family members, and the physical strain and subsequent threat to the health of the caregiver.

Table 1.1

Percent of Persons 65 Years of Age and Over Who Have Difficulty Performing Selected Personal Care Activities (by Sex and Age): United States

Sex and Age	Personal Care Activity						
	Bathing	Dressing	Eating	Trans-ferring	Walking	Getting Outside	Using Toilet
Both Sexes							
65 years and over	9.8%	6.2%	1.8%	8.0%	18.7%	9.6%	4.3%
65–74 years	6.4	4.3	1.2	6.1	14.2	5.6	2.6
65–69 years	5.2	3.9	1.2	5.3	12.2	4.9	2.2
70–74 years	7.9	4.8	1.1	7.1	16.6	6.6	3.0
75–84 years	12.3	7.6	2.5	9.2	22.9	12.3	5.4
75–79 years	9.8	6.4	2.1	7.5	19.5	9.9	4.1
80–84 years	16.8	9.7	3.2	12.4	29.0	16.8	7.8
85 years and over	27.9	16.6	4.4	19.3	39.9	31.3	14.1
Male							
65 years and over	7.6	5.8	2.0	5.6	15.5	6.3	3.1
65–74 years	5.7	4.4	1.5	4.8	12.9	4.5	2.4
65–69 years	5.3	4.1	1.7	4.7	11.5	4.3	2.3
70–74 years	6.1	4.9	1.4	5.0	14.9	4.7	2.4
75–84 years	9.2	7.3	2.5	6.0	18.3	7.5	3.6
75–79 years	7.8	6.7	2.3	4.7	15.6	6.3	2.7
80–84 years	12.3	8.5	3.0	8.7	24.2	10.2	5.6
85 years and over	23.1	14.1	4.3	12.7	32.2	21.9	10.0
Female							
65 years and over	11.2	6.5	1.7	9.7	20.9	11.8	5.1
65–74 years	6.9	4.2	0.9	7.0	15.1	6.5	2.7
65–69 years	5.1	3.7	0.9	5.7	12.9	5.3	2.2
70–74 years	9.1	4.8	1.0	8.6	17.8	8.0	3.4
75–84 years	14.2	7.7	2.4	11.2	25.7	15.3	6.5
75–79 years	11.1	6.2	3.3	9.3	22.2	12.3	5.0
80–84 years	19.2	10.2	3.4	14.3	31.4	20.2	9.0
85 years and over	30.1	17.7	4.4	22.2	43.3	35.4	15.9

Financial Costs

Caregiving includes many financial burdens. The obvious costs relate to medical needs such as physician services, nursing assistance, medications, food, and clothing. Some people also need physical therapy, psychological assistance, or special equipment to allow them to function independently. Others may need to be enrolled in a nursing home. Although 80–90 percent of caregiving is in-home care, sometimes placement in a nursing home becomes a necessity. Yearly expenses for nursing homes can run upwards of $30,000 per year. The total average nursing home costs in the United States from 1986 to 1990 was $33 billion per year, with over $120 billion projected by the year 2020.

There are additional costs associated with caregivers' having to decrease the hours they work outside the home and, consequently, the income they generate. For example, in a survey of caregivers it was found that 22 percent had quit jobs because of their relatives' needs, and 55 percent had had to reduce the number of hours they worked. Those who continue to work may experience conflicts between the needs and expectations of the job and those of the care-receiver. When asked, over half of caregivers who worked 20 hours a week or less said they would work more hours if they were not giving care.

Emotional Strain

Symptoms of depression, anxiety, feelings of helplessness, lowered morale, and emotional exhaustion have all been associated with caregiving. Unfortunately, too many caregivers resort to ineffective means to resolve these feelings. For example, caregivers are two to three times more likely to use mood-altering drugs than the general population, and 12 percent admit to using alcohol as a way of coping. These means of coping do not really relieve the situation— it is still there when the substance wears off—and may result in ill health for the caregiver. Consequently, they are not recommended. More effective ways of coping are presented in chapter 7.

Interestingly, women caregivers seem to experience more emotional strain—or at least admit to more—than do males. Over half of wives report that caregiving is an emotional burden, compared to only 40 percent of husbands. Similarly, almost one-half of daughter caregivers studied reported emotional strain, compared with under one-third of sons. Perhaps women caregivers should be especially targeted for psychological assistance, male caregivers should be helped to recognize and acknowledge their feelings, or both.

Family Strain

Caregiving can have a significant impact on family relations. Approximately 25 percent of people caring for elderly parents and one-third of other caregivers (other than spouses) have children under 18 years of age living at home. You can imagine—if you don't already experience it—the competition for the caregiver's time in these situations. Given the demands of child care and elder care, it is not surprising that many caregivers experience "caregiver overload."

In addition to conflicts with dependent children, caregivers may argue with brothers or sisters about the quality or type of care provided Mom or Dad. Disagreements with siblings seem to be exacerbated when one of them is the primary caregiver and the others are relatively uninvolved. For example, when one sister takes her parent into her home to live and resents the lack of time or financial assistance the other sister devotes to the parent's care, conflicts may be expected.

Not to be forgotten in this discussion of family strain is the relationship between the caregiver and the care-receiver. Unfortunately, the frustrations of caring for an elderly parent are too often played out in elder abuse, whether physical or psychological. You may be surprised to learn that daughters make up a substantial portion of elder abusers. Yet given that daughters are most often the caregivers, perhaps this is predictable. When elder abuse has been studied closely, an interesting observation has been made: it occurs frequently when the caregiver is financially dependent upon the care-recipient. It seems that the resentment of having to rely on one's elderly parent for financial support can be acted out in abusive behavior.

Physical Strain and Health Status

In recognition of caregiving's potential negative effects on health, the caregiver has frequently been referred to as the "hidden patient." However, the data to support this contention are sketchy at best. For example, when asked, only 16 percent of caregivers report that caregiving has contributed to a decline in their health. Caregivers in one category do, however, report physical strain and subsequent ill health from caregiving: 25 percent of caregiving wives say that their health has worsened as a result of caregiving responsibilities. Some researchers have suggested that caring for another person may help the caregiver shift attention from his or her own health problems to the needs of the care-recipient; in this process, caregivers feel healthier than they otherwise might.

The Benefits of Caregiving

Whereas discussions of caregiving often focus on its negative aspects—its costs—there are many benefits of the caregiving experience.

Finances

Although caregiving can be financially draining, most caregivers report it is not. For example, in a study of long-term nonspousal caregivers of disabled elders, more than half reported spending *nothing* extra per month. Furthermore, 20 percent reported spending less than $50 per month, and 15 percent $50–$100 per month. Only 8 percent of these caregivers said they spent more than $100 per month on caregiving. Figure 1.6 summarizes these data. Other researchers have found fewer than 20 percent of caregivers responding that the care costs more than they can afford. Although

Figure 1.6: Average Monthly Cost of Caregiving Reported by Nonspousal Caregivers

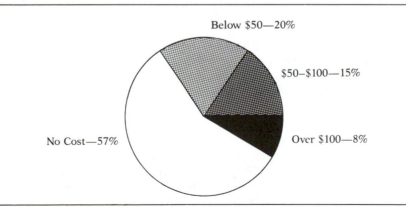

Below $50—20%

$50–$100—15%

Over $100—8%

No Cost—57%

the financial burden appears to be greatest among spouses, still only 25 percent report high levels of financial strain.

These data on the lack of financial strain should be interpreted cautiously, however. Many caregivers feel a sense of responsibility to the care-recipient and are uncomfortable reporting that the financial burden is excessive. Also, the data cited above refer to the *perceptions* of the caregiver; the *reality* may be quite different. Nevertheless, it seems that the financial burden may be more manageable than it seemed at first glance.

Emotions

Although depression, anxiety, and feelings of helplessness are associated with caregiving, so are more positive feelings. Earlie Washington, the director of the Elder Support Project (a group at the University of Chicago devoted to identifying the positive side of caregiving), investigated the benefits derived by caregivers. She found that caregivers felt good about fulfilling an obligation, felt useful, and felt more worthy of care from others when they become frail and aged. Washington also found that those who reported very little stress from caregiving responsibilities were those who perceived caregiving in terms of *fulfillment* rather than *sacrifice*. They felt *privileged* rather than *burdened*.

Caregiving, then, has many positive aspects. You will feel better and be healthier if you focus upon the rewards rather than the difficulties. The discussion of selective awareness techniques in chapter 7 will show you how to do that.

Family Life

If you are now providing care, you know the strain it can put on family life, especially if you have dependent children still living at home. However, you also are well aware of the benefits your family derives from providing this care. For example, elders living with you can help care for younger children, thereby actually relieving—rather than causing—family strain. In cases involving a divorced daughter or son, elders in the home can not only serve child care needs but may also provide companionship for the adult. If the caregiver is an elderly spouse, the new role may compensate for the loss of other roles (such as that of "paid worker") and may provide a renewed sense of usefulness. Furthermore, care-recipients may help with household chores and may actually contribute financially to the family's income. As shown in figure 1.7, caregivers obtain many benefits from care-recipients.

In Conclusion

The number of caregivers in the United States is huge and still increasing—estimated right now at seven million. That is a direct result of the significant increase in our elderly population. You can hardly go through the day without bumping into someone who is caring for an elderly parent or spouse. Some businesses, recognizing the potential negative effects of caregiving responsibilities on workers in terms of absenteeism and decreased productivity, have developed elder care programs, similar in some ways to the child care programs they instituted earlier. In fact, some elder care programs are combined with child care programs (these are called "intergenerational"), with elders and children interacting to the benefit of both.

You should know that if you are experiencing financial burdens, emotional strain, or family problems associated with caregiving, you are not alone. However, also know that there are many positive aspects of caregiving, and if you focus upon these you will feel better, maintain your own and your family's health, and realize

Figure 1.7: Benefits of Caregiving: Contributions of Care-Recipients

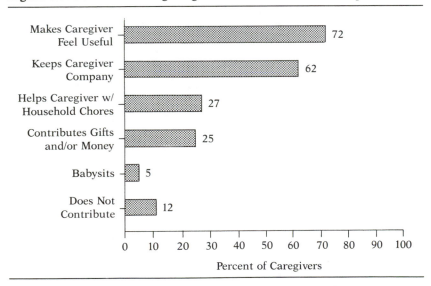

the honor afforded you to care for a loved one who, at some earlier time, cared for you.

This book is devoted to helping you derive the significant benefits of caregiving while diminishing its costs. This is no easy task but one we know we can accomplish. Since you're reading this book, you are already motivated. Having spent considerable time researching and writing this book, we're also ready. Now let's proceed together down the road of caregiving fulfillment.

2

Coming Home/Staying Home

It took a lot of work, creativity, and help from friends, family, and the community, but Mom was able to live with us until the end. She died at peace, in an environment in which she was comfortable, happy to be surrounded by family. It was a wonderful experience for the children, and we have warm memories of Mom and a better understanding of her history and her life. We feel good about our decision and the time that she lived and shared with us. We miss her.

In the beginning it wasn't easy, but it's amazing how it all turned out. I am a single parent, rearing two children alone, working one full-time and one part-time job to make ends meet. I was able to obtain some financial assistance to make changes to the house to accommodate Mom's wheelchair and to add grab bars and safety bars to the bathroom and to the stairs. We changed all the doorknobs to handles, so that even with her arthritic hands she could easily open the doors; we also wrapped foam rubber around her eating utensils so she could grasp them and feed herself. Because of her hearing impairment, the telephone company installed a special ringer and amplifier on Mom's phone. Muffin, our York-shire terrier, was her constant companion and would sit on her lap in the wheelchair for hours while Mom read or watched television.

While I was away at work each day, "Meals-on-Wheels" delivered a hot meal. Mom looked forward to that. The meals were good, and she liked the brief visits from the delivery folks. Our neighbor had young children at home, so she would come by in the middle of the morning and again in midafternoon to check on Mom. She always brought the baby with her, and Mom enjoyed their visits. Two afternoons a week, the senior center van would pick up Mom along with her wheelchair and take her to the senior center for bingo and a snack. The people from the senior center were wonderful to her and treated her like a princess. We were very touched when even the van driver and the delivery folks for Meals-on-Wheels came to the memorial service to say good-bye to Mom.

It's understandable that Mom wanted to remain at home. A home provides continuity, a background that has existed for many years where everyone knows and understands one another's ways. It has a relaxing familiarity. Anything new brings profound ambiguity and uncertainty and creates anxiety. A new environment (a different home, apartment, hospital, nursing home) creates internal and external chaos, so that the elder feels like a stranger in a foreign land. In almost every case it is the urgent wish of the older person to remain at home, or at least in his or her own community.

Maintaining elders in the community can be both challenging and rewarding. Involving the family and the elder, along with the appropriate community resource people, will facilitate making these decisions. It is important to keep in mind the need for all of us, elders included, to maintain control over our own lives. As long as elders are able to take care of some of their personal management needs and maintain a voice in the decision-making and planning process, they will retain a sense of independence. In so doing, they will likely be healthier and happier and will maintain their self-esteem.

This chapter discusses the matter of bringing the care-receiver home, either to his or her own home or into the home of the caregiver. There are questions to consider regarding the needs and capabilities of the care-receiver. There are also safety considerations to address, a variety of health-promotion factors, and community resources that could significantly enhance the quality of life for both you and your loved one. The general concepts we present apply whether the care-receiver is coming from the hospital, from another type of care facility, or from his or her own home.

Deciding on Home Care

Congratulations on your decision to help provide care for an elderly relative or friend. You probably made this decision very carefully and deliberately. Many individuals have been inappropriately placed in nursing homes when what they really needed was a much more independent environment in which they could thrive. Your decision to provide that kind of setting for your loved one was probably not an easy one. In some locales comprehensive, multidisciplinary evaluations and follow-up are available to help older persons and their families make determinations regarding home care versus institutionalized care; the majority of us, however, have to make these decisions without the benefit of such professional assistance. We hope that these multidisciplinary groups, sometimes called geriatric assessment teams, will become more readily available in the future. For now, you may feel that you are entirely on your own. Well, we're here to help, so let's proceed.

Hospitalization and Discharge

The elderly are the largest single group of consumers of hospital care. Their readiness to be discharged and their caregivers' readiness to bring them home rarely influence when they are *actually* discharged. This is because the *early discharge concept* has been created to contain health care costs. Reduced length of stay and more aggressive discharge policies have become important features of hospital treatment for all health care consumers. Since 1983, Diagnostic Related Groupings (DRGs) prescribed by Medicare limit the number of days a person can stay in the hospital based on the patient's diagnosis. If the patient is not discharged within the allowed number of days, the hospital loses money. If the patient is discharged before the allotted number of days, the hospital makes money. You can see how this system has a significant impact on when patients are discharged. As a result of Medicare policy, elders may be discharged before they and their caregivers feel they have recuperated adequately. This payment system has led to a strain on both health care agencies and family caregivers. The early discharge concept adds 21 million days of care per year to home and community programs.

When the elderly are admitted to the hospital, the experience can be very disorienting and may result in their losing contact with services received before admission. The subsequent discharge can be equally traumatic, as they go from a protective environment to a less protective one. For these reasons, discharge from the hospital should be carefully planned and coordinated by the hospital and the community service providers. Discharge planning should begin on the day of admission to the hospital, to encourage an active plan of rehabilitation and reintegration into the community. Giving patients adequate notice of their discharge, discussing with them arrangements for their return home, and arranging the provision of appropriate services are all part of discharge planning.

Because of difficulties experienced in making a transition to the hospital and then back to the community, some elderly patients may simply refuse to be hospitalized again. There are a number of reasons for such a response. First, they may prefer to die in surroundings familiar to them without intrusive medical intervention. Additionally, cultural or religious beliefs or practices, financial considerations, fear of hospitals, a desire to remain with the family, fear of death, and fear of having the dying process prolonged in the hospital may all be factors. If your loved one resists hospitalization, seek some insight into her or his motivation to facilitate a discussion of and solution to the problem.

Readying the Home Environment and the Caregiver

As you prepare to address the home health needs of your care-receiver, you need to weigh several factors. First of all, it is essential to determine the level of disability and its potential for causing dependency. The inability to perform daily self-care activities without the *regular* help of another person is considered the point of no return for independent living. The following questions will help you understand what the multiple needs of your care-receiver may entail. When asking yourself these questions, keep in mind how *much* or how *little* assistance your loved one needs to accomplish the activity. For example, can he or she do it completely alone, or does the elder need help getting set up? Once set up, can he or she then do it independently? Does your elder need assistance only to complete the act, or must you do it all? Throughout, we provide approaches and ideas that we hope will help you through this period.

Evaluating the Care-Receiver's Abilities/Disabilities

The first consideration in evaluating your loved one's abilities is her or his degree of mobility—that is, the ease with which the care-receiver can get around on her or his own, and the potential for falling (the major threat to the mobility of elders). In addition, you need to assess whether chest pain, leg pain, breathlessness, dizziness, or fatigue affects the elder's performance of daily tasks. Table 2.1 provides a checklist.

If your loved one is not self-mobile, what assistance is required? Those not self-mobile are at risk of acquiring pressure sores and also of falling. A mobility aid, such as a walker, cane, tripod, or wheelchair, can make elders more self-sufficient and decrease their susceptibility to pressure sores. Sometimes grab bars

Table 2.1
Assessing Mobility

Activity	Needs No Help	Needs Some Help	Needs Complete Assistance
1. Walking without aid (e.g., cane or walker)	_____	_____	_____
2. Walking with aid	_____	_____	_____
3. Standing without aid	_____	_____	_____
4. Standing with aid	_____	_____	_____
5. Maintaining balance when walking	_____	_____	_____
6. Standing erect when walking	_____	_____	_____
7. Lifting feet evenly	_____	_____	_____
8. Sitting without aid	_____	_____	_____
9. Sitting with aid	_____	_____	_____
10. Rhythmic, even gait	_____	_____	_____

and rails placed strategically around the house can assist with mobility as well.

For elders who are less mobile, who are bedridden, or who spend a significant amount of time in bed, you may want to consider purchasing certain equipment or making changes in the home. Special equipment can be purchased or rented through hospitals, surgical/medical supply stores, or pharmacies. Sometimes the local branches of the Salvation Army, the Red Cross, the March of Dimes, the American Cancer Society, and other disease-specific organizations donate or give discounts on medical equipment. They may be able to help you obtain used medical supplies or arrange for you to borrow the equipment for the time you need it. Depending on your loved one's condition, Medicare and Medicaid may pay for the purchased or rented items.

Activities of Daily Living

Closely related to mobility is the care-receiver's independence in carrying out the activities of daily living. Can he or she wash, bathe, dress, eat, and use the toilet without assistance? Does your loved one have problems with urine and with bladder control? Table 2.2 provides a checklist that will help you evaluate how much assistance your loved one needs in meeting the tasks of everyday life. Once you have completed that checklist, assess how

Table 2.2
Assessment of Ability to Perform Activities of Daily Living

Activity	Needs No Help	Needs Help Starting	Needs Complete Assistance
1. Bathing	———	———	———
2. Getting dressed	———	———	———
3. Oral hygiene	———	———	———
4. Using toilet or pot	———	———	———
5. Eating	———	———	———
6. Using telephone	———	———	———
7. Cooking meals	———	———	———
8. Shopping	———	———	———
9. Taking medication	———	———	———
10. Grooming	———	———	———

you can assist your loved one. Then evaluate resources available to you in providing this assistance. Appendices 1 and 2 contain a list of additional resources that might be of help.

Safety Considerations

Among the most important considerations when you are bringing an elderly person home from the hospital, or into your home to live, is safety. It makes no sense to bring your loved one home only to place him or her in danger because of your failure to take certain precautions. To assess your home's safety, refer to table 2.3

Fire and Security

Assessment of fire hazards and security in your home is vital. In many communities, the local fire department will inspect homes for fire hazards, and sometimes local police will evaluate homes for safety from intruders, ensuring that doors, windows, and other means of entry are adequately secured.

Reports of the elderly using old favorite appliances that lead to fires or other serious accidents are all too common. Poor circulation or efforts to save on utility bills by keeping the thermostat set low in winter may induce the elderly to use electric blankets or heating pads. These appliances must be periodically replaced, and new appliances should have automatic overheating protection.

If your loved one smokes, he or she might doze off and drop a lighted cigarette in bedcovers or on bedclothes. Common sense safety measures can prevent this and other types of fires.

- Smoking should be allowed only in designated areas or with someone in attendance.
- Flame-retardant nightwear must be worn at bedtime.

Table 2.3
Evaluating Your Home's Safety

Safety Feature	Present	Absent
1. Handrails on both sides of stairs	———	———
2. Reflective tape on edges of steps	———	———
3. Stairwells well lighted	———	———
4. Nightlights	———	———
5. Reflective tape on light switches	———	———
6. Floors free of scatter rugs, toys, plants, etc.	———	———
7. Electrical cords out of pathways or taped down	———	———
8. Pathways clear of frail furniture	———	———
9. Handrails beside the tub and toilet	———	———
10. Skid-proof mats in shower and tub	———	———
11. Hot water temperature less than 110° F.	———	———
12. Chairs with arms	———	———
13. Phones within easy reach	———	———
14. Large dial and lighted dial phones	———	———
15. Levers for doorhandles	———	———
16. Low-pile carpeting	———	———
17. Plastic drinking glasses		
18. Smoke detector in kitchen, living room, and bedrooms	———	———
19. Elevated toilet seat	———	———
20. Toilet paper and towels within easy reach of commode and tub	———	———
21. Bell, whistle, or monitor available	———	———
22. Locks on doors to stairs	———	———
23. Glasses, dishes, and flatware within easy reach	———	———

- Use of candles should be discouraged.
- Smoke detectors should be in place and operating properly.
- Adequate ventilation should be provided in winter, and the chimney should be routinely cleaned.
- Lightbulbs may need to be of higher wattage to assist the elderly to see and to prevent falls. Outlets must be wired to accommodate these higher-wattage bulbs.
- Loose-fitting flammable clothing—e.g., bathrobes, nightgowns, and pajamas—should not be worn when one is cooking.
- Water-heater thermostats must be set low enough (below 110°F) to prevent hot water from burning the skin.
- Emergency exits should be identified for use in case of fire.

Agencies and publications that help with safety issues are listed in appendices 1A and 1B under "Safety."

Falls

Falling is the most common cause of fatal injury in the aged. Indeed, for people of any age, injuries from a fall can limit the ability to lead an active, independent life. The frailty of elderly bones and the ease with which these bones can break are of particular concern. Each year, falls cause hip fractures in about 210,000 older persons, 20 percent of whom die within a year of the injury. Those elders most at risk of falling are over seventy-five, have an abnormal gait, and have difficulty walking. Many falls occur at night, when the person's balance may be affected by medications, diminished muscle tone, or lessened alertness.

Falls can be prevented. Table 2.4 provides suggestions for limiting the dangers of falling, while figure 2.1 depicts some mobility aids that can help prevent falls.

Structural Modifications

The actual structural environment of your home may need modification to accommodate your loved one's needs. The modification may be as simple as changing doorknobs to levers, which are more easily grasped by arthritic hands. In some cases, however, major structural remodeling may be required: widening doorways, installing ramps, or enlarging bathroom facilities. Contact your local or state housing authority to determine the availability of special grants and loans for these modifications. Relevant organizations and publications are listed in appendices 1A and 1B under "Home Modifications and Remodeling." The American Association of Retired Persons (AARP) also offers a variety of publications to assist with home repairs. Additional assistance may be offered by:

Table 2.4
How to Prevent Your Loved One from Falling

- Clearly identify stairs. Mark the first and last steps in a series of steps with white or bright contrasting tape at the tops of the treads.
- Provide ample lighting, especially on bedside tables and in halls and stairways.
- Place light switches at the top and bottom of stairways.
- Place handrails on both sides of stairways.
- Place grab rails in the shower and tub and next to the toilet.
- Place a bench or a chair in the bathtub.
- Avoid the use of bath oils, because they make both the feet and the bathtub very slippery.
- Use nonskid adhesive strips on bathtubs.
- Equip bathrooms with nightlights.
- Place a nightlight or a light switch beside the bed.
- Place the telephone where it can be reached from the bed.
- Arrange frequently used articles on lower shelves, so the elderly person need not reach or climb for such items as food, cooking utensils, and clothing.
- Provide a cane, walking stick, or walker as an aid in maintaining balance.
- Insist on extreme caution on wet or icy pavement.
- Provide a wheelchair for those who consistently need help moving from place to place or for those who are unsteady on their feet.
- Provide well-fitting, supportive, low-heeled shoes with rubber soles. Warn the elderly person not to walk in stocking feet, slippers, or smooth-soled shoes, especially on stairs or waxed floors.
- Encourage your loved one to rise slowly from a sitting position. When lying down, he or she should sit up and wait a few minutes before attempting to stand.
- Use nonskid floor wax on linoleum floors.
- Be sure that floor surfaces are level and free of clutter.
- Install plain carpets, rather than shag.
- Secure area rugs firmly to the floor with nonskid rubber backing. Avoid using throw rugs.
- Check the elder's vision and glasses prescription regularly.
- Insist on regular tests of the care-receiver's hearing. Sometimes simply removing ear wax can improve balance.
- Limit your loved one's intake of alcohol. Even a little alcohol can further disturb already impaired balance.
- Keep the temperature in the home no lower than 65° F. Prolonged exposure to low temperatures can cause dizziness and falling.
- Encourage regular physical exercise (walking and swimming, for example). Improvement in strength and muscle tone will help prevent falls.

Figure 2.1: Walking Aids

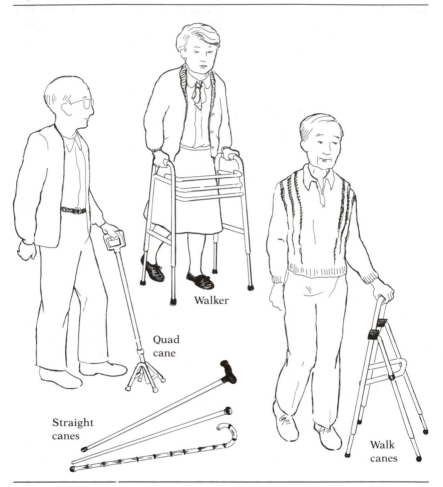

Walker

Quad
cane

Straight
canes

Walk
canes

- Farmers Home Administration
- The U.S. Department of Housing and Urban Development (Contact your city or HUD field office. Ask about Community Development Block Grants)
- The Veterans Administration (provides low-interest loans to veterans to modify their homes)
- The Internal Revenue Service (may allow you to deduct equipment, furnishings, and permanent changes as medical expenses on your tax return; keep all relevant bills and invoices)

You may wish to consider ECHO housing. ECHO stands for "elder cottage housing opportunity," a small, self-contained, portable home unit that can be placed in the yard of a single-family home. The idea for these homes originated in Australia, where they are called "granny flats." American companies offer completely installed one-bedroom units with more than five hundred square feet for less than $20,000; some two-bedroom models are also available. These homes are barrier-free, energy efficient, and portable. Their placement generally requires a special-use permit which often has a termination date. ECHO housing is *not* restricted by the same zoning laws as mobile homes. For resources related to ECHO, consult the section titled "Housing Alternatives" in appendix 1B.

Hygiene

The hygienic habits of your loved one will influence his or her quality of life. In this section, we consider such habits as bathing, caring for the teeth and gums, and caring for the hair and nails.

Bathing and Care of the Skin

Daily bathing is not usually recommended for elders, because their skin tends to be dry. Elders need to bathe only a couple of times a week. "Spot washing" can be done wherever and whenever needed. In general, tub baths should be discouraged because of the potential for falls and injuries. Showers or sponge baths are better. For those who insist on a tub bath, a tub transfer seat can be bought or rented at a medical equipment store or at a pharmacy. A plastic desk chair with arms and nonskid leg bottoms offers another alternative. Using a hose with a nozzle allows you to assist your loved one taking a tub bath without getting wet yourself. Figure 2.2 shows a bathroom equipped with several important safety features.

You can employ other strategies in special situations. For example, if your loved one is embarrassed to be naked but needs assistance with the bath, he or she can wear underwear. To make your elder feel more secure, place a bell within reach of the bath. In addition to alerting you of an emergency, the bell can let you know when your elder is through bathing. A twenty-dollar nursing home-monitor will allow you to hear the care-receiver and also to tell when the bath is over.

Getting out of the bath requires close attention because of the tub's slippery surface and the elder's stiff joints. Provide your loved

Figure 2.2: Bathroom with Safety Aids

one with nonskid shower shoes and advise her or him to grasp rails tightly and to rise slowly from the bath seat. Assist the elder in getting her or his feet over the side of the tub and standing securely on the floor. Place a chair covered with a large towel near the tub so your elder can sit down to dry off—this decreases the risk of falling or of becoming dizzy while bending over.

Warm, not hot, water is recommended, and soap should be used sparingly, especially if the elder has dry, flaking, or itching skin. Such dry skin is common, so use a mild lotion- or lanolin-based soap. Usually dry skin is simply a result of aging; however, it may develop in reaction to soaps, cleaning products, cosmetics, or dry air in overheated rooms. Likewise, some laundry detergents can cause itching skin. Treatment of dry skin is essential to prevent scratching and the resulting sores with their potential for infection. Persistent dry skin and itching should be evaluated by your physician.

Here are a few helpful hints:

- Use moisturizing skin lotions that contain petroleum or lanolin. Apply lotions right after bathing while the body is still damp to seal in extra moisture.
- If necessary, use lotion several times a day to combat dryness and irritation.
- Do not use heavily perfumed products or after-bath colognes and splashes that contain alcohol; they can be drying.
- Apply sunscreens when out in the sun.
- Encourage your elder to wear loose, soft clothing and to avoid wearing wool next to the skin.
- Avoid using harsh laundry detergents and bleach. Double rinses for clothes and bed linens will help ensure that all soap is removed.
- Avoid fabric softeners; they too can be irritating to the skin.
- Use a humidifier or vaporizer in the care-receiver's room to help keep skin and nasal passages from becoming dry and irritated. To prevent the growth of bacteria, remember to clean the humidifier or vaporizer periodically according to the manufacturer's directions.
- Place a shallow pan of water under the bed to evaporate and moisturize the room. To avoid bacteria growth, wash the pan with hot soapy water between fillings.
- Wash all new clothing and linens several times before the elder uses them.

Dental Health

Because aging gum tissue is especially susceptible to injury and infection, treating dental problems can be difficult. It is best to avoid such problems in the first place. Elders with their natural teeth intact should clean them daily with a soft-bristled toothbrush designed for the adult mouth, using a fluoride toothpaste and following with dental floss. Brushing should be done after meals and snacks when possible, and before going to bed. Flossing should be done once a day. The fineness of the floss and the coordination required, however, may make flossing too difficult for the elder to do alone. In this case, floss aids can be purchased for under a dollar at most drugstores. Even with a floss aid, you may have to assist your loved one. A mouthwash will eliminate bacteria that can cause tooth decay and will make your loved one's breath feel and smell fresher. Mouthwashes should be swished in the mouth for several minutes.

Although many elders have maintained some of their natural teeth, approximately 50 percent have not. Daily care is no less important for elders with dentures. Full or partial dentures should be removed every night, cleaned, and placed in a clean container with cool water freshened with a tablespoon of mouthwash. This allows gum tissue to recuperate from the pressure of the denture, and the denture will last longer if it is removed daily. Use a soft-bristled toothbrush, paste, and tepid running water to clean dentures. A denture-cleaning solution may also be used. Be careful never to allow the dentures to dry out; drying out will ruin them.

A regular dental checkup, at least every six months, is a must. Through the normal aging process, mouth tissues can change dramatically in just a few months. This can cause poor-fitting dentures, irritations, lesions, or chewing problems which, in turn, cause poor eating habits or jaw pain. If you notice swelling or a small cut that might have been caused by the dentures, remove them for twenty-four hours. Then have the elder attempt to wear the dentures again. If discomfort persists, see your dentist. Also consult the dentist if your loved one complains of a mouth sore, especially one that doesn't heal within a week or two. Oral cancer is more prevalent in the elderly, so sores that do not heal should be evaluated by a health professional.

Hair Care

As does skin, hair becomes dryer and more brittle with aging. Therefore, your loved one's hair should be washed no more than necessary, usually once or twice a week. Frequent brushing helps to keep the natural oils distributed. Use a brush that is as soft-bristled as possible while still penetrating the hair. Hard or plastic bristles can rake and scratch the scalp. Use a good conditioner and avoid hair sprays—they can be drying. If your loved one uses pins or other hair accessories, check periodically to make sure the rubber coating is still intact so the scalp won't be scratched.

Hairstyle is an individual preference. If your elder is a woman, however, she might consider keeping her hair relatively short. Shorter hair is easier to wash, natural oils can be more easily distributed, and it can air-dry more quickly.

Nail Care

With aging, the nails become dry, brittle, and thick and may turn yellow. Dry nails are likely to crack, split, and tear, but good nail care can prevent many potential problems. Fingernails and hands should be moisturized daily. Trim the nails after bathing when they are softer and easier to cut. File nails in an oval shape—don't cut down into the sides of the nail—and gently push the cuticle back with an orange stick. Avoid using nail polish and polish removers, which tend to dry the nail even more.

Toenail care is very important for the elderly. Because circulation in the feet is decreased, injuries can go unnoticed and infections can set in. Toenails are particularly dry, brittle, and thick in the aged. Purchase a pair of large, strong clippers made for use on toenails. Never try to trim dry toenails; always cut them after bathing or after soaking them in warm water. Cut the nail straight across and not too short.

The elderly often have problems with their feet. For some, particularly women, callouses, corns, and bunions result from having worn ill-fitting shoes for years. The feet tend to spread, necessitating a larger shoe; yet for reasons of vanity, many women refuse to buy larger sizes. Also, shoe styles and brands vary in their fit. Each time new shoes are purchased, the foot should be remeasured. Buy shoes in the late afternoon or after the elder has been walking for several hours, because at such times the feet are somewhat swollen. Buy shoes that allow room for the toes to wiggle but are not so big as to cause slipping. New shoes should be worn for only thirty minutes at a time. If red, irritated areas develop and don't go away after twenty-four hours, call the doctor. Because of the chance of an infection, never open blisters or cut away callouses or corns. Should these occur, limit the amount of time the shoe is worn, soak

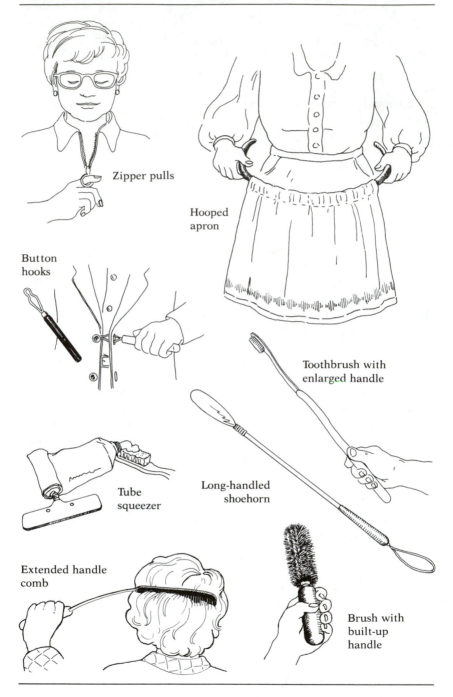

Zipper pulls

Hooped apron

Button hooks

Toothbrush with enlarged handle

Tube squeezer

Long-handled shoehorn

Extended handle comb

Brush with built-up handle

feet in warm water, and apply moisturizers. Over-the-counter products such as moleskin, pumice stones, and toe pads can help alleviate discomfort.

Nutrition

We all require a balanced diet, but the elderly typically need fewer calories because of a decrease in both metabolic rate and levels of activity. Caloric intake for a normal-weight elder engaging in normal activities should be approximately 1200 to 1600 calories per day. As a rule of thumb, elderly men should weigh 106 pounds for the first five feet of height plus 6 pounds for each additional inch; elderly women should weigh 100 pounds for the first five feet of height and 5 pounds for each additional inch.

The elderly are more likely to be malnourished, anemic, or dehydrated and to have vitamin deficiencies, osteoporosis (weak and brittle bones), and electrolyte imbalances. The fact that your loved one's weight is normal doesn't necessarily mean that he or she has good nutrition. Watch what your loved one eats. Does he or she get some of each of the four basic food groups each day? (See table 2.5). Is his or her diet balanced, or does one type of food predominate? What about the ratio of carbohydrates, proteins, and fats? Does he or she consume a lot of empty calories (such as candy, chips, ice cream, alcohol) that do not provide sufficient levels of nutrients? Do poor-fitting dentures cause your loved one to avoid foods such as meat, fresh vegetables, and fruits?

If the care-receiver doesn't eat enough meat, vegetables, fruits, or other iron-rich foods, he or she may become anemic (deficient in iron in the blood). Because of difficulty chewing or digesting certain foods, such vitamin deficiencies are prevalent in the elderly. Remember that overcooking foods to make them more chewable or digestible may deplete their vitamin content. It is important

Table 2.5
Four Basic Food Groups

Milk and Dairy Products	2 servings a day (8 oz. milk, ½ oz. cheese, 1 cup yogurt)
Meats, Poultry, Seafoods, Legumes	2 servings a day (two eggs, 2–3 oz. hamburger patty, ½ cup beans, etc.)
Fruit and Vegetable Group	4 servings a day
Bread and Cereal Group	4 servings a day (1 slice bread, ½ cup cereal)

that elders ingest adequate vitamin C (such as in orange juice) and vitamin D (such as in milk). Vitamin C deficiency can result in weak gums, and vitamin D deficiency can cause osteoporosis, a weakening of the bones that makes elders susceptible to fractures. However, do not give your loved one vitamins without consulting your physician. Large doses are not usually necessary, can cause stomach upset and constipation, and may result in other unforeseen problems.

There are many reasons elders may not have an adequate diet. They may have eaten the same way for many years, feel comfortable with their set routine, and refuse to alter it. Some foods may cause them to feel gassy, become constipated (e.g., milk products), or have an upset stomach. Others, as noted earlier, may be difficult to swallow or chew. In spite of these limitations, a well-balanced diet is attainable for everyone. Try steaming or pressure-cooking vegetables and fresh fruits to make them easier to chew while maintaining their flavor and nutrients. Similarly, you can pressure-cook or "crock-pot" meats to make them more tender without sacrificing their nutritional value. Eliminate any strong seasoning and encourage your loved one to do the same. This may present a problem, since the sense of taste diminishes with age, causing the elderly to use more seasoning. In this case, use lemon and lime juices, garlic, paprika, and herbs (e.g., tarragon, thyme, parsley, and oregano) to add zip to foods.

If your loved one has difficulty eating or swallowing because of mouth sores, use a blender or food processor to chop or grind the food. Likewise, soft foods—mashed potatoes, tomatoes, squash, and applesauce—can perk up a bland diet.

It may sometimes be necessary to assist your loved one with meals. However, try to keep her or him as independent as possible. Figures 2.4 and 2.5 show various helpful utensils, and these tips may help lessen the frustration and mess of mealtimes:

- Use a cafeteria tray with sections for foods, utensils, and beverages to keep everything in its place. Sectioned trays will also help your loved one push food onto the utensils.
- Use cups with large handles—they are easier to grasp.
- Don't fill glasses completely. Provide a straw or a "sippy cup" lid to prevent spills.
- Use a placemat or plastic tablecloth to simplify the clean-up.
- Place a towel instead of a napkin in your loved one's lap.
- Build utensils up with tape or foam padding to make them easier to grasp.

Figure 2.4: Eating Aids

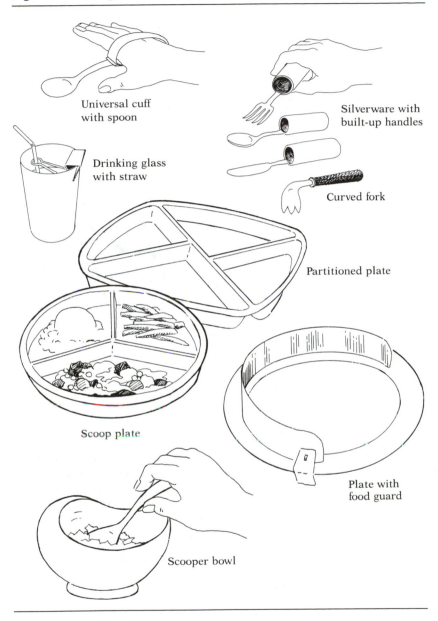

Universal cuff
with spoon

Silverware with
built-up handles

Drinking glass
with straw

Curved fork

Partitioned plate

Scoop plate

Plate with
food guard

Scooper bowl

Figure 2.5: Aids for Kitchen Work

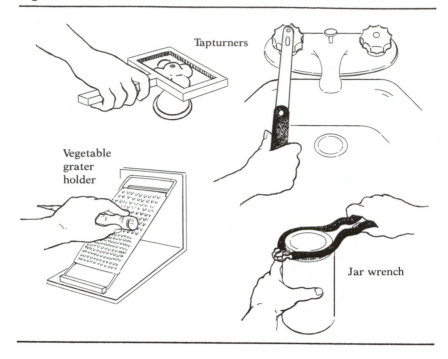

Tapturners

Vegetable
grater
holder

Jar wrench

• Bend forks and spoons to an exaggerated angle to help your
loved one feed him- or herself.

Loss of appetite, a common problem for the elderly, can herald
illness. Periodic disinterest in food for a day or two shouldn't cause
concern; however, if it persists for more than a few days and weight
loss occurs, call your physician. If your loved one experiences loss
of appetite, make sure that plenty of fluids are ingested. Juices,
milk, and milk products provide nutritional benefits as well as
fluid. If there are no signs or symptoms of illness, increased activity may boost appetite. Encourage your loved one to move about
and to get some fresh air if possible. Since constipation can cause
loss of appetite, find out if your loved one's bowel habits have been
normal for the past week or two.

Dehydration (insufficient body water) and electrolyte imbalance (imbalance of body chemicals) are common health concerns
for the elderly. Because the elderly often have a decreased thirst,

they may not drink enough fluids. Some medications have a diuretic effect (i.e., they increase urination) and thus can further deplete the body of needed fluids. In addition, some of the elderly purposely limit the amount of fluids they drink so they won't have to go to the bathroom as often, ask someone for assistance, or risk bladder incontinence. Unless instructed otherwise by a health care professional, encourage your loved one to drink a minimum of eight 8-ounce glasses of fluids a day, at least half of these in the form of water. Coffee, tea, and carbonated beverages do not supply the minerals necessary for the body to function adequately.

Sleep and Exercise

Let your loved one's body dictate how much rest and sleep are needed. It is not unusual for elders to have difficulty sleeping, to awaken often, or to have shorter periods of restful sleep. In addition, some medications can cause sleep disturbances, as can anxiety, depression, and other emotional disorders. If your loved one complains of sleep problems or if you have noticed a change, investigate. Is your loved one taking any new medication? Has anything happened to cause your elder to be depressed, anxious, or overly worried? Has his or her activity level decreased? Is he or she sleeping more during the day? If the sleep problem continues, consult your physician.

Exercise is a must for all of us, the elderly included. Without routine exercise the body literally wastes away. All normal bodily changes of aging are exaggerated with inactivity. Physical activity helps to maintain and improve not only physical well-being but also mental and emotional health. Regular exercise maintains muscle strength, flexibility, coordination, and endurance. Daily exercise can help keep your loved one alert, independent, and happy. Activity can decrease the chances of bowel problems, varicose veins, appetite loss, and circulatory problems.

An activity need not be taxing to qualify as exercise. A fifteen- or twenty-minute walk combined with activities of daily living is enough to keep the body functioning at an optimal level. Remember that a slow walk for the elderly is equivalent to much more vigorous exercise for younger people. Rest periods should be spaced throughout the day, with activity periods not to exceed an hour without at least a fifteen minute rest.

Feeling Healthy and Maintaining Quality of Life

When you plan for caregiving, consider the results of a recent study which asked elders, "What makes you feel healthy?"[1] Results showed that the most important element in feeling healthy was having company—that is, family, grandchildren, pets, young friends, and volunteer workers. Knowing that others care about them helps the elderly to feel better about themselves. Elders also cited the importance of some regular activity. These activities included eating a balanced diet, knitting, showering, doing housework, listening to music, watching television, and reading, as well as such outdoor activities as swimming, walking, and gardening. Adequate sleep was also identified as important. Further, these elders expressed a need for independence, which they described as freedom—having their own routine, looking after themselves, having control over their own lives, living in their own homes if possible, and having easy access to transportation.

Pets

Pets have proven to be very therapeutic for elders. Petting dogs and cats can lower blood pressure, heart rates, and anxiety levels. Caring for the animal also helps the elderly person feel valuable and responsible. Pets can provide a feeling of protection and can be ears for the hearing impaired, if the animal is taught to bark or otherwise alert the elder when someone comes to the door or the telephone rings. Animals have also been known to warn their owners when they smell smoke or fire.

Obviously, the pet should not be too rambunctious and should be house trained and capable of understanding instructions. A puppy may not be the best choice. If you want an older animal that meets the criteria, your local Society for the Prevention of Cruelty to Animals (SPCA) can be an excellent resource. See appendix 1A for resources related to pets.

Medical Screenings

In addition to immunizations, routine screenings and physical exams are recommended. Screenings can detect problems early, when they can more easily be treated. Yearly physical examinations should include vision and hearing tests, dental exams, and

---

1. Personal communication with Dr. Laura Wilson, Director of the Center on Aging at the University of Maryland, College Park, MD, 1990.

monitoring of blood pressure and blood-sugar levels. Recent researchers have concluded that as we age, our blood-sugar levels may automatically rise; thus, it may be normal for elders to have higher blood sugar than younger adults do. Health care providers should continue to monitor these research findings to prevent overdiagnosing or overmedicating diabetic conditions in the elderly. In addition, at least once a year, three different stool specimens should be evaluated for hidden blood in the gastrointestinal tract (digestive system).

Women's Health

Elderly women have some specific health needs. For example, women over sixty-five should continue their monthly breast self-examinations and undergo a yearly mammogram and pelvic exam with a Pap smear. Since postmenopausal women produce limited amounts of estrogen, they are subject to weakened bones (osteoporosis), increased incidence of urinary leakage or urgency, and vaginal dryness and atrophy. Urinary and sexual dysfunction and the associated distressing local symptoms can often be adequately relieved with estrogen prescriptions. Estrogen replacement prevents postmenopausal osteoporosis, which contributes to the broken hips and fractured bones too often experienced by older women.

All women should evaluate their daily dietary intake of dairy products to assure consumption of at least twelve hundred milligrams of calcium per day. When calcium intake is too low, calcium supplements (preferably calcium carbonate with vitamin D) should be considered. Adequate calcium intake cannot reverse bone loss that has already occurred, but research indicates that adequate calcium in the bloodstream may slow the subsequent rate of bone-mass loss.

Community Resources

In planning for home care, identify local sources of assistance. This is not always easy. First, check with the discharge personnel at the hospital. Ideally, they will have anticipated posthospitalization needs and made some arrangements. However, hospitals are in competition, and one hospital's staff may be reluctant to refer patients to services offered by other hospitals. Personally contact information services in other health care organizations, even those not suggested by your hospital. You might also call agencies on aging, such as the American Association of Retired Persons, the National Association for Home Care, the National Association of Area Agencies on Aging, the National Council on Aging, and the Older Women's League. Addresses and telephone numbers for these agencies and many others are listed in appendix 1A. Such agencies exist in every state and offer services that include home-delivered meals, transportation, and home health care. In addition, their staff will know what services are available or will soon become available in your area. The telephone number for the area agency on aging is usually in the phone book's government listings (blue pages) or in the yellow pages under "Senior Citizens." State offices on aging are listed at the end of appendix 1A. Other information resources include: support groups, senior centers, churches and synagogues, and physicians.

Most larger communities offer a variety of assistance. These include home health care organizations, adult day care centers, adult day health centers, respite care, small group homes and house sharing, and assisted living. Each is briefly described below.

Home Health Care

With adequate support from family and friends, home health care may be the ideal alternative for many elderly. A variety of services—psychological, social, personal, and medical—can be provided in the home to individuals with moderate to severe incapacity. These programs are usually sponsored by visiting nurses' organizations or by hospitals.

Visiting nurses' associations (VNAs) are established in most states. VNAs traditionally offer medical care services, including in-home nursing, with specialties such as speech, physical, and occupational therapies, hospice care, Alzheimer's and AIDS care, and sometimes personal care assistance.

Adult Day Care

Some programs care for elders at a central site during the day, returning them to their residences at night. Adult day care in most cities is a community-based program operating through hospitals, churches, nursing homes, city and county governments, or senior centers. These centers usually operate during normal working hours, five days a week. Elders can attend on a full- or part-time basis to give caregivers a break. Typically, these programs offer socialization, group activities, hot meals and snacks, wellness checks, and sometimes transportation and rehabilitation. Group activities may include crafts, chair exercises, trips, games, and discussions of current events. Some programs have special groups for people with Alzheimer's disease. The programs are highly variable; therefore, no generalizations can be made about client characteristics, services, staffing, or costs. Find out what type of adult day care is available in your community, and determine whether it meets your needs.

Adult Day Health Center

These centers offer medical, restorative, and support services seven days a week, but participants spend the nights at home. Adult day health centers are an option for the frail elderly, who might otherwise have to be placed in a nursing home because of the complexity of their medical conditions. Services may include prescription drugs, dentistry, optometry, audiology, podiatry, psychiatry, outpatient laboratory and X-ray services, in-home services, physician services, inpatient medical services, hospice, and skilled nursing.

Respite Care

Respite care meets the needs of the elder while the usual caregiver takes some time off. Services may include personal care, help with walking, housekeeping, grocery shopping, preparing meals, and pet care. Respite care may be offered through businesses, home health agencies, home care organizations, or visiting nurses' associations. It relieves the caregiver for a period ranging from a few hours to several days or weeks. Sometimes respite care sends an employee into your home, while other programs offer temporary lodging and care at another facility. Services are provided on a part-time or short-term basis while the primary caregiver is away—for example, on a vacation or a business trip.

Small Group Homes and House Sharing

Sometimes elders choose an arrangement in which they live in a regular home with others of their age. Minimal care is provided in these facilities. Depending on state laws, a group home may be able to offer services to one or two elderly people without requiring licensure. These homes are for individuals who do not require twenty-four-hour nursing supervision for care and nutrition.

Homemaker–Chore Services and Personal Care Services

These services are specific to home management needs. Home-maker services may include routine light housecleaning, laundry, and meal preparation. Chore services include running errands and shopping. Personal care services focus on basic daily living—bathing, toileting, feeding, dressing, and personal hygiene. These programs are usually implemented by paraprofessionals under the guidance of professional supervisors. The care-receiver is visited two or three times a week for one to four hours.

Assisted Living

Assisted living is an arrangement whereby elders live in their own apartments but are helped with various daily activities and are monitored twenty-four hours a day. This arrangement works for frail, chronically ill, or socially isolated elders. It allows them to live independently while providing them with social opportunities, meals, and transportation. They receive assistance with daily activities and with taking medications. In addition, assisted living provides round-the-clock protection through communication devices (pull chains or call lights) installed in the elders' apartments. These can be invaluable in emergencies or when assistance is needed.

In Conclusion

In summary, there is much to consider when you bring an elderly loved one into your home for care. This chapter presented a variety of considerations and suggestions. We believe that these will help you better prepare your home and yourself for the arrival of your loved one. Appendix 1 lists organizations and publications that can assist you. Do not hesitate to contact the listed agencies. They are there to help you. Again, congratulations on your decision to provide home care for your loved one. You are a special person!

3

Health Care Issues:
Being an Advocate

Did you ever hear of a physician who actually visits with a hospitalized patient? We mean *visits*—doesn't just perform medical tests or ask about symptoms, but actually sits and talks about the patient's family and the latest current events. Did you ever hear of a physician who spends time feeding hot cereal to a patient unable to feed himself because he is incapacitated by a stroke? I know of such a physician, a cardiologist. She was my father's doctor when he was hospitalized for his second stroke, and she actually did everything mentioned above.

Did you ever hear of a physician so busy that patients aren't even given time to ask all their questions about their conditions? Or a physician so concerned with treating the patient's medical problems that other related problems are ignored—for example, a doctor who prescribes drugs to lower a patient's blood pressure without considering the effect those drugs might have on the patient's libido and, consequently, his or her marital relationship? This physician might cure the condition, only to see the patient die of complications. I know of such a physician, also a cardiologist. He was the doctor who "cared" for my father after two heart attacks, and he actually did the things I mentioned. My family still maintains a relationship with the cardiologist I described first. The uncaring, insensitive one may be selling shoes for all I know.

This chapter will help you identify both types of physician early on, so you can advise the care-receiver to stay with the effective one and kiss the other good-bye. In addition, we will identify other health services that can help you perform your caregiving duties, and we will show you how to get the most out of those services. Finally, we will help you determine when a nursing home might be necessary and how best to select one.

In other words, this chapter will help you be a better advocate for your loved one, particularly in relation to health care.

Selecting a Physician

One of the most important caregiving functions is ensuring that your loved one receives the quality of health care she or he deserves. Vital to that assurance is the selection of a physician capable of responding to the care-receiver as a whole person—a physician who will see more than a heart or lungs, a doctor who will treat the physical symptoms but also be concerned with nonmedical aspects of the patient's life, a physician who knows that those nonmedical aspects have an impact on the person's health.

Such a physician is more easily described than discovered. Doctors are trained to cure medical illnesses, and many have specialized in order to keep abreast of the latest, most effective treatments. For example, if you have a kidney problem, you probably want to see a nephrologist—a kidney specialist—rather than a general practitioner who seldom treats patients with kidney problems, doesn't regularly read medical journal articles about kidney problems, and hasn't seen a kidney (healthy or otherwise) since medical school. The problem is that the nephrologist may not know or care about your psychological reactions to your condition (that's the specialty of the psychologist) or about your inability to pay for services (that's the specialty of the social worker). Nevertheless, psychological reactions and financial concerns may diminish the effectiveness of any treatment prescribed.

Physicians are trained to cure people's physical ills, not to help people change the behaviors that lead to these physical ills. Consider the hypertensive patient who is overly stressed. The doctor may order the person to relax more frequently. If so, the patient ought to ask, "How?" Most physicians would be at a loss to respond. Similarly, the patient who is told to stop smoking ought to ask, "How?" because wanting to stop smoking and actually stopping are two different things.

Finally, the reimbursement mechanisms in the U.S. health care system reward physicians for time spent on medical procedures, particularly those performed in the hospital, not for time spent discussing the patient's health risk behavior or how to change that behavior. Physicians who do spend time counseling patients—

treating them as whole people—do so at their own expense. They could be seeing other patients and being reimbursed by Medicare, Medicaid, or a health insurance carrier. It takes an exceptionally caring and sensitive doctor to provide the type of care you want for yourself and your care-receiver. Studies show that elders, in particular, need this type of medical interaction.

This network of obstacles between the need to treat patients as whole people and the reality of doing so means that you need to be extremely cautious in choosing a physician and to maintain a vigilant assertiveness as that relationship proceeds.

How to Find a Doctor

In seeking a physician, explore some or all of the following suggestions:

1. Ask family and friends for recommendations, explaining all the criteria that are important to you.
2. Ask your family physician to recommend specialists who treat patients the way you want to be treated.
3. Telephone the local medical society and request the names of physicians who are certified, qualified, and concerned with patients.
4. Telephone your local hospital and ask to speak with the resident on call in the emergency room. First-year residents have an opportunity to evaluate doctors in various situations and will usually be happy to suggest names.
5. Consult doctors at "teaching hospitals" (those associated with medical schools), since they tend to have the most advanced care, equipment, and facilities; patients at these hospitals generally receive considerable attention from medical personnel.
6. Telephone recommended doctors' offices to inquire about fees, acceptance of new patients, office hours, and how long you will have to wait for an appointment.
7. Seek a recommendation from organizations and agencies with an interest in the patient's specific medical condition (for example, the Alzheimer's Disease and Related Disorders Association).
8. If all else fails, get the name of a family practice physician from your local or state medical society. Family practice physicians have special training in counseling patients and may be board-certified in geriatric medicine.

Your Rights

The American Hospital Association has developed a "Patient Bill of Rights" (table 3.1) to help hospitalized people obtain the kind and quality of medical care they deserve. When interacting with your care-receiver's physician, use the following revised Patient Bill of Rights to ensure that he or she is treated appropriately.

If any of these rights are violated, speak with the physician immediately. If you do not get satisfaction, look for another doctor.

How to Speak to the Doctor

When you need to communicate with the doctor, use the assertiveness skills presented in chapter 5 to help you express your point of view and wishes clearly but not aggressively. The goal of your communication should not be to antagonize the physician, but rather to lead to meaningful improvement in the services provided or the manner in which the physician interacts with your loved one.

Chapter 5 also discusses the need to speak in "I statements." Do not refer to what the physician is or is not doing; instead, speak in terms of what you prefer in patient-doctor interactions. For example, rather than "You treat my mother like a child," say, "I prefer

Table 3.1
Patient Bill of Rights

Each patient is entitled to:

1. Considerate and respectful care
2. The right to obtain complete information concerning his or her diagnosis, treatment, and prognosis, in terms that he or she can understand
3. The right to all the information he or she needs to give informed consent (risks, benefits, alternative treatments) before treatment
4. The right to refuse treatment, once he or she is aware of the facts, to the extent permitted by law
5. Privacy and confidentiality (refusal to be examined in front of people who are not involved in the case, confidentiality of records)
6. A reasonable response when asking for help, including evaluation, service, and referral, as indicated by the urgency of the case
7. Information about conflicts of interest (ownership or interest in labs evaluating tests, professional relationships among doctors involved in the treatment)
8. The right to be told if his or her treatment is to be made part of a research project or experiment
9. The right to an explanation of the physician's bill
10. The right to expect follow-up care

to have doctors speak to patients as adults rather than as children." The physician's response to the latter will probably be less defensive and more accommodating.

It may be wise to prepare written questions for the doctor in anticipation of the visit. Then you won't forget what you want to ask, and your questions will be phrased in a thoughtful manner to elicit the information you really want. Encourage the care-receiver to write out questions in advance too. You or your loved one might want to know how to take certain medications (with food? with water?), what the potential side effects of these medications are, or what other options exist. You might want a fuller description of the long-term implications of the illness or conditions. Writing down the questions in advance will help you get the answers you seek.

When You Need a Specialist

Although the care-receiver should have a primary physician who supervises her or his general medical care (usually a general practitioner, internist, or family practice physician), there are times when a specialist is needed to treat a particular condition:

1. *Allergist*—specialist in allergies
2. *Cardiologist*—heart specialist
3. *Dermatologist*—skin specialist
4. *Endocrinologist*—gland disorders specialist (for example, to treat diabetes)
5. *Gastroenterologist*—digestive tract specialist
6. *Geriatrician*—specialist in problems of the elderly
7. *Geriatric psychiatrist*—specialist on psychological and mental problems of the elderly (for example, Alzheimer's disease)
8. *Gynecologist*—specialist in the female reproductive system
9. *Neurologist*—specialist in disorders of the nervous system
10. *Oncologist*—specialist in the treatment of cancer
11. *Ophthalmologist*—specialist in the treatment of eye disorders
12. *Orthopedist*—specialist in bones, joints, and muscles
13. *Podiatrist*—specialist in foot care
14. *Proctologist*—specialist in disorders of the rectum and colon
15. *Psychiatrist*—specialist in mental, emotional, and behavior disorders
16. *Rheumatologist*—specialist in arthritis and rheumatism
17. *Urologist*—specialist in the urinary system in both sexes and in the male reproductive system

Consult your primary care physician for recommendations when a specialist is needed. In addition, a number of other health care personnel may become part of the medical care team from time to time:

1. *Nurse practitioner*—has more training than the registered nurse and may perform physical examinations and diagnostic tests, counsel patients, and develop treatment plans.
2. *Occupational therapist*—helps disabled patients function more independently.
3. *Physical therapist*—provides treatment for movement disorders, to improve patients' range of motion.
4. *Physician's assistant*—performs some of the more routine medical procedures so as to free the physician for more specialized care.
5. *Registered dietitian*—provides information about nutrition and develops nutritional treatment plans.
6. *Registered nurse*—has two to four years of education in nursing schools and may be involved in patient education, administering medication, and supervising treatments prescribed by the physician.
7. *Social worker*—counsels patients regarding services available to finance treatment and to meet physical and emotional needs.
8. *Speech pathologist*—works with patients to improve their speech (for example, after a stroke).

Nursing-Home Care

Although only 5 percent of people over sixty-five years of age spend their last years in nursing homes, 20 percent live in such a home at some time in their lives. They may be between hospital care and full recovery, or their caregiver may be unavailable due to long-term travel or illness. Two-thirds of nursing home residents are women, half are eighty-five years of age or older, and almost half are childless.

At some time you may want or need to consider housing your loved one in a nursing home. This can be a very difficult decision, fraught with the potential for enormous guilt. Nursing-home care is admittedly an imperfect solution to an unwelcome situation—the deterioration of your loved one's physical or mental health and the realization that home care is insufficient. However, there are situations in which a nursing home is best for the care-receiver and for your own family.

When Nursing-Home Care Is Warranted

When your loved one is either physically disabled or mentally in-competent to the extent that home care is impossible, a nursing home may be the answer. When home care would be devastating for the family because of family members' attitudes or lifestyles (for example, extensive traveling), a nursing home may be the an-swer. And if for any other reason home care is judged to be inappro-priate, nursing-home care may be the answer.

Although admission to a nursing home can be disturbing, there are many benefits about which your loved one should be aware. One of these is greater access to others of his or her own age with whom to socialize. Eating meals together, sharing a room, doing arts and crafts projects with a group, and participating in recrea-tional activities all have the potential to enhance elders' social lives.

I'm reminded of a presentation I was asked to make to a group of "senior citizens" at a local school. The buses brought more than two hundred people to hear my presentation, "Feeling Comfortable Talking about Sexuality." I was well-prepared. I had slides, pro-duced at significant cost, on which appeared sexual terms in white letters on a red background, and, as I showed each slide on the screen, the participants were instructed to shout out the term. The first term was "KISS," and when it appeared, the group shouted so loudly that I was delighted. The next word was "HUG," and this time they shouted so loudly it seemed as though the ceiling and walls would come down. This continued through several words— until the word "PENIS" appeared on the screen. At that point it became so quiet that I could hear the beads of perspiration from my forehead as they hit the floor. The same thing happened when "VAGINA" was projected.

I found out later that the participants had not been notified of the topic of my presentation. They had simply been offered the op-portunity to take a field trip and had jumped at it. Using the sur-vival skills I had gained through years of sharing a bedroom with two brothers, I eventually managed to salvage the presentation and to prevent any long-term psychological scars. However, I did learn how important peer contact is for elders, even if that contact is for a vaguely understood purpose. Nursing homes provide an op-portunity for regular peer contact.

In addition, numerous services are easily accessible to resi-dents in nursing homes. Clergy, barbers, beauticians, physical therapists, and nurses may be part of the home's staff.

Further, the stress and frustration of living in the caregiver's home may be so great and, consequently, so unhealthy for all concerned, that moving into a nursing home is a relief.

When it is determined that your loved one should enter a nursing home, you and the care-receiver must find one that is affordable and comfortable and provides the type and quality of care needed. If your loved one is mentally incompetent you must choose a nursing home without consulting her or him. *In all other instances*, however, the person who will be living in the nursing home should be involved in selecting it.

Locating a Nursing Home

The first step is to find a home that meets your criteria. Begin by getting recommendations from your physician, visiting nurses, relatives, and friends. In addition, each state has Area Agencies on Aging and, by federal regulation, a Long-Term Care Ombudsman (someone to receive and investigate complaints about nursing homes). Consult these sources. Check your local phone book for addresses.

Other nursing homes can be located by purchasing the membership directory of the American Association of Homes for the Aged (write to the AAHA at 1129 20th Street N.W., Washington, DC 20036). If you live in or near a major city, you may find useful an article published in the August 1985 issue of *Good Housekeeping* that lists information about the best nursing homes in ten metropolitan areas (available in local libraries; a reprint can be purchased by writing to the Back Issues Department, Good Housekeeping Magazine, 250 West 55th Street, New York, NY 10019).

Selecting a Nursing Home

Once you have generated a list of nursing homes, decide which type of home best suits your loved one's situation. Begin this process as early as possible. Most nursing homes, especially the better ones, have waiting lists. Once you select a home, get your loved one's name on that waiting list. If you are called before he or she is ready to be admitted, you can request an extension.

There are three basic types of homes: *homes for the aged* offer minimum care and are for elders able to function independently; *intermediate care facilities* provide daily nursing supervision and care; and *skilled nursing facilities* serve the chronically ill who require continual medical attention. Often—but not always—these three types of care are available in one nursing home.

All nursing homes and their administrators are licensed by the state. Those that receive Medicare payments (skilled nursing facilities) or Medicaid payments (skilled nursing facilities or intermediate care facilities) must also be certified by the federal government. However, most nursing-home care costs are not reimbursable by Medicare. This may be an important consideration in choosing a home. Many nursing homes charge more than $30,000 per year. Only after the care-receiver's financial status has been reduced to the Medicaid-eligible level does financial aid for nursing-home care become available. Each state defines this eligibility level differently, so find out what your state's definition is.

In addition to cost, consider other criteria. A visit to the home will give you an impression of its facilities and, perhaps, its programming. There are certain things to evaluate during this visit. One is whether a "Nursing Home Resident's Bill of Rights" is prominently posted. These rights have been developed by the federal government and represent the *minimum* to which your loved one is entitled in that setting. Table 3.2 lists these rights.

Your evaluation of potential nursing homes should include acquiring answers to the following questions:[1]

Residents
• Are the residents similar to your loved one?
• Are they of similar educational and socioeconomic levels?
• Are they similar in their health status?
• Are they friendly, or do they seem isolated and distant?

Safety Considerations
• Is the building fire-resistant or fireproof?
• Is there an automatic sprinkler system?
• Are smoke detectors installed throughout the building?
• Are there portable fire extinguishers?
• Are all exit doors clearly marked?
• Are they easy to open from inside?
• Are fire drills held on a regular basis?
• Are hallways properly lighted and free of obstructions?
• Are hallways equipped with handrails on both sides?
• Are grab bars installed in all bathing and toilet areas?
• Are call bells installed at all beds and in all bathrooms?
• Are they in good working order?

1. Helene MacLean, *Caring for Your Parents: A Sourcebook of Options and Solutions for Both Generations* (New York: Doubleday, 1987) 230–33.

Table 3.2
Nursing Home Resident's Bill of Rights

Each resident who is admitted:

1. is fully informed, as evidenced by the resident's written acknowledgment before or at the time of admission, of these rights and of all rules and regulations governing the exercise of these rights;
2. is fully informed, before or at the time of admission and during stay, of services available in the facility, and of related charges, including charges for services not covered under Medicare or Medicaid, or not covered by the facility's basic daily rate;
3. is fully informed of his/her medical condition by a physician (unless the physician notes in a medical record that it is not in the patient's interest to be told) and is afforded the opportunity to participate in planning his/her medical treatment and to refuse to participate in experimental research;
4. is transferred or discharged only for medical reasons, or for his/her welfare or that of other residents, and is given reasonable advance notice to ensure orderly transfer or discharge;
5. is encouraged and assisted, throughout his/her period of stay, to exercise his/her rights as a resident and as a free citizen. To this end, he/she may voice grievances and recommend changes in policies and services to facility staff and/or to outside representation of his/her choice without fear of coercion, discrimination, or reprisal;
6. may manage his/her personal financial affairs or be given at least a quarterly accounting of financial transactions made on his/her behalf if the facility accepts the responsibility to safeguard his/her funds for him/her;
7. is free from mental and physical abuse, and free from chemical and physical restraints except as authorized in writing by a physician for a specified and limited period of time, or when necessary to protect the patient from injury to himself/herself or to others;
8. is assured confidential treatment of his/her personal and medical records, and may approve or refuse their release to any individual outside the facility;
9. is treated with consideration, respect, and full recognition of his/her dignity and individuality, including privacy in treatment and in care for his/her personal needs;
10. is not required to perform services for the facility that are not included for therapeutic purposes in his/her plan of care;
11. may associate and communicate privately with persons of his/her choice, and send and receive his/her personal mail unopened;
12. may meet with and participate in activities of social, religious, and community groups at his/her discretion;
13. may retain and use his/her personal clothing and possessions as space permits, unless to do so would infringe on rights of other patients, or constitute a hazard to safety;
14. is assured privacy for visits by his/her spouse; if both are inpatients in the facility, they are permitted to share a room.

Source: Health Care Finance Administration, U.S. Department of Health and Human Services, Washington, D.C.

Institutional Matters

- Is the facility run for profit?
- Is it licensed for the current year?
- Is it accredited by the Joint Commission of Accreditation of Health Care Organizations?
- Is a statement of patients' rights conspicuously posted?
- Have you been able to examine the most recent state inspection report?
- Does the admissions agreement require that a new resident be given a complete medical examination immediately before or immediately after acceptance?
- Does the facility provide the special services required by your loved one's condition?
- Are the mentally incompetent or mentally disturbed residents housed on a separate floor or in a different wing of the building rather than with patients whose mental faculties are functioning normally?
- Is it close enough to a good hospital to facilitate emergency transfer to intensive care?
- Is the atmosphere bright and cheerful or drab and underlit?
- Are residents alert and communicative, or do most appear to be withdrawn or overtranquilized?
- Are there more than four beds in a room?
- Do most rooms have two beds?
- Does every bedroom have a window?
- Do all bedrooms open out onto a corridor?
- Are wheelchair ramps provided for easy access to essential areas?

Professional Services

- Are a physician and registered nurse readily available on a twenty-four-hour basis?
- Are dentists, eye doctors, podiatrists, and other specialists available on a regular schedule?
- Are rehabilitation programs conducted on a full-time basis or only one or two days a week?
- Are rehabilitation programs supervised by professionally accredited personnel?
- Does the number of nurses and nurses' aides appear to be adequate for the needs of the residents? (Ask residents if help is available when they need it.)
- Are all drugs stored in a room set aside for that purpose?
- Does the pharmacist keep a record of each person's drugs?

• Have individual drug records been computerized so that potentially dangerous combinations can be promptly brought to the doctor's attention?

Finding Out about Food

• Is the kitchen clean, and is all garbage properly contained?
• Does a dietitian supervise meal preparation for residents with special requirements?
• Are meals nutritious, varied, and attractively presented?
• Are the portions large enough?
• Are the menus prepared a week in advance? Does the meal being served conform to the menu entry?
• Are nourishing snacks available between meals and at bedtime?
• Is there an attractive dining area for ambulatory residents?
• Is it accessible by wheelchair?
• Are sufficient staff members available at mealtime to help those who need it before their food gets cold?
• Are individual food preferences taken into account?

Recreation

• Is the recreation program organized by a paid professional?
• Are cultural and educational resources of the community an integral part of this program?
• Are residents taken on group outings to special events?
• Are social and recreational activities planned for patients confined to their own rooms?
• Is there a choice of activities for each day and evening?
• Are attractively equipped rooms set aside for socializing, playing cards or word games, sewing, and the like?
• Is there a library on the premises, and is it constantly replenished?
• Are the grounds safe and well-maintained, so that patients can spend time out of doors?
• Is good use made of community volunteers for visiting, intergenerational activities, and celebration of religious holidays and birthdays?
• Does the Residents' Council participate in recreational planning?

Personal Matters

• Is every resident's room area provided with a comfortable chair, a good reading light, a chest of drawers, some shelf space, and a closet for personal possessions?

- Are residents permitted to bring a favorite piece of furniture from home?
- Are residents assured of privacy in toilet and bathing facilities, and while dressing and undressing?
- May residents wear their own clothes?
- Are there facilities on the premises for keeping these clothes clean?
- Are the services of a barber and hairdresser regularly available?
- Can outgoing calls be made in complete privacy?
- Can visitors be received in complete privacy?

Once you have determined the answers to these questions, compare nursing homes and choose the one most appropriate to the needs of your loved one.

In Conclusion

As a caregiver you have already demonstrated your concern. You have given your time, effort, and finances to allow someone you love to live her or his remaining years with optimum health and quality of life. You are important to the care-receiver in many respects, not the least of which is as an advocate on health-care issues. You can help assure that she or he receives necessary health services and that those services are offered in a manner that acknowledges her or him as a total person. If residence in a nursing home is warranted, you can help make an appropriate placement by generating a list of potential homes and evaluating them in terms of their residents, safety considerations, institutional matters, professional services, meal and food offerings, recreation facilities and policies, and personal matters.

No one needs to encourage you to perform this advocacy role well. You know its importance. This chapter and others that follow will allow you to meet this obligation by teaching you certain skills (for example, assertiveness) and providing checklists to help you. When in doubt about what to do or how to do it, refer to these chapters. We continue in the next chapter with a discussion of some common medical-care skills.

4

Common Medical Caregiver Skills: What You'll Need to Be Able to Do

After several minutes of listening to me review what I considered routine care instructions for Dad, my mother started crying. Surprised, I asked her, "What in the world is wrong?" She replied, "You forget, I don't have a nursing degree like you. I don't know all this stuff. It may seem easy to you, but I'm scared to death. What if something goes wrong and I don't know what to do? Your daddy could even die and it could all be my fault."

She was right. I was overwhelming her with a lot of information, and, yes, it did seem pretty simple to me. But when I gave her a written guide, answered her questions, and provided ample encouragement, she was able to review what to do for many of the problems she might experience in caring for my predominantly bedfast elderly father. During the two years that my father needed constant care, she found that she could do things she had never thought possible. She provided tender loving care and unbounded devotion. As my father's health declined, my mother felt good about what she was able to do for him, and her care brought them even closer together.

Normal Aging Changes

All of the body's systems change with age. Hearing, vision, smell, taste, touch, mental processes—they all slow down. Many problems you will face in caring for your elderly loved one will be due to normal aging changes and not to medical problems at all.

The following are changes that you might expect.

Vision

Visual acuity starts to decrease with age. In particular, the abilities to discriminate fine detail and to discriminate between colors such as blue and violet diminish. Depth perception and peripheral vision also decrease, leading to more falls. These changes often require the elderly to take more time to read, which may lead others to assume incorrectly that they are confused or "slow." Because of their decreasing ability to discriminate color, elders may choose clothes that clash, and make-up application or other uses of color may seem "off." Some suggestions can help your loved one cope with these changes in vision:

- Schedule yearly eye examinations. Visual changes are gradual and progressive and can best be treated when diagnosed early.
- Make sure glasses are clean, readily available, and used when appropriate.
- For any level of visual impairment, consider obtaining large-print magazines and newspapers or talking books from your local library.
- Purchase an electric magnifying glass that provides a light. Use a soft-white lightbulb to reduce glare.
- Urge your elder to avoid watching television in a dark room or walking from a dark room into a brightly lit room. It takes aging eyes several minutes to adjust to light changes.
- If your loved one is legally blind, seek assistance from the appropriate organizations. These are listed for you in appendices 1A and 1B under "Visual Impairment and Blindness."

Hearing

One of the most common signs of increasing age is a decrease in hearing. Normal changes include losing the ability to discriminate sounds—particularly words beginning with the letters *S, Z, T, F,* and *G*—and to hear higher-pitched sounds. That's why older people often have difficulty hearing women's voices but can hear most men's voices. Below are some useful tips for helping your loved one hear more easily.

- Because hearing may diminish gradually, make sure your loved one has at least a yearly hearing evaluation. Some hearing impairments can be improved by the use of a hearing aid; however, don't buy a hearing aid until it has been recommended by a licensed professional. Certain kinds of hearing loss cannot be improved with a hearing aid.

• If your loved one has a hearing aid, check the batteries at least once a month. Clean the earmold often, depending on how much earwax builds up. Make sure that the earmold and tubing are dry before they are reinserted, since water can impede sound conduction.

• Remind your elder to turn off the hearing aid when it is not in use and to store it in a safe, dry place.

• Remind your loved one not to shower, apply hairsprays, or use a hair dryer with the hearing aid in place.

• Call your local telephone company and ask about special services for the hearing impaired. Special bells, flashers, volume controls, and amplifiers for ear pieces are available.

When speaking with the hearing impaired,

• Sit to the side of the elder's "best" ear, but never speak directly *into* the ear.

• Speak distinctly; don't shout. A normal pitch or slightly deepened voice may help.

• Face your elder—lip reading may help him or her better understand what you are saying. Likewise, facial movements, expressions, gestures, and situational cues can provide hints about the content of your speech.

• Decrease extraneous noise, such as the television or radio.

• Speak from a distance of three to four feet with good lighting on your face so that facial expressions can be seen clearly.

• Avoid chewing gum, eating, or covering your mouth when speaking.

Organizations to contact for assistance are listed in appendix 1A under "Hearing Impairment." Publications are listed under the same title in appendix 1B.

Smell, Touch, Taste, Thirst, Vibration, and Temperature

All of the senses decrease with age. Because of this, the elderly may have difficulty realizing that food is spoiled or that they've forgotten to flush the commode. They may need to be reminded to drink fluid throughout the day, because thirst also diminishes. Because their sense of touch is less acute, elders should be particularly careful with hot water, heating pads, hot water bottles, or putting hands or feet near heating vents. Teach your loved one to test hot water with a thermometer and to use a kitchen egg timer to time the use of any source of heat. Check the skin often to make sure it is not becoming red or blistered. Fragile elderly skin burns easily.

Because the sense of touch and vibration are decreased, the elderly may have difficulty taking their own pulse. Many heart medications require that pulse count be measured before the medication is taken. Although the radial (wrist) pulse is the most common pulse point, the carotid (neck) pulse is much stronger and easier to find. Figure 4.1 shows how to take both of these pulses.

Neurological/Mental Changes

Dealing with the normal mental changes associated with aging can be very frustrating for both the elderly person and the caregiver. Decreases in mental functioning are gradual and progressive. Most often you will notice an increasing inability to remember recent events. For example, your loved one may forget where she or he laid her or his glasses just moments ago, who just called on the phone, or what the caller said. A decrease in short-term memory *is* normal. Other normal changes include a slowing of the ability to think (the elderly can think and respond appropriately; it simply takes them a little longer).

Try not to second-guess your elder's responses, and do not assume that you aren't understood just because those responses are slow. Give small amounts of information at a time, slow your speaking pace, and decrease distractions such as background music, television, and other people's conversations. Use information-bearing sentences, telling, for example, the date of the month, the day of the week, the time of day, the season, or the weather. These may need to be repeated often to help reorient the confused or disoriented person. Likewise, you may periodically need to orient your loved one to you by name or by your relationship to him or her. The elderly also start to lose their ability to think abstractly. Try using analogies and examples to convey abstract information.

Musculoskeletal Changes

Common changes of aging include increased muscle flaccidity and decreased muscle tone, sense of balance, and fine motor coordination. Shorter strides and a slower pace during walking are com-

Figure 4.1: Taking a Pulse

An accurate pulse can be taken using either the radial (wrist) site or the carotid (neck) area.

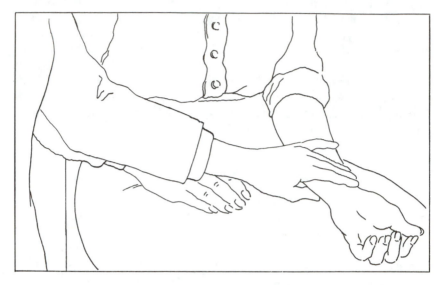

To measure the *radial pulse*, slide your finger down from the thumb to the wrist. Gently press with your third finger until you feel the pulse. If you have trouble feeling the pulse, turn the hand over, facing palm down, to get a stronger pulse.

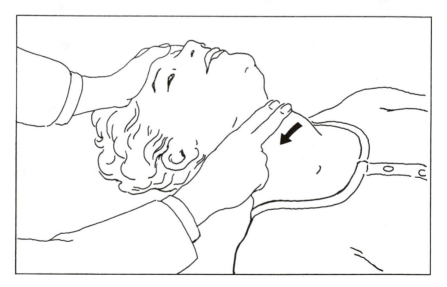

To measure the *carotid pulse*, gently place your second and third fingers on the side of the neck across from the "Adam's apple." Adjust your touch so that you can feel the pulse without putting too much pressure on the artery. Be careful not to massage or compress the pulse site for longer than a minute and a half. Always count a pulse for one full minute.

mon. What do these changes mean for your loved one? You may expect her or him to tire more easily and to need more frequent periods of rest. Chairs with arms should be stationed throughout the house to permit rest stops. If your elder is using a walker or other device, there is a greater risk of falling or tripping on rugs, toys, furniture legs, or other objects on the floor. Try to keep unstable objects like lamps, coat racks, and large plants out of your loved one's most frequent routes. If your care-receiver tires and tries to gain support by grabbing one of these, a serious injury might occur.

Because of your elder's decreased fine motor coordination, you may notice that he or she has trouble picking up small objects, winding a watch, or putting on a hearing aid or eyeglasses. Sometimes using a mirror can help the elderly person accomplish these tasks. Your tactful offers to help with these seemingly simple tasks can help lower your loved one's frustration level.

Respiratory and Cardiovascular Systems

One reason your loved one tires more easily is decreased circulation in the lungs, providing the body with less oxygen. Similarly, the blood circulation in general is slowed. The results can be dizziness when your elder rises too quickly and a rapid heartbeat after even minimal activity. The lesson to be learned from all this is, *take it slowly.*

Genitourinary and Endocrine Systems

Common but embarrassing changes in the genitourinary system of the elderly include prostate enlargement in men and loss of muscle tone in the perineal floor for women. Both conditions can cause difficulty with starting, urgency, and increased frequency of urination. Ten million Americans have some form of incontinence—that is, the inability to refrain from urinating. Stress incontinence is perhaps the most common and the best known type. With stress incontinence, coughing or straining can cause urinary leakage. It is estimated that one woman in three has some degree of incontinence after menopause and that one in every five older men is incontinent to some extent. Nevertheless, incontinence is not normal, and it is not something that every older person should expect to experience. When incontinence is first apparent, it should be recognized as a medical problem and brought to the attention of a physician.

There are several causes of incontinence, and some of them can be successfully treated. Should incontinence persist after a medical evaluation is made, you may encourage your loved one to wear adult diapers and to go to the bathroom on a regular schedule (every hour). Pelvic muscle exercises, called Kegel exercises, can also help. These exercises need to be practiced at least one hundred times a day (instruct your loved one to do ten contractions ten times a day). "Kegels" involve strengthening the pelvic muscles by simply contracting and loosening the same muscles that one would use to start and stop urine flow. Remarkable improvement has been noted in as little as six to twelve weeks with daily Kegel exercises.

Finally, aging of the endocrine system results in changes in the regulation of body heat, so that the elder has an increased sense of being cold. Comfort is really the main concern here. Keep rooms warm, and provide sweaters, lap robes, and socks. Help your loved one choose warm and practical clothes, such as warm-up suits and other fleece-lined garments. Be sure to watch the elder's use of heating pads, hot water bottles, and the like. Elderly people burn easily and may not know that the device is too hot or has been in use for too long.

Psychological and Emotional Changes

Many of the normal changes of aging can lead to depression or despair in the elderly. A loss of independence is a primary cause of such feelings among elderly who have lived independent, active lives. Changes in relationships with others because of retirement, the death of a spouse, or a move may cause feelings of sadness. Another common reason for depression is changes in the body due to aging. Think of how many times you have heard your loved one say, "I used to be able to . . . but no more. I'm too old." And, of course, the awareness that one is coming to the end of one's life can be sobering.

It is important to share with your loved one that it is normal to feel down or depressed from time to time. Acknowledge that it can be hard adjusting to all these changes—even the good ones, like staying with you. Try to facilitate her or his independence as much as possible. Assign your loved one daily chores (setting the table, making the coffee). Give praise for good work and good suggestions. Let your elder know that she or he is important, helpful, and needed. Try not to interfere with daily routines. These provide comfort and orientation for the elder.

How to Know When Something Is Wrong and What to Do about It

Although many troublesome discomforts of the elderly are simply a part of aging, many others are not. This section covers some common medical problems and how you can handle them.

Pain

A common misconception about the elderly is that they complain of pain all the time, and often complain needlessly. This is not usually the case. There are two basic types of pain: acute and chronic. Acute pain usually appears suddenly, is of short duration, and can be relieved with the appropriate therapy. Acute pain often means that the cause of the pain has just happened or has reached its worst potential. Chronic pain, on the other hand, is ongoing, may start suddenly or come on gradually, and can last months or years. The intensity of the pain may vary or remain constant. The pain may be in a very defined location, or it may be vague and diffuse. Chronic pain may or may not be helped by medication or other therapies. It is important to remember that even if it cannot be lessened by usual methods, the elder's pain is real.

Pain is a very important symptom for gauging health in the elderly. Elders should not expect pain with aging, nor should they accept it as normal. Pain should be evaluated by a physician. Likewise, physical complaints can be caused by emotional distress or stress. In this case, those emotional needs should be addressed.

To prepare to consult with the physician, gather as much information about the pain as you can. Some of the questions you will want to ask your loved one include:

- When did the pain start? Were you involved in an activity at the time? Can you think of anything that might have caused it (fall, slip, etc.)?
- Describe the pain. Where is it? Is it constant, or does it come and go? Is it sharp, dull, or aching? Does anything make the pain worse (movement, changing positions, breathing, etc.)? Does anything ease the pain?
- How long have you had the pain? Has the pain changed in any way since it first began?
- Have you ever had this pain before? When?

Any new physical complaints must be communicated to a physician. If the complaint is a long-running one and there is nothing new about it, however, try tried-and-true remedies. Try to make your elder more comfortable, give medication as prescribed by the doctor, and let your loved one know that you understand he or she is uncomfortable and that you care. Should this old, familiar pain change in any way, call the doctor.

Falls, Cuts, and Bruises

Falls, cuts, and bruises are all too prevalent for the elderly. This section discusses how to respond to these mishaps:

1. Falls

Falls are a common threat to the elderly. Nearly half of people over sixty-five experience a fall. Some of these accidents result in minor injuries like cuts or bruises, while others can cause major injuries and even death. Falls are commonly caused by dizziness, losing balance, and muscular weakness. As discussed earlier in this chapter, physical changes include gait changes (uneven walking pace), shuffling or not picking up the feet, swaying, slowed reflexes, weakened muscles, and loss of vision. All these factors contribute to the risk of falls.

The best strategy is to try to prevent a fall. Chapter 2 outlines how to reduce the risk by preparing your home for your loved one. Additionally, remind your loved one to rise slowly, holding on to some type of sturdy support. Once the elder has gotten up, he or she should stand for a moment to regain a sense of balance and to "clear the head." Moving should then proceed slowly, with a support close by (wall, chair, railing, or the like). If your elder feels faint, cannot go on, or for some other reason questions being able to remain standing, he or she should lean against a wall and ease down to the floor.

If your loved one falls, stay calm, and proceed as follows:

- Sit down next to your loved one so that you can determine the extent of the injury.
- Look for any obvious signs of injury (nonresponsiveness, bleeding, unnatural shape of an arm or leg).
- Check for signs of pain, confusion, swelling, bruises, or other signs of injury.
- If any of these are present, call your doctor or emergency ambulance at once.
- When help is needed, leave your loved one lying on the floor, keeping her or him as comfortable and calm as possible.

If you do not find any signs of major injury, devise a plan to get your elder up and into a bed or chair. If a bed or chair is not nearby, push a chair (preferably one with arms) as close to your fallen elder as possible. Call for additional help from a family member or a neighbor. As you lift your loved one, you can reduce the chances of another fall by grasping his or her arm near the armpit, having the elder hold on to your forearm, and bracing your foot in front of his or her feet. If your loved one isn't too heavy, you can reach under the arms and around the chest from behind, slowly pulling him or her up to a sitting position.

Keep looking for any signs of swelling, bruising, or bleeding, and check for pain. Watch for changes in the eyes, confusion, or sleepiness. If any of these signs appear, call the doctor.

2. Cuts

You can easily take care of simple, shallow cuts. Immediately rinse the cut with cold, clean water, apply pressure for a minimum of five minutes, and then put on an adhesive bandage. Remember that the elderly may bleed more readily and longer than younger people do because elderly blood vessels are more fragile and break more easily. Similarly, the elderly's skin is often very fragile and breaks and tears easily. Do not stretch the adhesive strip or tape across the skin, and most important, when removing tape or a bandage, pull very slowly and moisten the skin with petroleum jelly or a greasy lotion. Remove the adhesive strip within twenty-four hours or so to allow the wound to be exposed to the air to dry. Never leave a bandage on longer unless instructed to do so by a health care provider, because the darkness and moisture under an adhesive strip provide a fertile climate for infection.

If a cut is deep or if bleeding does not slow or stop after five minutes of constant pressure, continue to apply pressure to the cut and take your elder to a health care center to have the cut treated. It may require stitches.

3. Bruises

Bruises are caused by bleeding under the skin, usually due to a blow to the area (a fall, a bump, or the impact of a dropped object). The elderly bruise easily because they often have diminished protective fat over blood vessels, and their blood vessels are more easily broken. Most bruises can be minimized by the prompt application of ice to the injured area. Make a simple ice pack by placing about a third of a cup of cold water in a top-closing plastic bag and adding a few ice cubes (or even better, crushed ice). Place a cold, wet cloth over the area, and place the ice on the cloth. Leave the ice pack on for at least fifteen minutes. Bruises that continue to swell or grow larger despite the use of ice should be checked by a health care provider.

Infections

The elderly are much more prone to infections than are younger people. They may also have more difficulty fighting off an infection once it occurs. Signs of infection include pain, swelling, fever, and redness. Infections may develop over a period of a few hours to several days. Infections of wounds are usually easily identified, but the

Figure 4.2: Taking a Temperature

Although there are several different ways of taking a temperature, the most common is the oral method. To take an oral temperature:

1. Obtain a thermometer made of some material other than glass. The elder, in his or her confusion, may bite the thermometer.
2. Shake the thermometer until the reading indicates it is below 96° Fahrenheit (F.) or 35° Centigrade or Celsius (C.).
3. Clean the thermometer with alcohol, making sure to wipe off the excess alcohol with a clean cotton swab.
4. Insert the thermometer under the care-receiver's tongue and have him or her close the mouth.
5. Remove the thermometer after 3 to 4 minutes to read the temperature. Use the chart below.

A normal temperature can vary from person to person but is approximately 98.6° F. or 37.0° C. To convert degrees F. to degrees C., subtract 32, then multiply by ⅝. To convert degrees C. to degrees F., multiply by ⅖, then add 32.

Centigrade (Celsius)	Fahrenheit
0	32.0
36.0	96.8
36.5	97.7
37.0	98.6
37.5	99.5
38.0	100.4
38.5	101.3
39.0	102.2
39.5	103.1
40.0	104.0
40.5	104.9
41.0	105.8
41.5	106.7
42.0	107.6

symptoms signaling respiratory, urinary, or other types of infections may be vague. If your loved one complains of feeling tired or depressed, is confused or irritable, or has vague, nonspecific complaints, she or he may have an infection. As usual, look for signs of change: mood, level of alertness, eyes, skin color, cough, fever, strong-smelling urine, or any other changes. If these signs or symptoms persist for over forty-eight hours without improvement, or if they get progressively worse over a period of eight to twelve hours, call your elder's doctor. Figure 4.2, "Taking a Temperature," outlines how to take a temperature—an important piece of information to have *before* you call the physician.

Pressure Sores

Perhaps the most upset my mother ever got while caring for my bedfast father was the day she discovered a pressure sore on his right hip. With tears in her eyes, she asked me what she had done wrong and how she could help it heal. She had been following my instructions for preventing a bedsore, but because of his extensive weight loss and his poor nutritional state, her best efforts weren't enough. She was able, however, to prevent the pressure sore from getting any larger, and it did start to heal.

Pressure sores are a major problem for those elderly who are primarily bedfast or chairbound. Pressure sores are areas of skin—usually over bony areas like the hips, backbone, or inside of the knees—which, because of pressure, become red. Blisters or broken skin may or may not appear. The good news about pressure sores is that they are the most easily preventable and treatable afflictions of the elderly. Although bedsores or pressure sores can be prevented, they do require some vigilance on the part of both the elder and his or her caregiver.

The three factors needed to produce a pressure sore are pressure, friction irritation (often from sheets), and moisture. Again, the elderly's skin is fragile, easily damaged, and slow to heal. Prevention is the key:

- Decrease pressure, friction, and skin folding as much as possible.
- Help your loved one remain as mobile as possible.
- Help your loved one change positions at least every two hours, more often if possible.
- Have her or him sit or lie on an egg-crate mattress, a water mattress, or a sheepskin.

65

- Keep your elder as dry as possible. Change adult diapers frequently. Be sure to have her or him wipe dry after urination, dry the skin well after bathing, and use a lotion gently rubbed in. Change clothes as often as necessary to avoid the buildup of perspiration, particularly on the back and buttocks. Avoid pajamas with buttons or snaps in the back, and get all-cotton sleeping garments to allow the skin to breathe and get rid of moisture.
- Avoid tight-fitting panties, briefs, girdles, and bras, which can cause pressure and friction.
- Obtain sheepskin booties from pharmacies or medical supply houses to protect heels and ankles. Place pillows between knees to prevent pressure, and don't align the knees directly over each other.
- Use soft cotton or flannel sheets, and wash them in baby detergent to keep them as soft as possible. Use fitted sheets to decrease wrinkling, and straighten the sheets at least every two hours.
- Discourage your loved one from eating in bed; crumbs and spilled liquid can contribute to pressure sores.
- When you bathe, help dress, or otherwise have the chance to observe your elder's skin, check to see whether there are any depressed areas. Is there any redness? If so, try to relieve pressure on these areas and watch them carefully. Skin can break down in a matter of just a few hours.
- If you do notice a depressed or reddened area, call your physician and ask whether you can obtain medication to help toughen the skin and slow the breakdown.

Constipation

Constipation and the resultant use of laxatives by the elderly create a cycle that is not easily broken. Aging can lead to a decreased sensation of fullness in the lower bowel. Decreased activity levels and changes in diet toward softer foods and less water and fiber can contribute to constipation.

Many of the elderly believe that they should have a bowel movement every day. It is helpful to know what has been normal in terms of your elder's bowel habits. Keeping a calendar of bowel movements and their type—diarrhea, loose, formed, or hard—can help the elderly person understand his or her own normal bowel rhythm and avoid unnecessary use of laxatives or enemas. Encourage your loved one to move about and walk when possible, for activity can stimulate the bowel. Including adequate fluids—eight glasses or more daily—and roughage such as fresh fruits and vegetables in the diet can help your loved one maintain normal bowel habits.

If constipation persists for more than five days after fiber and fluids have been increased, a glycerin suppository can be used. If the suppository is ineffective, then try giving a Fleet enema (follow package instructions). Should the constipation continue after the Fleet enema, the elder's doctor should be notified. Avoid laxatives. They are habit forming, inhibit normal bowel function, and can cause dehydration.

Some people find that rocking back and forth or elevating their legs with a low stool while sitting on the commode can help stimulate a bowel movement. Going to the bathroom at set times, such as right after breakfast, can also help set bowel routines. It is also important to remind your loved one that everyone has her or his own routine; bowel movements need not occur every day. It's not abnormal to miss a day from time to time.

Bowel Incontinence

Bowel incontinence is the inability to control bowel movements. (It does not mean diarrhea or more frequent stools.) This condition, which afflicts more than two million Americans, is the single most common reason for putting the elderly in nursing homes. The elderly usually react to their own uncontrolled bowel movements with embarrassment, anger, and depression, while their caregivers often respond with anger, frustration, irritation, disgust, or nausea. Yet bowel incontinence can be dealt with successfully at home if one understands its causes and follows certain management tips.

Bowel incontinence can have one or more causes. Some medications, infections, cancer, poor circulation, or senility can contribute to incontinence. Other causes include poor bowel habits (not going to the bathroom when the bowel feels full), chronic use of laxatives, stress and anxiety, respiratory problems (not being able to hold the breath long enough to push out the stool), poor diet and low fluid intake, and immobility. The onset of uncontrolled bowel movements is a sign that something has changed for your loved one. Like all other changes in body functions, bowel incontinence should be evaluated by a physician. In many instances it can be resolved or at least diminished.

If your loved one has received a thorough medical evaluation yet continues to have a problem with bowel incontinence, try the following to help you both cope with this unpleasant and embarrassing condition.

- A balanced diet with plenty of fresh vegetables, fruits, and grains as well as eight glasses of liquid a day can assist in regulating the bowel.
- Regular exercise, such as walking, can help.
- A routine bathroom time, such as right after breakfast, is often helpful.
- Instruct your loved one to insert a glycerin suppository before trying to have the bowel movement.
- If incontinence persists after these efforts, your loved one will need some type of protection such as adult diapers, large maternity pads, or cotton pads and plastic pants.

If bowel incontinence persists after your best efforts and those of your physician, don't be overly discouraged. Bowel incontinence often waxes and wanes. There may be periods of months when your loved one will once again be able to control the bowels.

Medication

There are several questions you should be able to answer regarding medications used by your loved one:

- What medications is the care-receiver taking?
- Are all the medications necessary?
- How does each one contribute to the health and welfare of your loved one?
- What are the potential side effects of the medications?
- Can the elder administer them by him- or herself?
- Is there any chance that the dosages are too strong, or that the various medications are incompatible with one another? The best person to determine potential interactions among drugs is a physician who specializes in the care of the elderly.
- Does your loved one's doctor know about all the medicines your loved one is taking? (These include both prescription and over-the-counter drugs.)
- If your elder is being treated by more than one health care provider, is each of them aware of what medications the others are prescribing?

Because aged kidneys and livers function significantly less effectively than those of a younger adult, problems of dosages, interactions, and frequency of administration are more likely to occur in elderly persons. For this reason, here are a few hints to facilitate medication management:

- Write down the names of any drugs that have caused an allergic reaction or any adverse side effect, and remind health care providers at each visit.
- For each drug prescribed, know the name, why it is prescribed, how often it should be taken, and for how long.
- Know what side effects to watch for.
- Clarify any special instructions. Some medications must be taken according to specific directions—for example, "Take with meals," "Take on an empty stomach," or "Do not take within two hours of eating or drinking dairy products."
- Never stop a medication simply because the symptoms are gone unless a physician so advises. Remember also that you should not discontinue medications even when side effects appear unless a physician advises you to do so. This is especially important when the elder is taking high blood pressure medicine, heart medications, antibiotics, or steroids.

Medications can be quite confusing, especially if the elder is taking several a day, at different times of the day. An organized system can improve safety by helping you keep track of them. Try the system below:

- For each week, make a written chart (see figure 4.3) listing the drugs' names and when they should be taken during the week. Then show the times each medication is to be taken each day. Each time a medication is taken, cross a line through the appropriate time designation. At the end of the week, start a new chart.
- If labeling is a problem, code both the bottle of medicine and the drug name on the chart by color or by letters of the alphabet, written in large, dark lettering.
- As a daily reminder of medications to be taken, all the medications can be placed in a cup. This is useful only if a few pills are taken each day at the same time, or if it is easy to tell the differences among them by their shapes or colors. This system

Figure 4.3: Medication Chart

Name of Drug/ Directions	Sun	Mon	Tue	Wed	Thu	Fri	Sat

Name of Drug/ Directions	Sun	Mon	Tue	Wed	Thu	Fri	Sat
DRUG A— 3 times a day	8 12 5	8 12 5	8 12 5	8 12 5	8 12 5	8 12 5	8 12 5
DRUG B— once a day in A.M.	8	8	8	8	8	8	8
DRUG C— 3 times a day	8 12 5	8 12 5	8 12 5	8 12 5	8 12 5	8 12 5	8 12 5

Source: U.S. Department of Health, Education, and Welfare—Public Health Service: Alcohol, Drug Abuse, and Mental Health Administration.

ensures that no more pills than are required for the day will be ingested.

- When many pills are prescribed for each day, you can organize them with an egg carton. With a large pointed marker, write a different hour on each egg cup. For each hour, place the pills that are to be taken in the appropriate cup. Since the egg carton holds a dozen eggs, there are enough cups for twelve different times.

Be cautious if there are small children in the house—they may become curious and decide to try medications that are left open and accessible. In addition, leaving pills out will not work for medications that must be kept tightly sealed, such as nitroglycerin, or for those that need to be refrigerated, such as antibiotics. For these drugs, place a reminder in the appropriate egg cup, so that the care-receiver is alerted to take the medication at the designated time.

In Conclusion

Although we can expect many normal changes in our loved ones due to aging, not all the changes that occur are related to aging. Knowing your loved one's usual personality, habits, and lifestyle can help you pinpoint changes that result from illness or disease. Moreover, even if you do not have a background in health care, you can learn to manage many of the problems encountered when caring for elderly loved ones.

5

Common Nonmedical Caregiver Skills: Dealing with the Whole Person

Doris was a coauthor, a coworker, and a good friend. Several years after being diagnosed with breast cancer and undergoing a mastectomy, she became weak and unsteady when she walked. Fearing that she might have experienced a small stroke, Doris scheduled an appointment with her physician, who conducted numerous tests and consulted several medical specialists. It turned out that Doris's problem was actually much worse than she had suspected; she had a malignant brain tumor. After the surgery the doctors hoped that all the cancerous matter had been excised. Unfortunately, that hope soon faded, and Doris's condition became worsened in spite of radiation treatments and experimental medications.

Long proud of her appearance—a regular at the beauty parlor, and known by name to many department store clerks—Doris became embarrassed by her loss of hair and loss of weight. So ashamed was she that even her good friends were discouraged from visiting. Except for those occasions when she needed to travel for radiation treatments or to see one doctor or another, she remained indoors. Doris's body was being treated, but her spirit and mind were being neglected. Her husband and daughter did their best to keep her spirits up, but they were limited by their lack of skills and knowledge. Then Rob came along.

Rob, a minister trained in counseling, has counseled many dying people and provided solace to their families. Rob had known Doris professionally for many years, but now he was in a new role. He was there to help Doris die well and to suggest ways her family could help her achieve that goal. Soon Doris was receiving visitors, writing good-bye notes to her friends, and planning her funeral. At last, she was being cared for as a person rather than as a tumor.

The point of this story is not to discourage you from striving to meet the medical needs of the person for whom you are caring. Rather, we want to encourage you to consider also the *other* needs of that person, and we wish to provide you with some skills to respond to those needs. Acquire the skills to respond to the *medical* needs of the person for whom you are caring—but also respond to that person's *nonmedical* needs. The latter are just as vital. People cannot be divided into pieces; the mind, spirit, and body coexist within the person.

This chapter presents skills to help you communicate better with the person for whom you provide care (as well as with others with whom you interact), resolve conflicts more effectively to maintain positive relationships, and be assertive so your rights are not violated, and you can obtain that to which you are entitled.

Communication Skills

Learning how to communicate more effectively will help you get along better with the person for whom you are providing care, as well as with friends, family, and coworkers.

Nonverbal Communication

Notice the body posture of people with whom you come into contact. During an interesting activity—for instance, a well-presented lecture—most of them will lean or look toward the lecturer or the center of the group, indicating that they are involved in what is going on. During a boring lecture, they will lean away from the lecturer or group. We call this physical behavior *body language.* Body posture often says as much as the spoken word. When people are uncomfortable about expressing their thoughts or feelings verbally, body language may be their only form of communication.

We all recognize the importance of communicating *nonverbally*—we smile when we say hello; we scratch our heads when we're perplexed, we hug a friend to show affection. We also use an array of body terms to describe nonverbal behavior: "Keep a stiff upper lip," "I can't stomach him," "She has no backbone," "I'm tongue-tied," "He caught her eye," "I have two left feet," and "That was spine-tingling." We show appreciation, affection, revulsion, and indifference with expressions and gestures. We tell people we are interested in them merely by making eye contact, and, like the male peacock displaying his feathers, we display our sexuality by the way we dress, the way we walk, and the way we stand.

Verbal Communication

Unfortunately, nonverbal expressions of feelings and thoughts are easy to misinterpret. Consequently, to depend on nonverbal communication alone is to risk being misunderstood. Furthermore, if another person is using nonverbal communication to express feelings to you, it is up to you to ask—verbally—whether you are getting the right message. Without such a "reality check," the other person may be totally failing to connect but assuming that she or he is communicating effectively.

For example, imagine that a man and woman on their first date begin hugging, kissing, and caressing each other after a movie. The woman's breathing speeds up, and the man, taking this as a sign of sexual arousal and interest, presses onward. When the woman suddenly pushes free and complains that he is too impatient, the man is confused.

The problem is one of interpretation rather than of incompatibility. The rapid breathing that the man took as a sign of arousal was really a sign of nervousness. If the couple had been more effective verbal communicators, they could have clarified the situation at the start. Instead, they reached a silent impasse, with him confused and her resentful.

Check your impressions of someone's nonverbal communication, and improve your communication by making your nonverbal and verbal messages as consistent as you can.

Planning Time to Talk

The television set is a common barrier to communication. We are often so busy watching it that we don't take time to talk with those around us. To improve your communication with others, you may need to plan time for discussions. In setting up such times, it is wise to do the following:

1. Allow *sufficient* time to have a *meaningful* discussion.
2. Disconnect the phone, and don't allow other people to interrupt you.
3. Accept all feelings and the right to the verbal expression of these feelings. For example, it is just as appropriate to say, "I feel angry when . . ." as to say, "I feel terrific when. . . ."
4. Take a risk and really describe your *thoughts* and *feelings*. Don't expect the other person to guess what they are.
5. Approach your discussions with the mutual understanding that the goal is to improve your relationship.

Think of someone with whom you'd like to communicate better. Perhaps it is the person for whom you provide care, your supervisor at work, a coworker, or a family member. To plan a meaningful discussion with this person, write your answers to the following questions:

1. When is the best time to engage in a meaningful discussion?
2. Where is the best place to have this discussion?
3. What thoughts will you express?
4. What feelings will you express?

Listening

This seems obvious and yet is often ignored. Before saying anything, listen *carefully* to what the other person is saying. That sounds easy. Yet too many of us focus on what *we* want to say and how to phrase it so it comes out just right, and we don't listen to what the other person is saying. How can we expect other people to listen to us if we aren't listening to them? The listening and paraphrasing (active or reflective listening) skills you will learn below, in our discussion of conflict resolution, are effective in regular conversation as well. All of us can do a better job of listening. Try to pay more attention to this aspect of your communication.

Beginning with Agreement

You will be surprised at how much better you can communicate with someone with whom you disagree if you start your message with a point on which you *do* agree. Of course, this requires you to listen carefully and identify something with which you can agree. For example, if you are disagreeing about who should do the dishes, you might begin by saying, "I agree it is important that the dishes be washed. . . ." If you look and listen intently, you can always find a point of agreement.

To test your understanding of how to begin discussions on points of agreement, write in the letter of the "agreeing" response for each grouping below:

_____ 1. a. You may know a lot about some things, but in this instance you're dead wrong.
   b. Certainly the police are overworked. However, I still think they are paid too much.
   c. I couldn't disagree with you more. You don't know what you're talking about.

_____ 2. a. Yes, women are more apt to seek medical care; but perhaps that's because they are ill more often.
   b. It's obvious that in this case you're misinformed.
   c. Maybe I'm wrong, but my experience leads me to believe that a college education doesn't have any influence on one's salary.

_____ 3. a. Stress really can be harmful. On that we're in agreement. However, I don't think anything can be done about stress.
   b. You're totally wrong! Stress cannot be managed.
   c. I wish that I could agree with you, but your argument is so absurd that I can't find a single point of agreement.

The agreeing responses are (1) b, (2) a, and (3) a. Can you see how each of these statements begins with a point of agreement first and then goes on to disagree? This is a skill worth practicing.

"And," Not "But"

The word "but" is like an eraser; it erases everything that precedes it. When someone says, "Yes, your needs are important, but . . ." he or she is actually saying, "Your needs may be important, but let's forget about them, because I'm about to tell you what's *really* important." In other words, your needs are being erased so that we can focus on the "real issue." Listen to how people use the word "but" and you will get a real insight into communication. Listen to how *you* use "but"!

Substituting the word "and" for "but" is so simple and yet so significant. "And" leaves what preceded it on the table and *adds* something to it. "Your needs are important, and . . ." means that we will not discount (erase) your needs; we will consider them in addition to considering what will be presented next. Use more "ands" and fewer "buts."

"I" Statements

Too often we try to get other people to behave or believe as we do. Others naturally resent that, just as we resent it when they try to get us to behave or believe as they do. Part of this problem relates to the words we use to communicate.

Consider a woman whose boss expects her to work on Saturdays. If she wants to object to that, she should do so with "I" statements. For example, she shouldn't say, "When *you* expect me to

76

work on Saturdays. . . ." Instead, she should say, "When *I* am expected to work on Saturdays. . . ." In this manner, she places the focus not on the boss's behavior but on her situation. Consequently, the boss need not get defensive, and they can more easily discuss and resolve the situation. When we say "you," we make the other person feel that she or he is being criticized and must defend her- or himself. When we say "I," we are focusing on *our* feelings, beliefs, and interpretations. Feeling less defensive, the other person is more likely to listen to us, and the result will be more effective communication.

Practice this skill by rewriting the statements below as "I" statements. The first one is done for you as an example.

1. When you make me work on Saturdays, I resent it.
   Rewrite: When I'm expected to work on Saturdays, I feel resentful.
2. When you call me names, I feel terrible.
   Rewrite: _____
3. You make me so angry when you don't listen to me.
   Rewrite: _____
4. You are always late for meetings, and I'm getting fed up with it.
   Rewrite: _____
5. When you speak critically of me to the other employees, I get so embarrassed that I'd like to hide in my office the rest of the day.
   Rewrite: _____

Avoid "Why" Questions

As with statements that focus on "you" instead of "I," questions that begin with "why" make the other person defensive. "*Why* did you leave so early?" challenges the other person to justify leaving early. "Why" questions are often veiled criticisms. The person who asks, "Why don't you spend more time with me?" may be seeking an answer but is probably making a statement ("You don't spend enough time with me!"). Avoid "why" questions.

USING THESE SIMPLE COMMUNICATION techniques, you can interact better and improve your relationship with the person for whom you care, as well as with people at work, your family, and your friends. The result will be a happier, healthier you.

Conflict Resolution

One set of communication skills worth learning involves settling conflicts effectively. If you can become effective in resolving conflicts, your interpersonal relationships will be improved and both parties to a conflict will feel that their needs have been met.

Resolving conflict can be relatively simple. What usually complicates the situation is a lack of listening, an attempt to win, an inability to demonstrate understanding of the person with whom one is in conflict, and a rigidity that rejects alternative solutions. Consider this example:

John has worked all day and is very tired. His wife, Mary, has been stuck in the house with the kids all day and is bored to tears. John wants to spend a quiet, relaxing evening at home. Mary wants to get out of the house for some excitement.

Mary: Let's go shopping tonight.
John: Are you kidding? I had a hard day at work. I wasn't home relaxing all day like you were. I want to stay home, plop down in front of the TV, and take it easy.
Mary: I was home all day relaxing? Are you serious? It's boring to spend all day with four-year-olds and without an adult to talk with. I need to get out.
John: Forget it. No way. I'm staying home.
Mary: You inconsiderate jerk. You don't even care about me.
John: Just leave me alone.

The result might be that John agrees grudgingly to go with Mary but complains the whole time. The shopping will not be enjoyable for either of them under these circumstances. Or John and Mary may stay home, with Mary sulky and complaining. In this case, even though John has gotten his way and is staying home, he will not be able to relax. In neither case do John and Mary get what they need; they both lose. There *must* be a better way!

There *is* a better way. The three-step conflict resolution technique we present has proved effective in resolving conflicts so that everyone gets to win. Here are the three steps:

1. *Reflective or Active Listening:* reflect or paraphrase back to the other person his or her *words* and *feelings*.
2. *Identifying Your Position:* state your *thoughts* and *feelings* about the situation and describe why you feel this way.
3. *Exploring Alternative Solutions:* brainstorm other possibilities

so all have their needs met, although those needs may not be met exactly as the individuals had initially expected.

Listen to how John could have responded to the conflict.

Mary: Let's go shopping tonight.
John: Sounds as if you had a rough day and need to get out.
Mary: Rough? It was miserable. It's boring spending time with four-year-olds who are playing together when I have no adult to talk with.
John: You don't feel very stimulated during the day, do you?
Mary: No, I don't.

To this point, John has been using "reflective listening." That is, he has been paraphrasing the words and the feelings of Mary as he has understood them. He has not even discussed what he wants or needs. This demonstrates to Mary that John is paying attention to her and trying to identify her needs. When Mary comes to realize this—as she will, since John is doing such a good job of listening rather than arguing his point of view—she will be more willing to listen to John and identify what *he* needs. Now John is able to explain his position.

John: I had a rough day too. It seemed to be nonstop. I'm very tired and feel like an overwound spring. I was looking forward to coming home and relaxing. Going shopping wouldn't be relaxing for me.
Mary: It sounds as though one of us is out of luck.
John: Well, hold on a second. Let's see if there is some way we can go out and still make it relaxing.
Mary: Maybe we could go out for dinner. Or to a movie.
John: Yeah, or we could go to that concert at the high school, or ask Frank and Betty over to play bridge.

Note that the conflict ended with John and Mary exploring alternative solutions that would allow John to get what he needs (relaxation) and Mary to get what she needs (stimulation). Whether they stay in or go out is irrelevant. The real needs can be met to everyone's satisfaction.

In every conflict situation—with the person for whom you are caring or with your boss, coworkers, friends, or family members—this technique for resolving conflicts so everyone gets what he or she needs (although not necessarily as they originally planned) can be effective. But employing the technique, especially when you find yourself in a conflict, takes some practice.

There is no substitute for practicing this method during real-life disagreements, but practicing in advance of using it in the "real world" is a good idea. One way to start is for you to rearrange a dialogue consistent with this positive way of resolving conflicts. To help you do this, a conflict between an elderly mother and her caregiver daughter is presented below. On a separate sheet of paper, rewrite the dialogue so that both Beth and her mother get what they need. Do this before reading how *we've* rewritten the dialogue. See if your way is more effective than ours.

> *Beth:* I'm heading out to have lunch with Lynn. I'll be back in about two hours. Do you need anything before I go?
> *Mom:* You're always leaving me alone! I want you to stay with me today. That's what I need.
> *Beth:* You've got to be kidding! Always leaving you alone? I spend most of my time with you. In fact, I don't have any time for myself.
> *Mom:* Time for yourself? How would you like to be in the condition I'm in? Then you'd realize that time for yourself isn't very important.
> *Beth:* Well, I'm not in your condition. I am healthy and normal, which means that I need to spend time with my friends and get away by myself sometimes. You're being unreasonable and selfish. I'm sick and tired of your attitude.
> *Mom:* One of these days when I'm gone, you'll feel sorry you didn't pay more attention to me!
> *Beth:* I'm going. Good-by!

Now, before reading further, rewrite this dialogue consistent with the three steps for conflict resolution presented above.

Here is one way the dialogue might go if Beth uses the techniques for conflict resolution.

> *Beth:* I'm heading out to have lunch with Lynn. I'll be back in about two hours. Do you need anything before I go?
> *Mom:* You're always leaving me alone! I want you to stay with me today. That's what I need.
> *Beth:* You're feeling lonely today?
> *Mom:* Lonely? Today? I'm always lonely, cooped up as I am.

Beth: It must be tough being ill and not able to go out as often as you'd like.

Mom: Tough? You'd better believe it! I'm getting sick and tired of it.

Beth: And I can help you feel better by spending more time with you?

Mom: Yes, you could.

Beth: I feel frustrated at times too. I feel cooped up taking care of you. Not that I don't want to or that I don't feel honored to be able to help you, but at times it is just too much for me. At those times, I need to get out and be with my friends.

Mom: I can sure understand that, but it doesn't help me out much.

Beth: It sounds as if you need to have someone to be with you more often, and I need to get out periodically. Let's see if we can find a way to satisfy us both—to have someone with you more often and to let me get out when I need to. We could hire someone to come in and spend time with you every couple of days.

Mom: Maybe we can schedule times of the week to plan on being together. That way I'll know when to expect your company, and you can schedule around our times together.

Beth: And you could join a regularly scheduled activity at the senior citizens' center—and while you're there, I can go out with my friends.

Mom: Maybe we could ask another relative to visit me more often so you can get out.

Beth: Those are all good solutions. Which one should we try first?

In our rewritten dialogue, we've tried to show that both Beth and her mother have legitimate needs that can be met concurrently. When this technique for resolving conflicts is used, the relationship becomes better, because both people listen and demonstrate that they are concerned enough about each other to try to help satisfy these important needs.

Keep in mind that the purpose of this technique is *not* to convince someone that your point of view is correct. It is not a technique for manipulation. The intention is to find an *alternative* solution that makes both you and the other person happy. A student of mine asked, "What happens if I use the steps you outlined and my daughter says, 'There you go with that psychology crap again'? What do I do then?" I told her to tell her daughter, "You're right. This is something I learned at school to help resolve conflict. I love you, and I value our relationship, so I decided to try this technique. I hope we can both use it so that when we disagree we can come to a solution both of us are happy with. Would you like me to teach it to you?" How can anyone object to the use of a system designed to help find a solution satisfactory to both parties in a conflict and, at the same time, help maintain an important relationship?

There are probably some conflicts that you can anticipate, perhaps between you and the person for whom you care. Why not try to achieve positive resolution of those conflicts rather than give in or be so stubborn that, although you get your way, you're not happy? Why not try a system that lets both you and the other person win? Anticipating that conflict, on a separate sheet of paper, write a dialogue reflecting the way you'd like to see it resolved.

Next, rehearse the dialogue.

Now, when the conflict presents itself, you will be ready to resolve it so that both you and the other person are satisfied and, as a result, your relationship improves.

Assertiveness

Before we begin a discussion of assertiveness and its relationship to caregiving, let's assess how assertively you usually act. For each statement below, write in the number on the scale which best represents how characteristic that statement is of you:

+3 = very characteristic of you, extremely descriptive
+2 = rather characteristic of you, quite descriptive
+1 = somewhat characteristic of you, slightly descriptive
−1 = somewhat uncharacteristic of you, slightly nondescriptive
−2 = rather uncharacteristic of you, quite nondescriptive
−3 = very uncharacteristic of you, extremely nondescriptive

_____ 1. Most people seem to be more aggressive than I am.
_____ 2. I have hesitated to make or accept dates because of shyness.
_____ 3. When the food served at a restaurant is not done to my satisfaction, I complain about it to the waiter or waitress.
_____ 4. I am careful to avoid hurting other people's feelings, even when I feel that I have been injured.

_____ 5. If a salesperson goes to considerable trouble to show me merchandise that is not quite suitable, I have a difficult time saying no.

_____ 6. When I am asked to do something, I insist upon knowing why.

_____ 7. There are times when I look for a good, vigorous argument.

_____ 8. I strive to get ahead as much as most people in my position.

_____ 9. To be honest, people often take advantage of me.

_____ 10. I enjoy starting conversations with new acquaintances and strangers.

_____ 11. I often don't know what to say to attractive persons of the opposite sex.

_____ 12. I will hesitate to make phone calls to business establishments and institutions.

_____ 13. I would rather apply for a job or for admission to a college by writing letters than by going through interviews.

_____ 14. I find it embarrassing to return merchandise.

_____ 15. If a close and respected relative were annoying me, I would smother my feelings rather than express my annoyance.

_____ 16. I have avoided asking questions for fear of sounding stupid.

_____ 17. During an argument I am sometimes afraid I will get so upset that I will shake all over.

_____ 18. If a famed and respected lecturer makes a statement that I think is incorrect, I will let the audience hear my view as well.

_____ 19. I avoid arguing over prices with clerks and salespeople.

_____ 20. When I have done something important or worthwhile, I manage to let others know about it.

_____ 21. I am open and frank about my feelings.

_____ 22. If someone has been spreading false and negative stories about me, I see him (her) as soon as possible.

_____ 23. I often have a hard time saying no.

_____ 24. I tend to bottle up my emotions rather than make a scene.

_____ 25. I complain about poor service in a restaurant and elsewhere.

_____ 26. When I am given a compliment, I sometimes just don't know what to say.

_____ 27. If a couple near me in a theater or at a lecture were conversing loudly, I would ask them to be quiet or to take their conversation elsewhere.

_____ 28. Anyone attempting to push ahead of me in a line is in for a good battle.

_____ 29. I am quick to express an opinion.

_____ 30. There are times when I just can't say anything.

To score this scale, reverse the signs (+ and −) before your answers to items 1, 2, 4, 5, 9, 11, 12, 13, 14, 15, 16, 17, 19, 23, 24, 26, and 30. Then total the minuses and the pluses as they *now* are and subtract to find the difference between the two. For example, if your pluses add up to +60 and your minuses add up to −45, your score is +15; if your pluses add up to +60 and your minuses add up to −80, your score is −20. Positive (plus) scores mean that you generally act assertively, and minus scores mean that you generally act nonassertively. The higher the score, the more assertive; the lower the score, the more nonassertive. We will soon make sense of these concepts for you, but first let's listen in on Gladys's phone call.

Ring! Gladys picks up the telephone to hear the dulcet sounds of her friend Sue. "Gladys, I have an appointment for lunch. Can you watch Billy from noon until three?"

"Sure, Sue. Take your time and enjoy yourself. I'll expect you at noon." But in Gladys's mind another conversation is being recorded: "I don't believe that Sue! She's always asking me to watch her kid. What am I, a babysitter? I was looking forward to playing tennis with Joan today. Well, there goes that idea!"

This scenario is not atypical and not exclusive to women. Men and women who find it difficult to say no when asked by the boss to handle one more chore or responsibility have the same problem Gladys does.

Before we proceed, then, some definitions are necessary:

- *Assertive behavior:* expressing yourself, satisfying your own needs, and not hurting others in the process. Feeling good about this.
- *Nonassertive behavior:* denying your own wishes to satisfy someone else's. Sacrificing your own needs to meet someone else's needs.
- *Aggressive behavior:* seeking to dominate or to get your own way at the expense of others.

In the phone conversation described above, Gladys was nonassertive. She put aside her need for recreation and did not express her feeling of being used and taken advantage of by Sue.

If she had been aggressive, Gladys might have said, "How dare you ask me to watch that brat of yours? I have more important things to do. You're selfish and self-centered. When was the last time you watched *my* children?" Acting aggressively, Gladys would have denied Sue's right to ask a favor of her. Gladys would have fulfilled her own needs but would have done so in a manner that was unfair to Sue. Sue has the right to ask, and Gladys should not deny that right.

However, Gladys owns her own behavior. She has the right to say no. In a more assertive response to Sue's request, Gladys might have replied, "I can appreciate your need for someone to watch Billy, but I've been so busy lately that I promised myself today I wouldn't take on any commitments. I really need some recreation time, so I'm going to play tennis with Joan. Perhaps Mary is free to watch Billy. Do you have her phone number?"

If you act assertively, you are usually meeting your needs while maintaining effective interpersonal relationships. If you act nonassertively, you are not satisfying your needs, and those unsatisfied needs will create stress. If you behave aggressively, your needs are met at the expense of your relationships with others. Poor interpersonal relationships make you feel alone, as though no one can share either the frustrations or the joys of your caregiving.

Assertion theory presumes that every person has certain basic rights. Unfortunately, we are often taught that acting consistently with our rights is socially or morally unacceptable. Certain attitudes taught to us in childhood can stay with us as adults and interfere with our ability to exercise these basic rights. These attitudes violate our rights, and we must discard them. Your basic human rights include the following:

You have a right to put yourself first sometimes.
You have a right to your feelings.
You have a right to your own viewpoints.
You have a right to protest unfair treatment or criticism.
You have a right to ignore the advice of others.
You have a right to say no.
You have a right to be alone.
You have a right not to have to justify yourself to others.

Verbal Assertiveness

Unwilling to deny your basic human rights, you may choose to become more assertive. An assertive response is made up of four components:

Describe the Situation

Paint a verbal picture of the other person's behavior or the situation to which you are reacting. Often such a statement will begin with the word "when." Be sure to use "I" statements or neutral descriptions of the situation rather than to criticize the other person's behavior.

State Your Feelings

Relate your feelings about the other person's behavior or about the situation you have just described. Again, use "I" statements here: "I feel. . . ."

Identify the Change You Would Like

Be specific by identifying several ways you would like the other person's behavior or the situation to change. Rather than saying, "You should . . .," again use "I" statements: "I would prefer . . . ," "I would like . . . ," "I want. . . ."

Expected Consequences

Select the consequences you will apply to the behavior or situation. What will you do if the other person's behavior or the situation changes to your satisfaction? "If you do, I will. . . ." What are the consequences if nothing changes, or if the changes do not meet your needs? "If you don't, I will. . . ."

To demonstrate how to organize an assertive response, let's use the situation we described earlier: A woman's boss has been requiring her to work not only Monday through Friday but also on Saturday. An assertive response to this situation would be as follows:

> (*Describe the Situation*) When I am expected to work six days a week, (*State Your Feelings*) I feel tired and abused. (*Identify the Change You Would Like*) I would prefer working only Monday through Friday. (*Expected Consequences*) If I am scheduled to work only those five days, I will be conscientious about doing my work well and finishing it on time. If need be, I'll work through some lunch hours, stay later when necessary, or take some work home.

However, if I'm required to work on Saturdays, I will resign and look for another job. That is how strongly I feel about my right to have the weekends for myself.

Organize your own assertive response! Think of a situation related to your caregiving that has been of concern to you and for which an assertive response would be helpful. Below, write in what you would say if you responded assertively.

(Describe the Situation) _____

_____

_____

(State Your Feelings) _____

_____

_____

(Identify the Change You Would Like) _____

_____

_____

(Expected Consequences) _____

_____

_____

_____

Nonverbal Assertiveness

Assertiveness is not a matter only of *what* you say but also of *how* you say it. Even if you make an assertive verbal response, you will not be believed if your body language is nonassertive. To express yourself assertively:

1. Stand straight and steady, directly face the person to whom you are speaking, and maintain eye contact.
2. Speak in a clear, steady voice, loud enough for the person to hear you.
3. Speak fluently, without hesitation, and with assurance and confidence.

Stop for a moment and practice assertive *nonverbal* behavior as you recite the assertive response you wrote in earlier.

In Conclusion

Using the communication, conflict resolution, and assertiveness methods presented in this chapter, you can be a better caregiver. You will respond to more than the medical needs of the person for whom you are caring while ensuring that your own needs and those of other members of your family are met. And all the while you will be maintaining positive relationships with the people who are important to you. Practice these skills; they are extremely valuable!

6

Death and Dying

Fathers and sons. I thought I knew what that relationship meant after forty-three years of life—forty-three years with Dad. I remembered my father teaching me to ride a bicycle and placing the obligatory Band-Aid on my scrapes. I often crashed into the small iron chain protecting unsuspecting picnickers from people like me. Dad laughed, straightened the handlebars, and encouraged me to risk life and limb again.

Now the tables were turned. Dad lay in a hospital bed recovering from a stroke that had occurred on the very morning he was scheduled for quadruple bypass surgery. Now it was I who encouraged him—encouraged him to eat, to use his right hand, and to keep trying to communicate until he was understood.

Years ago Dad had helped me summon up the courage to protect myself against Butch, the neighborhood bully. Butch picked on me unmercifully, and finally Dad had had enough. To me, staying indoors when Butch was outdoors seemed an acceptable compromise. But my father insisted that I stand up for my rights. With courage instilled by Dad, one day I ventured into the courtyard while it was still occupied by Butch. Somehow Butch seemed to know I was coming, for he waited with hands on hips and a scowl on his face. As Dad watched from our apartment window, Butch started pushing me around, and I, with very little confidence but a great deal of bravado, found myself swinging my right fist toward Butch's left eye. To my amazement, knuckle found flesh and Butch reeled backward! More shocked than hurt, Butch nevertheless decided not to pick on Dad's son again.

Now I tried to help my father summon up *his* courage. He had to swing at his own "Butch"—his frustration at being able to think but not to express his thoughts, at being able to hear but not always to understand. I watched from a chair beside his bed, just as he had watched from our apartment window many years ago. I shouted encouragement to him as he had shouted to me. I held Dad's hand when the laboratory technicians drew blood or changed the I.V. Now it was I who stroked his forehead to calm him rather than the other way around. Just as he had tiptoed into my room when I was an infant to see if I was okay, I now checked to make sure that his chest was rising when he slept a little too silently for my comfort. I called the nurses to change his urine-soaked sheets as he had once called my mother to do the same for me.

When Dad's anguish surfaced at having come so close to obtaining the surgery he so badly needed, I felt that anguish. When Dad held me and thanked me for being with him, we both cried. And when one of us feared what the future might bring, the other sensed that fear as well.

I slept in his hospital room, offering the only things I could: my time, my love, my attention. The nurses, doctors, and technicians were terrific—most of them. The hospital staff were very caring—most of them. So I kept my evening vigil because of those exceptions. And because it was all I could do. And because Dad deserved it.

On one such evening I learned an important lesson. The nurse came to change my father's bedding just as I was placing together the four chairs that made up my bed. I watched to see whether she was one of the caring ones or an exception. As she fluffed up the pillows and tenderly covered Dad, all of a sudden my father incoherently, yet understandably, ordered her to find a pillow and a blanket for his son who was spending the night. In spite of his incapacitation, Dad was still watching over me. In spite of his dependence, Dad would make sure I had a pillow on which to rest my head. In spite of his own precarious state, Dad would ensure my warmth with a blanket and his caring and his love.

So we sat watching over each other, comforted by our closeness. Occasionally we hugged and cried, occasionally we laughed; but always we protected each other from life's uncaring exceptions.

Dad eventually had his bypass surgery, but unfortunately he suffered another stroke. It was only a couple of weeks afterward that he died.

That experience brought home what I had previously written about from a psychological distance: the need to prepare for death and to take as much control as possible of the dying process. This chapter aims to guide you in helping your loved one organize for death—an eventuality that we will all face.

Legal Papers

It is advisable to have certain legal papers in order long before death is anticipated. These include a will, a living will, a power of attorney (particularly for health matters), an organ donor card if one chooses to donate organs, and instructions regarding funeral and burial arrangements.

The Will

A proper will requires the assistance of an attorney. Without a will, your loved one will die *intestate*, meaning that the state will divide up the estate according to its laws rather than to the wishes of the person who has died. Dying without a will may also have tax implications, especially if there is no surviving spouse. In preparing a will, one must consider certain key issues.

1. *An executor should be chosen carefully.* The executor makes all decisions about the estate. Consequently, this person's ability to make wise decisions is vital. If the estate is under $600,000 (including life insurance policies, bank deposits, stock certificates, real estate, etc.), a relative may be chosen as the executor. However, if the estate is larger than that, it is recommended that a professional executor (for example, an attorney or banker) be hired.
2. *All assets should be specifically designated.* If jewelry is part of the estate, for example, and one desires to leave specific pieces to specific survivors, the jewelry and the persons to whom they are left should be identified in the will. If the will is not specific, the wishes of the deceased may be ignored, and the family may argue over the disposition of jewelry, furniture, sentimental objects, and the like.
3. *Beneficiaries of retirement programs and life insurance policies should be periodically verified.* Too often people do not recheck the beneficiaries listed on these instruments. In some cases, an ex-spouse acquires the assets because he or she is still the listed beneficiary.
4. *Keep the will in a safe place.* A safety deposit box is useful for

this purpose. Family members should know where the will is kept.

5. *Review the will regularly.* There may be reasons to change parts of the will. Perhaps new assets have been acquired, or there has been a change of wishes regarding the disposition of previously identified assets. Perhaps the tax laws have changed.

6. *Destroy previous wills.* This should be done to prevent any confusion about which will is current. *All* copies of old wills should be destroyed.

7. *Burial instructions should **not** be included as part of the will.* Since the will is usually read only after the burial, burial instructions should be kept separate but accessible to the family, who should know where to find them.

Living Will

Medical science has developed numerous technologies for prolonging life. There are respirators to maintain breathing, heart-lung machines to keep the heart beating and the blood circulating, and tubes inserted through the nose into the alimentary canal to feed patients unable to eat or drink. Some people argue that to be kept barely alive in this fashion is not to be "alive" at all. They would prefer to die as painlessly and in as dignified a manner as possible and do not wish their physicians to resort to last-minute "heroic" medical procedures. It is everyone's right to make that decision. However, if a patient is incapacitated—for instance, in a coma—and such a decision must be made—usually by the patient's family—a problem may arise. Since medical professionals are obligated by law and ethical codes to work to keep patients alive, they may hesitate to forego any actions to prolong life—even a comatose life—or perform any actions to shorten life (such as taking a patient off a respirator when the prognosis is that the patient will not be able to breath on his or her own).

If your loved one wishes not to prolong life with heroic medical procedures—some of which are painful, embarrassing, or costly—he or she should consider filing a *living will.* A living will is a written statement made by the care-receiver and witnessed by someone else; it instructs doctors not to use life-prolonging medical procedures when the person's condition is hopeless and there is no chance of regaining a meaningful life. A sample living will is presented in figure 6.1.

Modifications of this will can be made as one wishes. For example, your loved one might want to cross out words referring to

Figure 6.1: Living Will Declaration

To My Family, Doctors, and All Those Concerned with My Care

I, _____, being of sound mind, make this statement as a directive to be followed if for any reason I become unable to participate in decisions regarding my medical care.

I direct that life-sustaining procedures should be withheld or withdrawn if I have an illness, disease, injury, or extreme mental deterioration, such that there is no reasonable expectation of recovering or regaining a meaningful quality of life.

These life-sustaining procedures that may be withheld or withdrawn include, but are not limited to:

SURGERY   CARDIAC RESUSCITATION
RESPIRATORY SUPPORT   ARTIFICIALLY ADMINISTERED FEEDING AND FLUIDS
ANTIBIOTICS

I further direct that treatment be limited to comfort measures only, even if they shorten my life.

You may delete any provision above by drawing a line through it and adding your initials.

Other personal instructions:

These directions express my legal right to refuse treatment. Therefore, I expect my family, doctors, and all those concerned with my care to regard themselves as legally and morally bound to act in accord with my wishes, and in so doing to be free from any liability for having followed my directions.

Signed _____Date _____
Witness _____Witness _____

Proxy Designation Clause

If you wish, you may use this section to designate someone to make treatment decisions if you are unable to do so. Your Living Will Declaration will be in effect even if you have not designated a proxy.

I authorize the following person to implement my Living Will Declaration by accepting, refusing, and/or making decisions about treatment and hospitalization:
Name _____
Address _____

If the person I have named above is unable to act on my behalf, I authorize the following person to do so:
Name _____
Address _____

I have discussed my wishes with these persons and trust their judgment on my behalf.
Signed _____Date _____
Witness _____Witness _____

Courtesy of Society for the Right to Die, 250 West 57th Street, New York, NY 10107.

any life-sustaining procedures that she or he would like the doctors to try. "Comfort measures" referred to in the sample living will are medication, nursing care, and other treatments administered to keep a patient as comfortable and free from pain as possible. One section of the living will (designated "other personal instructions") allows it to be personalized with additional instructions. The living will should be signed and dated, witnessed by two people who are not blood relatives or beneficiaries identified in your property will, and renewed each year.

Some people may also want to include a "proxy designation clause" as part of their living will. This clause identifies someone who can make medical decisions in accordance with the wishes of the person signing the living will if that person is unable to make those decisions for him- or herself.

Once the living will is completed, several copies should made: one for the caregiver, one for the care-receiver's doctor to keep in his or her medical file, and one for the care-receiver's file of personal papers. In addition, a reduced copy should be kept in the care-receiver's wallet. Keeping the living will in a safety deposit box is not recommended, since it may not be readily available when needed.

Living wills are recognized by most states as representative of a person's wishes and are, therefore, legally binding. However, the specific form appearing in figure 6.1 may not be binding in your state. You can obtain your state's legally binding form by requesting one from The Society for the Right to Die, 250 West 57th Street, New York, NY 10107.

By the way, the fact that someone has a living will does not affect his or her life insurance coverage. Signing a living will, or terminating artificial life-prolonging treatment, is not considered suicide and will not negate an insurance company's obligation to pay on a life insurance policy.

Durable Power of Attorney

Living wills do have drawbacks. First, they are not uniform. As stated above, you must obtain your state's particular form. Second, they refer exclusively to the withholding of treatment and do not address the right to have treatment when that is appropriate. Third, some state laws require living wills to be reaffirmed periodically (something people may forget to do), other states require that the person be told that his or her condition is terminal before the living will can apply, and in still other states (five at last count) the living will must be filed with the court. Further, except in a few states, living wills cannot be written for a child or an incompetent adult.

These drawbacks have led experts to recommend the filing of a *durable power of attorney* instead of or in conjunction with a living will. The durable power of attorney can apply when a person is not terminally ill but temporarily incapacitated, protects a person's right to *have treatment* as well as to have it withheld, and avoids the need to anticipate all possible situations in which sensitive medical decisions might have to be made.

A *power of attorney* is a written instrument of agreement authorizing a person to act as the agent or attorney for another person. With the addition of the words "This power of attorney shall not be affected by my subsequent disability or incapacity," a durable power of attorney is created. Another option is the *durable power of attorney for health care decisions,* which limits a person's authorization to make decisions for another person to matters related to health. An example of a durable power of attorney for health care decisions appears in figure 6.2. An attorney should be consulted to ensure that the durable power of attorney is valid in your state.

Organ Donor Cards

In 1987 approximately 11,000 organ transplants were done in the United States; however, there were 13,000 people on waiting lists to receive organs. This 13,000-figure is considered low, since many potential recipients, knowing that organs are scarce, do not add their names to waiting lists. The shortage of organs for transplant is reflected in the following figures for 1987:

1. *Heart:* 1,512 transplanted, 900 persons on waiting list
2. *Liver:* 1,182 transplanted; 500 on waiting list
3. *Pancreas:* 127 transplanted; 100 on waiting list
4. *Heart-lung:* 43 transplanted; 200 on waiting list

There may be religious or other reasons the care-receiver does not want to donate organs upon her or his death (for example, orthodox Jewish law prohibits mutilation of the body, and thus organ donations and autopsies are forbidden). However, if the person for whom you provide care chooses to donate certain organs, an *organ donation card* should be completed and the family should be notified of this desire. An example of a uniform donor card appears in figure 6.3; such cards can be obtained from the National Kidney

Figure 6.2: Durable Power of Attorney for Health Care Decisions

---

I, (*your name*), hereby appoint: (*name, address, and phone numbers*) as my attorney in fact to make health care decisions for me if I become unable to make my own health care decisions. This gives my attorney in fact the power to grant, refuse, or withdraw consent on my behalf for any health care service, treatment, or procedure. My attorney in fact also has the authority to talk to health care personnel, get information, and sign forms necessary to carry out these decisions.

If the person named as my attorney in fact is not available or is unable to act as my attorney in fact, I appoint the following persons to serve in the order listed below:

(*Names, addresses, phone numbers of two persons*)

With this document, I intend to create a power of attorney for health care, which shall take effect if I become incapable of making my own health care decisions and shall continue during that incapacity.

My attorney in fact shall make health care decisions as I direct below or as I make known to my attorney in fact in some other way.

(a) Statement of directives concerning life-prolonging care, treatment, services, and procedures:

(b) Special provisions and limitations:

By my signature I indicate that I understand the purpose and effect of this document. I sign my name to this form on (*date*), at (*address*).

(*Your signature*)

Witnesses
I declare that the person who signed or acknowledged this document is personally known to me, that the person signed or acknowledged this durable power of attorney for health care in my presence, and that the person appears to be of sound mind and under no duress, fraud, or undue influence. I am not the person appointed as the attorney in fact by this document, nor am I the health care provider to the principal or an employee of the health care provider of the principal.

(*Date, signatures, and printed names and addresses of two witnesses*)

At least one of the witnesses listed above shall also sign the following declaration:

I further declare that I am not related to the principal by blood, marriage, or adoption, and, to the best of my knowledge, I am not entitled to any part of the estate of the principal under a currently existing will or by operation of law.

(*Signatures*)

Figure 6.3: Sample Uniform Donor Card

Print or type name of donor

In the hope that I may help others, I hereby make this anatomical gift, if medically acceptable, to take effect upon my death. The words and marks below indicate my desires.

I give: (a) _____ any needed organs or parts

(b) _____ only the following organs or parts

Specify the organ(s) or part(s)

for the purposes of transplantation, therapy, medical research, or education:

(c) _____ my body for anatomical study if needed.

Limitations or
special wishes, if any: _____
- -
Signed by the donor and the following two witnesses in one another's presence:

Signature of Donor	*Date of Birth of Donor*
Date Signed	*City and State*
Witness	*Witness*

This is a legal document under the Uniform Anatomical Gift Act or similar laws.

Foundation or your local motor vehicle bureau. The card should be copied, with one copy kept in the care-receiver's wallet and another copy with the care-receiver's personal papers. For many people, knowing that their death may mean that others can live is very comforting.

Other Important Papers

In addition to a will, a living will, a durable power of attorney, and an organ donation card, there are other papers and documents which the care-receiver should have in order and whose location the care-giver should know. These include:

1. Funeral and burial instructions (discussed in detail below)
2. Names, addresses, and telephone numbers of persons to be notified in case of death
3. Copies of trusts
4. Military papers
5. Marriage certificate
6. Birth certificate
7. Divorce or separation papers
8. Names, addresses, and telephone numbers of advisers such as clergy, attorney, banker, accountant, stockbroker, financial adviser, and insurance agent
9. Bank account numbers, location, and names of people authorized to sign
10. Safety deposit box location and list of its contents
11. Credit card numbers and billing address(es)
12. Stocks and bonds (names and numbers)
13. Other assets such as certificates of deposit, individual retirement accounts, and profit-sharing plans
14. Outstanding loans
15. Accounts, loans, and notes receivable with pertinent documents
16. Income tax returns for the preceding two years
17. Real estate holdings with loan information
18. Automobile information such as the make, model, license plate number, and location of title
19. Insurance policies with name and address of agent(s)

Having this information available in a central location will prevent confusion and frustration for the care-receiver's family. Documents should be stored in a safe place; a safety deposit box will serve this purpose. However, since a safety deposit box may be sealed upon the care-receiver's death, or the death may occur on a Friday night when the bank is closed, copies should be kept in a location to which the family has ready access.

Talking about Death

Perhaps the most important action caregivers and care-receivers can take is to discuss the inevitability of death. This discussion is often initially difficult and disturbing, but it can prove extremely meaningful. It allows adherence to the wishes of the care-receiver and lessens the confusion and frustration that often plague a family after the death of a loved one.

There are several reasons that discussing death is usually difficult. First, when a loved one dies, part of us also dies. We cannot rely on that person any longer, see that person again, or care for that person as we have done for so long. Second, a loved one's death forces us to confront our own mortality. Although there is no guarantee that our parents' deaths will precede ours, we usually expect that they will. When they do die, we are no longer insulated from death; our buffer is gone. We are next, so to speak. Because of our attitudes about death, we shy away from even mentioning the word and, instead, use euphemisms—"departed," "gone," "lost," "passed on," or "at rest." The result is what one author calls a "conspiracy of silence."

This is unfortunate, because there are many benefits derived from engaging in an open dialogue about death. Such a dialogue can reassure the care-receiver that his or her funeral and burial wishes are known and will be respected. Further, it provides an opportunity to articulate the significance of the care-receiver's life and of the influence that life will exert even beyond death. It also authorizes the care-receiver to share feelings about dying—feelings such as fear, or concern for surviving family members, and worry about those who will mourn the death when it does occur. In addition, discussing death and dying gives the care-receiver the comfort of knowing that the physician and other health care providers are sympathetic to his or her wishes regarding where death should occur (for example, in the home or the hospital) and what medical procedures should and should not be used. You see, it isn't only the family that should be involved. Health care providers should also participate in these discussions, even though many of them are not trained to do so.

A word of caution here: Often the elderly are willing to talk about death but are cut short by their friends and family. Remarks such as "I'm not going to be around forever" too often receive a response such as, "Oh, you'll probably outlive all of us." How many times have you heard an older person say something like, "When I'm gone I would like you to visit my grave on my birthday," only to hear a son or daughter remark, "We have plenty of time to consider that"? These statements by elders are attempts to face the reality of death and to help others do the same. To respond in a way that sidetracks these attempts is to act selfishly.

Here is an example of a more appropriate response: "I know you won't be around forever, and I have a lot of feelings about that. Let me share them with you, you can share your feelings with me." A good way to approach these situations is to accept the feelings and concerns of the care-receiver and ask for more information about them. Do not deny or criticize any feelings expressed. It's okay to feel fear, confusion, or any other emotion. Your role is to encourage the expression of these feelings and to offer any solace you can, realizing that often all you can do is express accessibility, since you can't control or prevent death or the feelings associated with dying. Just being available to discuss these feelings with your loved one will be welcomed.

Stages of Dying

If you can anticipate what a dying loved one can expect, you will be better prepared to recognize and respond to the stages of the dying process. The work of Elisabeth Kübler-Ross is often used as a guide to the stages of dying. Kübler-Ross identified five phases that most dying people experience: *denial* of impending death, *anger* at having to die, *bargaining* (for example, "If I could have one more month I'd spend it doing good"), *depression*, and finally, *acceptance* of death.

At the denial stage, you can help by discussing the medical evidence. Perhaps a second opinion will verify the care-receiver's condition. You can also acknowledge the value of denial as a protective device: "It must be difficult to accept that you're going to die."

At the anger stage, you can let your loved one know that she or he has a right to be angry and that the anger has an outlet; it will be encouraged, not suppressed. After all, wouldn't you be angry if you learned that your life would soon end?

Bargaining is a way of staving off the inevitable. Death is imminent regardless of any deals the care-receiver makes, and you must help him or her realize this: "I wish I could give one month of my life so you could live that much longer, but unfortunately neither of us can make such a deal." Such statements will help the care-receiver recognize the futility of bargaining.

Depression, too, is understandable. As with anger, the care-receiver should be encouraged to discuss feelings of depression, and these emotions should be accepted. Too often expressions of depression are denied by the family: "Come on, you don't really feel like that." It is better to acknowledge these feelings: "What a heavy burden you must bear. I can understand why you're feeling depressed. I'm sure I would too. Do you want to talk about it?"

Acceptance of death is the goal of the terminally ill. For those who reach this point, caregivers should be ready to help them organize their affairs so that they feel everything is in order.

These stages are guidelines. People move through them at different rates, move back and forth between stages, or do not go through all of them. The implication, though, is that dying people need different types of communication and relationships at different stages. Help your loved one through these stages by listening to her or him, encouraging open discussions and expressions of feelings, and respecting her or his special needs.

Needs of the Dying

Brent Hafen, a thanatologist (an expert on death and dying) has described the needs of dying people as follows:

1. The need to live to the end with dignity.
2. The need for hope; not necessarily the hope of preserving life, but the hope that accompanies faith and meaningful living.
3. The need to work through and ventilate feelings of guilt, denial, jealousy, anguish, and other emotions.
4. The need to be listened to without censure or anger and to be accepted, regardless of the use of defense mechanisms that may be bothersome to others.
5. The need to feel valued as a person.
6. The need to give and to be given to long after one is able to give.
7. The need to be remembered.
8. The need to function at some level, even if it is only to decide what to have for dinner.
9. The need for meaningful communication (verbal and nonverbal).
10. The need to maintain self-confidence, security, and self-esteem.
11. The need to receive "permission" from their loved ones to die.

If you keep these needs in mind when you interact with a dying loved one, you can better understand his or her actions and words and respond more helpfully.

Euthanasia

One need of some terminally ill people is to end their lives when they wish—usually short of extensive pain or disability. As you can imagine, this is controversial. Most of us would have great difficulty seeing a loved one end her or his life, even when that person has been in great pain. Death is so permanent! Nevertheless, when someone you love is in terrible discomfort, in a coma, or in some other situation she or he has difficulty defining as "living," and this condition is judged to be irreversible, you actually might consider a swift death to be in that person's best interest. Such an action is termed *euthanasia*.

Euthanasia is the putting to death, painlessly, of someone suffering from an incurable terminal condition. *Passive euthanasia* is the withholding of life-supporting treatments or measures to prolong life. Such withholding of treatment accelerates dying "naturally." Examples of passive euthanasia include the decision not to put someone on a respirator to maintain breathing and/or not to insert a feeding tube for nourishment. *Active euthanasia* is altogether different. It is an action taken to cause someone's death. Periodically we read of a distraught spouse who, following the wishes of his or her loved one, takes such action. A lethal dose of medication may be injected or a deadly poison placed in the spouse's drink. This is against he law, and people who have responded to their spouses' pain in this way have been prosecuted.

Many Americans oppose the active taking of life, but most support some form of passive euthanasia. If you and the person for whom you provide care agree that certain medical procedures should be withheld under certain circumstances, you must clearly state what those circumstances are and include them in the living will. In addition, you must be sure that your physician will accept these conditions. "The withholding of medical treatment" is not an excuse for providing suboptimal medical care nor is cost of care a justification for accelerating death.

Having faced such a situation with my father, I do not write of this subject lightly.

Grief and Mourning

When the death of a loved one occurs, a predictable process of grief commences. Even when the death is expected or even welcomed because of the pain or discomfort the loved one has suffered, it is still traumatic for the family. Although the exact nature of any one person's grief can differ markedly from another's, grief usually occurs in several stages. These are described in table 6.1. Each of these stages is necessary, and together they serve to return the grieving person to a normal life.

The first stage is shock and disbelief. The grieving person may feel numb and may weep for several days after the death. The second stage is a sense of profound sadness and longing for the de-

Table 6.1
Stages of Ordinary Grief

Timetable	Manifestations
Stage 1	
Begins immediately after death; lasts 1–3 days	Shock, disbelief, denial, numbness, weeping, agitation
Stage 2	
Peaks 2–4 weeks after death; begins to subside after 3 months; lasts up to one year	Painful longing, preoccupation, memories, mental images of the deceased, sense of the deceased being present, sadness, tearfulness, insomnia, loss of appetite, loss of interest, irritability, restlessness
Stage 3	
Usually occurs within a year after death	Resolution, decreasing episodes of sadness, ability to recall the past with pleasure, resumption of ordinary activities

ceased. The grieving person may be preoccupied with thoughts of the deceased and may even sense the presence of the dead person. Sadness, crying, loss of appetite, apathy, and difficulty in sleeping all characterize the second stage of grief. In the third stage, the grieving person becomes more accustomed to the reality of the death, and fewer episodes of sadness occur. This stage marks a return to normal activities, and the bereaved person learns to live with the loss of the loved one.

Psychologists recommend three steps for working out grief:

1. Face up to the death. Do not deny it or its impact.
2. Break bonds with the deceased (for example, dispose of his or her clothing).
3. Seek new interests, activities, and relationships.

It is very important to manage the grieving process well, for an array of literature attests to the danger that illness and disease will strike people who are bereaved. For example, a study of 4,486 widowers age 55 and older, found a higher than expected mortality rate during the first 6 months of bereavement. When data were examined more closely, the cause of these unexpected deaths was determined to be heart disease. The phrase "broken heart" acquired

103

a new and more fatal meaning. Other researchers have found that widows and widowers who live alone have a particularly high chance of dying while grieving. As a caregiver knowing of this danger, you must provide the understanding and social support necessary for a widow or widower under your care to successfully complete the grieving process.

If the normal stages of grief are prolonged, seek professional help for your loved one. Psychologists are trained to counsel bereaved people; a sensitive physician can assist as can another widow or widower who will spend some time with the bereaved person. Yet there is no substitute for a caregiver who can listen well, who is empathic since he or she is sharing the grief, and who encourages the bereaved loved one to share his or her thoughts and feelings.

Funerals and Burial Arrangements

By the time a death occurs, funeral and burial arrangements should have been decided upon, so that all that needs to be done is to put them into place. Whatever the funeral and burial plans may be, they are as important for the bereaved as for the deceased. Whether holding a wake, "sitting shiva," or attending a memorial service, the family and group support given to those in mourning at this time is an important component of their healing process.

In the United States, most people choose burial as the means of disposing of the body. Although a growing number of people select cremation, most desire to preserve the remains and to mark the spot of burial for surviving family members. Another increasingly popular option is cremation followed by a memorial service, or a memorial service alone (for example, for soldiers declared missing in action whose bodies are not available for either burial or cremation).

Memorial services can take many forms. Some involve objects from the deceased's life. For example, at one memorial service a father stood in front of a painting by his deceased daughter and spoke about her love of art. Another alternative is to structure the service around the biography of the deceased. In this case the family might research phases of the deceased's life and make brief presentations during the service. Often this approach results in the family's learning things about their loved one that they would never have learned otherwise. Other memorial services include the Jewish practice of lighting a yahrzeit candle one year after the death and the Catholic tradition of offering an anniversary mass for the repose of the soul.

Given enough time for planning, any memorial service that meets the needs of both the deceased and the bereaved family members can be arranged. For example, if friends from across the country want to participate, the service must be scheduled to allow them travel time. If a history of the deceased is to be presented, time must be available to do some research. Within these limitations, however, are many possibilities:

If a funeral and burial are chosen, several decisions must be made including the following:

1. Which funeral home will be used?
2. In which cemetery will the deceased be buried?
3. Will a casket be used? If so, what kind (wood, metal)? At what cost? Will you use a grave liner (a concrete container that lines the grave to prevent the earth from caving in when the casket deteriorates) or a vault?
4. Where will the grave marker be purchased? Some cemeteries require that you purchase it from them; others do not, but may charge exorbitantly for installing it if it is purchased elsewhere. How much are you willing to spend on a grave marker? What should it say?
5. Should the deceased be embalmed (replacing the blood with various embalming fluids to make the body more presentable)? Some states require embalming under certain circumstances (for example, if the body is transported over state lines, if the person died of a communicable disease, or if the body is held for over twenty-four hours before burial or cremation and adequate refrigeration facilities are not available).

In the past there were many complaints that funeral home directors deceived grieving, vulnerable family members about funeral and burial arrangements, charging them excessive fees and encouraging them—by playing on guilt feelings or incorrectly relating state regulations—to pay for unnecessary services. In 1984 the Federal Trade Commission responded by requiring funeral directors to observe the following practices:

1. Give customers an itemized list of prices at the beginning of any discussion of funeral goods or services.
2. Disclose prices over the telephone when asked.

3. Tell customers that, in most cases, embalming is not legally required.
4. Disclose in writing any mark-ups imposed on "cash advance items" such as flowers and death notices.

In addition, funeral directors were forbidden to:

1. Tell customers that they need a casket if they want a "direct" cremation.
2. Tell customers that there is a legal requirement to buy an outside burial container for the casket—unless state or local law or a cemetery does in fact require this.
3. Tell customers that laws or cemetery or crematorium rules require them to buy a certain item or service—unless this is actually the case.
4. Claim that funeral goods (such as sealed caskets) or services (such as embalming) will delay a body's decomposition for a long, or indefinite, time after burial. Customers cannot be told that a casket or vault will protect a body from water, insects, and so forth unless that is true.

The penalty for violating any section of the FTC regulations is a ten thousand dollar fine.

Other Necessary Procedures Following a Death

In addition to these decisions, other actions need to be taken at the time of death. Family members must be notified, the appropriate clergy must be called, the death certificate must be signed, the mortuary must be requested to transport the body, and the life insurance agent must be notified.

You must also file for death benefits. Several organizations may need to be notified: for example, the Social Security Administration and the Veteran's Administration. In filing for these benefits you may need copies of the death certificate, the birth certificate, the social security number, the income tax returns for the past three years, the marriage license, divorce documents, military records, or an itemized bill of funeral expenses. Gathering as many of these documents as you can *prior* to the death and keeping them with the care-receiver's personal papers will make filing for benefits easier when the time comes.

In Conclusion

Death is inevitable. It is also traumatic, even when it is expected. However, you can plan for the death of the person for whom you care by discussing his or her feelings and wishes about death and dying; preparing appropriate legal papers such as a will, a living will, a durable power of attorney, and a uniform donor card; getting other papers in order; recognizing the stages of dying and the needs of dying people; understanding the process of grief and mourning; and making as many funeral and burial arrangements as possible ahead of time. Doing these things will make the death of your loved one less threatening to your own health and the health of your family. It will ensure that the care-receiver's wishes are honored and that his or her dying will have the meaning and significance it deserves.

People tend to ignore such a "touchy" topic as death, thinking that to raise it will agitate the care-receiver. We argue that *not* to raise it is to be unresponsive to the person for whom you are caring—unresponsive because that person is already thinking about dying and may need to discuss these thoughts and feelings with you. Be open to such discussions so that you and your loved one can reap their benefits.

7

Managing Stress

Once upon a time there was a science teacher who conducted demonstrations to help his students grasp scientific concepts. One day, to the students' surprise, the teacher's pocket made a gulping sound. After two and a half gulps, one freckle-faced, red-haired student asked what was in the pocket, and whether it always made that disgusting sound.

The teacher reached into his pocket and, in the midst of the next "gulp," presented a frog. Placing the frog on the desk, the teacher yelled, "Jump!" Instantly the frog jumped. Instructing the students to observe carefully, the teacher again shouted "Jump!"—and again the frog complied.

Then, reaching into his other pocket, the teacher produced a pair of scissors and, before anyone could object, proceeded to cut off the frog's legs. "Now, closely observe the frog's reaction," the teacher told his shocked students. "Jump!" he ordered—but the frog did not move.

Since the students' minds were still full of the sound of scissors-against-frog-leg, when he asked them to draw a conclusion from the experiment, they were at a loss. Disappointed but undaunted, the teacher drew the conclusion for them: "You see, when you cut off a frog's legs, it loses its hearing."

We will make better sense of scientific findings than this science teacher did. In this chapter we will describe "stress," discuss some of its potential consequences, and show you how to prevent stress from making you ill or interfering with other aspects of your life. Our conclusion—that stress, in particular stress associated with caregiving, is manageable once you learn the requisite skills—is more sensible than the science teacher's and can make you healthier and happier.

Stress: What Is It?

Picture this: You're walking down a dark alley at night, all alone, and you have forgotten your glasses. Halfway down the alley (at the point of no return) you spot a big, burly figure carrying a club and straddling your path. Besides the thought, "Woe is me," what happens within you? Your heart begins to pound and speed up, you seem unable to catch your breath, you begin to perspire, your muscles tense. Your body prepares itself, when confronted by a threat, to either stand and fight or to run away. In the alley, that response is invaluable, because you need to mobilize quickly for some kind of action. We'll soon see, though, that in most situations in today's society the fight-or-flight response is itself a threat to your health.

One way of defining stress is to divide it into two components: the stressor and the stress reactivity.

The Stressor

A stressor is a stimulus with the *potential* to trigger the fight-or-flight response. Our bodies were evolutionarily trained for stressors that threaten our safety. The caveman who met a lion looking for its next meal had to react quickly. Cavemen who were not fast enough or strong enough to respond to this threat didn't have to worry about the next one. They became lion lunches. The fight-or-flight response, the body's readiness for physical action, was necessary, and its rapidity was vital for survival.

Modern men and women also find comfort and safety in the fight-or-flight response. Periodically we read about some superhuman feat of strength in response to a stressor: a person lifts a heavy car off another person pinned under it. We attribute this strength to an increase in adrenaline, and it is true that adrenaline secretion increases as part of the fight-or-flight response.

Other stressors we encounter can elicit this same fight-or-flight response, even though it would be inappropriate to respond immediately with physical action. These stressors are emotional ones—for example, the loss of status, threats to self-esteem, work overload, or overcrowding. When the boss overloads you with work, it is dysfunctional to punch her or him and equally ridiculous to run away. In the same way, when you experience physiological and emotional arousal—muscle tension, increased heart rate, perspiration, frustration, and anger—in response to the daily hassles of caring for an elderly relative, neither fight nor flight seems appropriate; that is, neither one will help you fulfill your caregiving responsibilities.

Stress Reactivity

The fight-or-flight response is called *stress reactivity*. This reaction prepares you for swift action when such a response is warranted. As we have noted, these bodily changes are not always harmful and may, in fact, be helpful. It is when your body is prepared for physical action but it would be inappropriate actually to do something physical that you may be harmed by the stress response.

Stress

Now that you know what stressors and stress reactivity are, it is time to define stress itself. Stress is the combination of a *stressor* and *stress reactivity*. Without the combination of these components there is no stress.

A stressor simply has the *potential* for eliciting stress reactivity. For example, a married couple have a parent for whom they are caring at home, and on a given day they both must work late; when they finally get home in the evening they have an argument with their children. However, one of these people may interpret these events as especially stressful—"I don't have enough time to myself," "I have too many responsibilities," "Life is unfair"—whereas the other might appraise the situation quite differently—"I do have a lot of responsibilities, but that makes me feel needed and important," "It's a good feeling to know that others think they can rely on me." The point is that stress includes an external component (the stressor) but also an internal component (your interpretation of the stressor). Therefore, you can short-circuit the stress response by reappraising the stressor so as to make it less stressful. Later in the chapter we will further develop this notion.

A Model of Stress

Stress begins with a life situation that knocks you (gently or abruptly) out of balance. It may be the need to care for a relative at home, the death of a loved one, difficulty meeting expenses, or the frustration of trying to find support services to help with or provide guidance in meeting your caregiving responsibilities.

You bring an interpretation to this life situation. We call that your *cognitive appraisal*. As we have seen, this perception of the life situation can be either positive or negative. If the situation is perceived as distressing, emotional arousal will occur. That is, you will become angry, frustrated, anxious, or nervous. These emotions can result in the bodily changes (physiological arousal) described above as the fight-or-flight response. As we have already discussed, the body's preparation to do something physical can lead to ill health or other negative consequences if something physical is not done. Below is a model (figure 7.1) to help you understand this process better.

Let's follow a person down this model to demonstrate how it functions. Imagine that an unexpected medical expense arises as you care for your mother (Life Situation). Now imagine that you interpret this situation as extremely distressing, since you had planned on buying a new car to replace the jalopy that is currently smelling up your neighborhood every time you leave for work (Perceived as Distressing). Being unable to buy that new car makes you angry and frustrated, and you are anxious about your ability to meet the full costs of your mother's medical treatment (Emotional Arousal). As a result, your heart races, the muscles of your back and neck tense, and your breathing becomes rapid and shallow (Physiological Arousal). After a while, you develop headaches and backaches, argue with your spouse, and perform less well at work (Consequences).

Now, let's imagine that a friend experiences the same crisis but interprets it differently. He or she says something like, "It's unfortunate that these medical costs are necessary, because I really do need a new car, but providing for my mother comes first." Or, "I

Figure 7.1: A Model of Stress

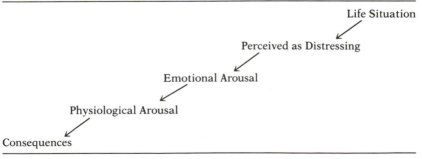

Life Situation

Perceived as Distressing

Emotional Arousal

Physiological Arousal

Consequences

really need a new car, but waiting another year will probably mean that I'll get a better car with better gas mileage and lower yearly upkeep." This different appraisal or interpretation means that emotional arousal will not occur, and physiological arousal and its negative consequences will also be curtailed. In other words, your friend's perception of the situation allows greater health and happiness for him or her.

Stress Management

Think of stress as a road that passes through the towns of Life Situation, Perception, Emotional Arousal, Physiological Arousal, and Consequences. As with other roads, we can set up roadblocks at various points to prevent anything from proceeding further. Stress management means setting up roadblocks along the course of stress, and the remainder of this chapter will show you how to create effective roadblocks. We will describe roadblocks to use at each point shown on the stress model, so that you can provide care while maintaining a manageable stress level. It doesn't make sense to become ill or to suffer other negative consequences if that is unnecessary, and the good news is that it *is* unnecessary.

Interventions as Roadblocks

Stress management interventions can occur at the life situation level, the perception level, the emotional arousal level, or the physiological level. We give examples of each below. Because of space limitations, however, only two examples of each type of intervention are provided. We encourage you to consider these merely as illustrations and to develop other roadblocks to use in managing the stress of caregiving.

Life Situation Interventions

Roadblocks at this level of the stress model require adjustments in your usual activities.

1. Support Groups
If you join a group of other caregivers with whom you can discuss your frustrations as well as your joys, you will be less likely to experience intense stress. Research reports are replete with findings that people can maintain physical and psychological health even in the face of extreme stress, if they have a social support group to

act as a buffer between the stress and its potential negative consequences. In Appendix 1A, we list support groups in more detail,
showing you how to find them, whether to join them, and what
functions they can serve. For now, let us say only that support
groups can be very effective life situation roadblocks.

2. Keeping a Diary (See figure 7.2)

It often helps to write down your feelings on a daily basis. The release is sometimes all you need to feel better. However, beyond
serving as a catharsis, a diary can help you assess the stressors you
experience and make changes in your life so that you experience
fewer of them in the future. To serve this function, the diary record
should have several components:

- *routine stressors*—experienced often
- *unique stressors*—seldom encountered
- *reactions to each stressor*—both physical and emotional reactions (for example, muscle tension or anger)
- *means of coping*—what you did at the time to manage the situation
- *better means of coping*—what you could have done that would
  have managed the situation better
- *relaxation methods tried*—what you did to try to relax that day
- *effectiveness of relaxation methods*—did they work? why? why
  not?
- *sensations experienced that day*—in your body (e.g., headache,
  stomachache) or in your mind (e.g., anxiety, insecurity)

At the end of each week reread your entries, searching for patterns and for changes you can make to reduce stress. Ask yourself
the following questions:

1. What stressors do I frequently experience?
2. Do I need or want to continue experiencing these stressors? If
   not, which can I eliminate?
3. How does my body typically react to stress?
4. How does my psyche (mind) typically respond to stress?
5. Can my body or mind's reactions to stress teach me ways to
   identify stress early so as to make it less harmful?
6. Are there certain coping techniques I use more than others?
   Are they effective? Do they work for or against me?
7. Are there coping techniques that I don't typically use but that

Figure 7.2: Daily Diary Form

Stressors	Reactions		Means of Coping	Means of Coping Better
	Physical	**Emotional**		
1. Routine				
a.				
b.				
2. Unique				
a.				
b.				

Relaxation Techniques Tried	**Effectiveness of Technique**
1.	
2.	
3.	

Sensations:

Body	Mind

would be helpful? How can I remember to use these techniques more often?

8. Are any particular relaxation techniques especially effective for me?
9. How can I organize my life to maximize relaxation?
10. Are there any body and/or mind sensations I usually experience either preceding or following stressful events? Are there ways to prevent these ailments from developing?
11. What will I *DO* as a result of what I've found out by keeping this diary? What adjustments will I make in my life? Whom else will I involve?

Keeping this diary can open your eyes to stressors to which you've become accustomed, to reactions that have become second nature but that are dysfunctional, and to means of coping at your disposal that are so far untapped.

Perception Interventions

Perception interventions require you to change your thoughts so that you can view stressors as less bothersome.

1. Selective Awareness

We are all free to choose what to think, although most of us don't exercise this control but, instead, allow our thoughts to ride the high seas rudderless. When we recognize that we are free to choose our thoughts and to focus our attention, we can take more control of that part of our lives. To take control of our thoughts, we employ "selective awareness." This technique requires us to focus on the good in the situation or the person. Once we learn to do that, we are healthier and we feel better.

I'm reminded of the story of the female college student who wrote to her parents, saying that she was in the hospital after a fall out of the third-floor window of her dormitory. She explained that she landed on the grass and, as a result, was only temporarily paralyzed. She noted that the good thing about her accident was that she met a hospital janitor with whom she had fallen in love. Because he was of a different ethnic and religious origin from hers and they knew this would alarm her parents, they had decided to elope rather than get married with their families present. She knew this marriage would work out, she said, since her future husband had learned from his prior marriage not to beat his wife when frustrated (it seems he had spent several years in prison because of his violent temper). Then she ended her letter by saying, "Mom and Dad, all of the above is untrue. I didn't fall out of the window, I'm not in a hospital paralyzed (not even temporarily), and I haven't met anyone I'm thinking of marrying. However, I am failing chemistry, and I wanted you to put that in its proper perspective."

This is selective awareness: putting things in their proper perspective. In every situation good and bad coexist. Some people are fortunate in that they naturally focus on the good, while others must work to develop that kind of focus.

Practice choosing to be aware of the positive. When finances are low, *consciously* remember that many people are homeless. When the person for whom you are caring is particularly irksome, remember those whose loved ones are no longer alive to bother them. When you don't seem to have any time for yourself, remember those who contemplate suicide because they are so lonely and lack people with whom to share their time. Practice selective awareness. It will change your perceptions of the stressors you encounter and allow you to live a more satisfying and fulfilling life.

Relative to caregiving, selective awareness will help you see the benefits to yourself, as well as to the person for whom you are caring, of the support you provide.

2. Locus of Control

Your perception of the degree to which you control events that affect your life is your "locus of control." To determine your locus of control, complete the scale in figure 7.3.

Figure 7.3: Locus of Control Assessment

Next to each number, circle the answer that best describes your beliefs:

1. (a) Grades are a function of the amount of work students do.
   (b) Grades depend on the kindness of the instructor.
2. (a) Promotions are earned by hard work.
   (b) Promotions come from being in the right place at the right time.
3. (a) Meeting someone to love is a matter of luck.
   (b) Meeting someone to love depends on going out often and meeting many people.
4. (a) Living a long life is a function of heredity.
   (b) Living a long life is a function of adopting healthy habits.
5. (a) Being overweight is determined by the number of fat cells you were born with or developed early in life.
   (b) Being overweight depends on what and how much food you eat.
6. (a) People who exercise regularly set up their schedules to be able to do so.
   (b) Some people just don't have time for regular exercise.
7. (a) Winning at poker depends on shrewd betting.
   (b) Winning at poker depends on good luck.
8. (a) Staying married depends on working at the marriage.
   (b) Staying married depends on being lucky enough to choose the right marriage partner.
9. (a) Citizens can influence their governments.
   (b) There is nothing an individual citizen can do to affect government actions.
10. (a) Being skilled at sports depends on being born well-coordinated.
    (b) Those skilled at sports work hard at mastering those skills.

Scoring: Give yourself one point for each of the following responses.

Item	Answer	Item	Answer
1	a	6	a
2	a	7	a
3	b	8	a
4	b	9	a
5	b	10	b

If you scored more than 5, you have an internal locus of control.
If you scored less than 5, you have an external locus of control.

If you have an external locus of control, you believe that events that affect your life are a function of fate, chance, luck, or powerful others (e.g., the doctor or your boss). If you have an internal locus of control, you believe that *you* are the one who most influences events that affect your life. Researchers have found that "internals" are more apt to seek information (to use in controlling their lives), whereas "externals" do not seek information, since they believe that nothing they can do with this information would have any significant influence on their lives. For example, hospital patients who are internals have more information about their medical conditions and about hospital resources than do external hospital patients; and internal prison inmates have more knowledge about the parole system and the prison rules and regulations than do externals.

The fact that you picked this book to read probably means you have at least some degree of internality. You believe that the information contained in this book can help you manage your caregiving responsibilities better. Externals would not see the value in such information since they believe that doing an adequate job of care-giving is a matter of luck or the help of powerful others (for example, the nurse or doctor).

The point of understanding locus of control is to be *realistic* about the control you exert as a caregiver. It is as stressful and unhealthy to believe that you have more control than you actually do as to believe that you have no control at all. You exercise a *limited* control over the health of the person for whom you are caring. That person's age, his or her condition upon coming under your care, and resources of time and finances all restrict the amount of control you exert. To believe otherwise would make you feel guilty about every setback in the person's health and about any limits on the time you can allot to caregiving. This guilt can make you ill and interfere with both family and work relationships. That, in turn, will cycle back to interfere with your caregiving. To prevent this vicious cycle, you must realistically assess the limits on the control you can exert—neither overestimating it nor using your assessment as a rationale for avoiding your responsibilities.

Take a minute right now to determine whether you have been lax in seeking information to help you provide better care (for example, finding out more about a certain medical condition or about certain medications), or whether you have been spending an inordinate amount of time and psychic energy on situations truly beyond your control.

117

Emotional Arousal Interventions

Roadblocks to emotional arousal from stress (which can lead to illness and other negative consequences) can be built through the regular practice of relaxation techniques. Regular relaxation can rejuvenate you so that you can manage the stress associated with caregiving. Learning a method of relaxation is relatively simple; practicing it on a daily basis may be more complex. The two relaxation techniques we have chosen were selected because they are both easy to learn and effective.

1. Meditation

Meditation requires a focus on something repetitive (such as a word repeated over and over again) or something unchanging (such as a spot on the wall). For our purposes, sit in a chair with your eyes closed and focus on your breathing by saying the word "one" in your mind every time you inhale and the word "two" every time you exhale. When you find your mind wandering, come back to focusing on your breathing, recognizing that no one can stay focused on anything for too long. To obtain the maximum benefit, meditate twice a day—upon rising and just before dinner. Do not meditate after ingesting a stimulant (such as coffee, cola, or tea) or after smoking a cigarette (nicotine is also a stimulant), since the purpose is to relax. And don't meditate after eating, since blood will be pooled in your abdomen to help with digestion instead of flowing increasingly to your arms and legs, as it does when you relax.

Researchers assert that meditation has many benefits. Meditators have been found to have decreased muscle tension, lower blood pressure, and decreased blood lactate (thought to be associated with lessened anxiety), and to be more self-actualized, have more confidence in managing stressors, and have a general state of more positive mental health. It is not difficult to see how far these benefits can go in helping you function more effectively as a caregiver while maintaining good physical and mental health.

2. Imagery

An excellent way to relax is to use visualization. Imagining relaxing scenes can release tension in muscles, decrease your heart rate, lower your serum cholesterol and blood pressure levels, and help you achieve a calm state of mind.

Begin by closing your eyes and rotating your eyeballs inward and upward, as if you were attempting to look at your own forehead. This procedure alone has been shown to result in increased alpha brain-wave activity (a sign of relaxation). The best relaxing imagery includes a very vivid scene. Use as many of your senses as you can to make the image as real as possible. You should smell the smells, hear the sounds, see the colors, feel the sensations, and even taste the flavors. Your preferred image might be of clouds, valleys, a willow tree, a field of wildflowers, a cool forest, a log cabin, a clear stream, a sloping hill—or just about any other scene that would relax you.

Although you would do best to develop your own relaxing imagery (different people find different things relaxing), I have chosen a sunny beach by way of example. Read this scenario and then follow the instructions above, recalling the scene described. You can also read the scene into a tape recorder and listen to it when you need to relax.

> You are driving to the beach with your car window rolled down. There is no radio on in your car. The wind is blowing through your hair, and the sun is beating down on your thighs. You can see people clad in bathing suits, walking with beach chairs and blankets, and carrying food in picnic baskets and coolers. You park your car. As you are walking to the beach, you hear the surf rolling onto the shore and smell the salt in the air. You find a quiet spot away from other people and spread your blanket. Tired from the drive, you are relieved to let your muscles relax as you lie on the blanket with your feet extending onto the sand.
>
> As you relax, you can taste the salt in the air. Droplets of ocean seem to fall on you as you hear the slap of the surf on the sand and its ever-so-gentle swish as it rolls back to sea. Everything seems light—yellow and tan and blue. The sun's bright yellow on the sand's soft tan contrasts with the ocean's vivid blue and seems the perfect combination for serenity. You close your eyes and take it all in through your other senses.
>
> The sun seems to move over your body. First your arms grow warm from the intensity of the sun's rays. You feel the heat pass through them, and loosen their muscles. Next your legs are caressed by the sun, as they too become warm. The sun moves to warm your chest now, and your whole chest area becomes heated and relaxed. Then the sun moves to your abdomen, bringing its relaxing warmth there. And, as though you had willed it, the sun next moves to your forehead, bringing warmth and relaxation there. Your whole body is now warm and relaxed. Your muscles are limp, and your body feels as though it's sinking into the sand, warm and heavy. You tingle from the sun's warmth.
>
> You hear the sea gulls flying over the ocean. They sound free and light and peaceful. Heading out to sea, they are carrying your

problems and worries with them, leaving you relieved and re-laxed. You think of nothing but your body's heaviness and warmth and tingling. You are totally soothed.

You have relaxed all day, and now the sun is setting. You feel the sun leaving and you slowly open your eyes, now wonderfully relaxed and content. You have no worries, no cares. You look up at the sea gulls who carried your problems and worries away, and you thank them. Feeling alert, you stand up and stretch, squishing the still warm—yet cooling—sand between your toes. You feel terrific. You feel so good that you know the car ride home will be pleasant. You welcome that time alone in your car, at peace, with-out problems or cares. You fold your blanket and leave the beach, taking with you your relaxation and contentment. You say good-bye to the beach as you walk away from it, knowing you can re-turn at any time.

Physiological Arousal Interventions

At this point on the stress model, your body is prepared to do some-thing physical—to fight or take flight. If you don't use that pre-paredness, you will retain such unhealthy conditions as high blood pressure, increased serum cholesterol, increased heart rate, and decreased effectiveness of your immunological system (making you less able to fight off diseases). You have an intense need to do some-thing physical to use up these stress by-products. Now you know why people under great stress throw dishes at one another, punch holes in walls, or beat up other persons (as in spouse and child abuse)—it feels good! Yet there are better and more socially ac-ceptable ways to use the body's preparedness. Two of these are briefly described below.

1. Exercise

I'm ashamed to admit it, yet it makes a point. I'm referring to the time I was in the upstairs bathroom and my son, who was four, was being a pain in the neck. As I was applying a very sharp razor to my very soft skin, Todd was using me as a tackling dummy. After repeatedly beseeching him to control his aggression, and after about half a pint of my blood had spilled into the sink, I was totally frustrated. Reacting reflexively, I did the only thing available to me at the moment—I kicked him.

Well, Todd had never even experienced a spanking in his first four years of life, and, in fact, his mother and I had emphasized that hitting was an inappropriate manner of solving problems. We had made that statement with such conviction and so often that when I kicked Todd, he looked as if his world had collapsed. Now mind you, this was not child abuse. The kick was pretty gentle. A judge in a court of law need only have looked at my mangled face to find self-defense. But Todd was deeply wounded anyhow. Staring at me with eyes wide open, he asked, "Why did you do that?" Without hesitation, I admitted, "Because it felt good." A few apologies, hugs, and kisses later, both of us realized that we had acted selfishly and vowed to learn from the situation.

Haven't you experienced situations in which you, too, would have liked to strike out at someone or something? A friend of mine punched a wall, only to find it surprisingly softer than his knuckles. His swollen hand finished healing several weeks before he was able to repair the hole in his wall.

When emotions build up, we seek physical outlets. It feels good to "let it out," so we slam doors, throw dishes, or kick four-year-olds. Now that you are familiar with the stress response and recognize that the body has been physiologically prepared to do something physical (fight or flight), you can appreciate the value of using your body in some active way.

There are more acceptable ways of using the stress products than those described above. I don't mean to make light of having kicked my son, because that was wrong. It was so wrong that, as I said, I'm embarrassed by the memory. Some people beat their spouses because they are distressed. Others beat their children. Still others act violently in other ways. The idea is to use stress products in a *positive* manner—a manner that will make you feel better and will not violate anyone else's rights.

Exercise is one option. Regular exercise has been shown to have psychological benefits (increased self-esteem, poise, and feeling of attractiveness, and decreased depression and anxiety) and physiological benefits (improved functioning of the lungs and circulatory system, delay of the degenerative processes associated with aging, strengthening of the heart muscle, and increased endurance). In addition, exercise can help you cope with stress, since it uses the stress by-products productively.

If you have been relatively inactive, before beginning an exercise program you should have a complete medical checkup. Once that is accomplished, how do you begin? Chapter 11 offers information to help you get started. In that chapter, you will learn how frequently, how intensely, and for how long you should exercise, as well as which exercises will best meet your needs. You might want to skip directly to chapter 11 if you have been motivated to begin a regular program of exercise. There's no time like the present!

2. Pounding the Pillow

Another way to use up the stress by-products and to feel better is to beat up your pillow or mattress. You will not hurt yourself or anyone else, and your pillow will be none the worse for the experience. Try it! You'll see how effective this simple release of tension is and how it helps you manage the stress associated with your caregiving chores.

In Conclusion

You *can* manage and cope with the stress you experience in general and with caregiving stress in particular. That stress need not make you ill or unhappy or frustrated. Using the stress model, you can set up effective roadblocks and improve the quality of your life. Remember, however, that there is no such thing as a "magic stress reduction pill." Managing stress takes work, but that work can pay off in big dividends. So why are you still reading this book? Put it down and begin to develop your stress management plan—*now!*

8

Time Management Skills: Fitting It All In

Time management—phew! I *know* this problem. As this is being written, one author is in the process of moving—not next door, not across town, but across the country, from the West Coast to the East Coast. That move necessitates finding a new job, a new place to live, continuing to support a daughter in college, coordinating schedules with a very busy spouse, monitoring the schoolwork of a dedicated ice-hockey-playing, high-school-girl-interested son, and writing this book. This chapter will certainly come in handy!

You, too, probably have trouble fitting it all in—especially since you are providing elder care while trying to manage your family life, perhaps working outside the home (and if not, working inside the home, which is no less taxing), and attending to your social needs by spending time with friends at the theater, ball games, club meetings, church or synagogue functions, and the like. So this chapter should also come in handy for you.

Recognizing the balancing act that elder care requires, this book not only offers advice on how to be an effective caregiver, but also devotes considerable space to explaining how you can care for your own needs. One of these needs is learning to manage your time effectively.

There are plenty of consequences of caregiving—both positive and negative—over which we have little control. Feeling overwhelmed by a lack of time, however, is *not* one of them, because there are effective time management techniques.

Several important realizations: Time is one of your most precious possessions. Time spent is gone forever. In spite of what we often profess, we cannot "save" time. Time moves continually, and is used—one way or another. If we waste time, there is no bank from which to withdraw time we saved to replace time we wasted. Coming to terms with our mortality means realizing that our time is limited. Nevertheless, we can invest time in ways that will free up more time than was invested. Realize, though, that you must initially spend some time to organize yourself in order to eventually give yourself more time. This investment will pay dividends; it will be worth it.

As you read the following suggestions, try to make direct application of these techniques to your situation. You will want to incorporate most of these techniques into your lifestyle; others, you will decide, are not worth your effort or the time. There is not one of us, however, who cannot benefit from many of the time management techniques described below.

Assessing How You Spend Time

The first step in managing time is to analyze how you spend your time now. To do this, divide your day into fifteen-minute segments, as shown on the chart titled "Daily Activity Record" (table 8.1).

Record what you are doing every fifteen minutes. Afterward, review this time diary and total the time spent on each activity throughout the day. For example, you might find that you spent three hours at your desk, two hours socializing, three hours eating meals, two hours watching television, one hour exercising, one hour shopping, two hours working around the house, seven hours sleeping, and three hours on the telephone, as shown on the sample "Schedule of Daily Activities" in table 8.2.

Next, evaluate your use of time. Did you spend too much time watching television and too little time doing housework? Based upon this evaluation, decide on an adjustment, but make it specific—for example, "I will watch one hour of television, and I will work around the house for two hours." A good way to make this change is to draw up a contract with yourself that includes a reward for success. You can photocopy the blank form below (table 8.3, "Summary of Daily Activities") to analyze how to spend your time.

Setting Goals

The most important part of time management is setting goals (see table 8.4): daily, weekly, monthly, yearly, and long-range. If you don't have a clear sense of where you are going, you cannot plan how to get there. Organize your time to maximize the chances of achieving your goals. List two goals for tomorrow, two for this

Table 8.1
Daily Activity Record

Time	Activity	Time	Activity
12:00 A.M.		12:00 P.M.	
12:15 A.M.		12:15 P.M.	
12:30 A.M.		12:30 P.M.	
12:45 A.M.		12:45 P.M.	
1:00 A.M.		1:00 P.M.	
1:15 A.M.		1:15 P.M.	
1:30 A.M.		1:30 P.M.	
1:45 A.M.		1:45 P.M.	
2:00 A.M.		2:00 P.M.	
2:15 A.M.		2:15 P.M.	
2:30 A.M.		2:30 P.M.	
2:45 A.M.		2:45 P.M.	
3:00 A.M.		3:00 P.M.	
3:15 A.M.		3:15 P.M.	
3:30 A.M.		3:30 P.M.	
3:45 A.M.		3:45 P.M.	
4:00 A.M.		4:00 P.M.	
4:15 A.M.		4:15 P.M.	
4:30 A.M.		4:30 P.M.	
4:45 A.M.		4:45 P.M.	
5:00 A.M.		5:00 P.M.	
5:15 A.M.		5:15 P.M.	
5:30 A.M.		5:30 P.M.	
5:45 A.M.		5:45 P.M.	
6:00 A.M.		6:00 P.M.	
6:15 A.M.		6:15 P.M.	
6:30 A.M.		6:30 P.M.	
6:45 A.M.		6:45 P.M.	
7:00 A.M.		7:00 P.M.	
7:15 A.M.		7:15 P.M.	
7:30 A.M.		7:30 P.M.	
7:45 A.M.		7:45 P.M.	
8:00 A.M.		8:00 P.M.	
8:15 A.M.		8:15 P.M.	
8:30 A.M.		8:30 P.M.	
8:45 A.M.		8:45 P.M.	
9:00 A.M.		9:00 P.M.	
9:15 A.M.		9:15 P.M.	

Note: Continue for a full 24-hour period.

Table 8.2
Schedule of Daily Activities

Activity	Total Time Spent on Activity
At the desk	3 hours
Socializing	2 hours
Eating meals	3 hours
Watching television	2 hours
Exercising	1 hour
Shopping	1 hour
Doing housework	2 hours
Sleeping	7 hours
On the telephone	3 hours

week, two for this month, and two for this year. Keep these goals in mind as you decide how to spend your time each day.

Prioritizing

Once you have your goals defined, prioritize them (see tables 8.5 and 8.6). Not all goals are equally important. Focus on those goals of major importance to you, and work on the other goals secondarily. Likewise, focus first on activities most important to the achievement of your primary goals. To guide this process, develop A, B, C lists.

On the A list are activities that *must* be done. For example, if the person for whom you provide care is feeling ill today and you need to take that person to the doctor, going to the doctor is on your A list today.

On the B list are activities that you'd like to do today and that do need to be done but that can be put off if necessary. For example, if you haven't spoken to a close friend recently and have been meaning to telephone, you might put that on your B list. You intend to call today, but if you don't get around to it, you can call tomorrow or the next day.

On the C list are activities you'd like to do if you get all the A and B activities done. If the C list activities don't get done, that is all right. For example, if a department store has a sale and you'd like to go shopping, put that on your C list. If you do all of the A's and B's, you can go to the sale; if not, you've suffered no great loss.

In addition, make a list of things *not to do*. For example, if you tend to waste time watching television, you might include that on your not-to-do list. That way you'll remember not to watch television today.

Scheduling

Once you have prioritized your activities, you can schedule your day. *When* will you go to the doctor? When will you shop for groceries? Remember to schedule some relaxation and recreation as well.

Maximizing Your Rewards

In scheduling your activities, remember that some time management experts say: "We get 80 percent of our rewards from only 20 percent of our activities and, conversely, we get only 20 percent of our rewards from the other 80 percent." That tells us that we should be sure we identify and engage in the 20 percent of activities that give us 80 percent of our rewards *before* we move to other activities. Maximize your rewards by organizing your time. In

Table 8.3
Summary of Daily Activities

Activity	Total Time Spent on Activity

Table 8.4
Goals

Tomorrow:
1. _____
2. _____

This week:
1. _____
2. _____

This month:
1. _____
2. _____

This year:
1. _____
2. _____

making your lists, give special consideration to those activities—the "20 percent." Try to place them on your A list or at least on your B list.

Saying No

I have a friend who says, "You mean I don't *have* to do everything I *want* to do?" What he means is that there are so many activities he would love to engage in that he overloads himself, feels overburdened, and winds up not enjoying himself as much as he expected. Because of guilt, concern for what others might think, or a real desire to engage in a given activity, we have a hard time saying no. The A, B, C lists and your schedule of activities will help you identify how much time remains for other activities and will make saying no easier—even to the person you are caring for, when that is appropriate.

Delegating

Whenever possible, get others to do the things that need to be done but do not need your personal attention. Conversely, avoid taking on chores that others try to delegate to you. For example, if the person for whom you are caring needs a bath but you have an appointment with a friend, ask your spouse or someone else with whom you live to give the bath while you keep your appointment. A word of caution: This advice does not mean that you should use other people to do work you should be doing or that you should refuse to help others when they ask. We are suggesting that you be discriminating regarding delegation of activities. Be quick to seek help when you are short on time and overloaded. Help others when they really need help and you have time.

Evaluating Tasks Once

Many of us open our mail, read through it, and set it aside to act on later. For example, your authors often receive questionnaires from graduate students who are doing a study. We tend to put the questionnaire aside and fill it out later. But that is a waste of time. If we pick it up later, we have to refamiliarize ourselves with the task.

As much as possible, look things over only once. When you pick it up, be prepared to finish working on it right then and there.

Using the Circular File

Another way of handling questionnaires is to file them in the wastebasket. How many times do you receive obvious junk mail? Though we know what is in those envelopes addressed to "Occupant," we still take the time to open them and read the junk inside. We would be better off going directly to the wastebasket. That would free up time for more important goal-oriented activities.

Limiting Interruptions

Throughout the day your planned activities will be interrupted. Recognizing this fact, you should schedule time for interruptions. That is, don't make your schedule so tight that interruptions would throw you into a tizzy. At the same time, try to keep interruptions to a minimum. There are several ways to do this. Accept phone calls only between certain hours. At other times ask your spouse or whomever you live with to take messages. Do the same with visitors. When you are busy, anyone who visits should be asked to return at a more convenient time or to schedule a visit for later.

If you are serious about making better use of your time, you must find some way of limiting interruptions. Adhere to your schedule as much as you can.

Investing Time

The bottom line of time management is that you must invest time initially in order subsequently to benefit by the good use of your

Table 8.5
List of Activities for Today

"A" List List below only those activities that you must spend time on today.	**"B" List** List below those activities that you would like to spend time on today but that could wait.
1. _____	1. _____
2. _____	2. _____
3. _____	3. _____
4. _____	4. _____
5. _____	5. _____
6. _____	6. _____
7. _____	7. _____
8. _____	8. _____
9. _____	9. _____
10. _____	10. _____

Table 8.6
List of Activities for Today

"C" List List below those activities to which you will devote time today *only* after you have completed all A and B activities.	**"Not to Do" List** List below those activities that you will avoid spending time on today.
1. _____	1. _____
2. _____	2. _____
3. _____	3. _____
4. _____	4. _____
5. _____	5. _____
6. _____	6. _____
7. _____	7. _____
8. _____	8. _____
9. _____	9. _____
10. _____	10. _____

time. Those who attend our classes or workshops often say, "I don't have time to organize myself the way you suggest. That would put me deeper in the hole." This is an interesting paradox. Those who feel they have no time to plan better use of their time probably need to take the time more than do those who feel they have the time. Confusing? Let us put it this way: If you are so pressed for time that you believe you don't have enough time to get yourself organized, that in itself signals that you need to apply time management skills. The investment of time in organizing yourself will pay dividends by allowing you to achieve more of what really matters to you.

People and Places Analysis

To further help you make decisions regarding how to spend your *limited* time, fill in the "People/Places Grid" in figure 8.1. (Its purpose and use will be explained.) In quadrant I list five people you like, in quadrant II list five people you dislike, in quadrant III list five places you like, and in quadrant IV list five places you dislike.

Now, identify the characteristics of the people you like and dislike and of the places you like and dislike. To do this, you must look for generalizations about the items in each quadrant. Perhaps there won't be total consistency in each quadrant, but look for characteristics shared by three or four of the people or places in a given list.

Take quadrant I first: What do the people you like have in common? Perhaps they have a good sense of humor, or they are caring and considerate. Perhaps they enjoy sports or are hard workers. On a separate sheet of paper, list these characteristics. Remember, don't limit yourself to characteristics that *all* of them possess; list characteristics that describe at least three of the five people you've listed. Make that list for quadrant I *now*.

Look at quadrant II next: What do the people you dislike have in common? Perhaps they are noisy or are poor listeners. Perhaps they are too serious or are selfish. On a separate sheet, list these characteristics. Again, don't limit yourself to characteristics that *all* of them possess, but choose characteristics applicable to at least three of the five people you've listed. Make that list for quadrant II *now*.

Do the same for quadrant III: What is it that places you like have in common? Perhaps they are busy and noisy, full of activity. Perhaps they are quiet and conducive to conversation. Perhaps they have a warm climate or an ocean or other body of water nearby. On your sheet of paper, list these characteristics. As before,

Figure 8.1: People and Places Grid

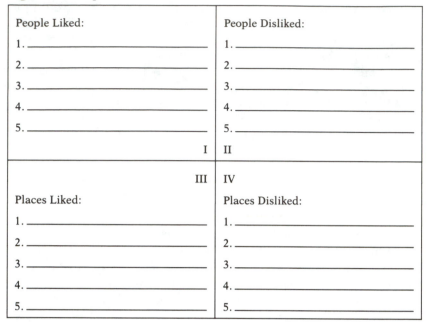

People Liked:	People Disliked:
1. _____	1. _____
2. _____	2. _____
3. _____	3. _____
4. _____	4. _____
5. _____	5. _____
I	II
III	IV
Places Liked:	Places Disliked:
1. _____	1. _____
2. _____	2. _____
3. _____	3. _____
4. _____	4. _____
5. _____	5. _____

list characteristics shared by at least three of the five places you've listed. Make that list for quadrant III *now.*

Last, do the same for quadrant IV: What is it that places you dislike have in common? Perhaps they are too quiet or lack interesting things to do. Perhaps they are in a cold, windy climate or too remote from a large city. Perhaps they are too "high-brow" and not "earthy" enough for you. Make that list for quadrant IV *now.*

Now that you've identified characteristics of people and places you like and dislike, you can use this information to organize your time better. For instance, make a plan to spend time with the kind of people you like and limit relationships with the kind of people you dislike. Spend time at the kinds of places you enjoy, and limit time at places that do not possess the characteristics you most appreciate. This seems obvious; however, most of us don't use this strategy when becoming acquainted with new people and don't understand why certain relationships are either so enjoyable or so unpleasant. We sometimes don't realize why we can't stand certain places or why other places appeal to us so much.

The "People and Places Analysis Questions" (figure 8.2) will help you sort out this information and develop a plan to use what you have learned from the grid to make better use of your time.

There are other ways to use this information about the people and places you like and dislike. For instance, ask yourself:

1. *What would happen if I took the people I like to the places I like?* Would I have a *great* time? Would I be unable to focus my attention on the people because of the characteristics of the place? Would I be unable to concentrate on the place because of the characteristics of the people?
2. *What would happen if I took the people I like to the places I dislike?* Would I like the people less? Would I like the places more? Would the places interfere with my relationships with the people, or would the people be so enjoyable that the places would be more tolerable?
3. *What would happen if I took the people I dislike to the places I like?* Would I like the people more? Would I like the places less because of sharing them with people around whom I feel uncom-

Figure 8.2: People and Places Analysis Questions

Who are the people with whom you want to spend more time?

_____   _____
_____   _____
_____   _____

Who are the people with whom you want to limit time?

_____   _____
_____   _____
_____   _____

At what places do you want to spend more time?

_____   _____
_____   _____
_____   _____

At what places do you want to limit time?

_____   _____
_____   _____
_____   _____

fortable? Could I ever enjoy these places again, or would they be forever ruined by the memory of having shared them with people I dislike? How would I feel if people I like found out I shared the places I like with the people I dislike?

In essence, you have just asked yourself whether you are a *people* person or a *places* person. Is whom you are with more important to you than where you are, or is your environment more important to you than your companions? There is no right or wrong answer. People simply differ in this regard. But figuring out which you consider more important will help you divide your time to be consistent with your preference.

A former graduate student of ours was also a flight attendant. On Tuesdays, Wednesdays, and Thursdays she attended classes, and on Fridays, Saturdays, Sundays, and Mondays she flew. Her route took her outside the United States, and when she listed places she liked they included Monte Carlo, Mexico City, and Paris. She found that she enjoyed places where there was much activity and where wealthy people congregated. And she found out that being at these places was more important to her than staying home and developing long-term relationships. Using that information, she maximized the time she spent at the places she most enjoyed and stopped worrying so much about her lack of a boyfriend or close woman friends at home. For her that was right. What is right for you?

Perception and Reality Check

Although you may sometimes feel overburdened and overloaded, there really is enough time to fit it all in. In a sense, a major element of time management is perception—realizing that with a little organization, everything you need to do and much of what you want to do can be done.

Consider the college students that your authors teach. When they attend their classes the first week of the semester and find out that they will have to write four term papers, take and pass eight examinations (four midterm exams and four final exams), and read at least four textbooks—all for just the four classes in which they are enrolled—they say they're "freaked out." Aware that they also wish to have a fulfilling social life and contribute as members of their families, our students perceive an overload and wonder whether they will find the time to do it all. Yet they experience this same situation each semester and pass enough classes to be allowed to register for subsequent semesters; clearly it *is* all manage-able. The problem is that they view all they need to do as one big package rather than as a number of small packages that need not be delivered the same day, the same week, or even the same month. To think of passing eight exams is different from thinking of taking one exam this week, another next week, and a third the following week.

You can see how your perception can influence your sense of time. Controlling your perception so that you look at parts of tasks and responsibilities rather than view them in their totality can be an important time management strategy.

In Conclusion

Be assured that in most cases you *can* fit it all in. You *can* be a good caregiver, an effective and full-functioning member of your family, and a productive worker, and still maintain an active social life. No one has said that caregiving won't change your use of time and im-pose some restrictions on your ability to pursue other interests. You are well aware that you face a new set of demands. Neverthe-less, if you use the time management techniques described in this chapter, you can expect to have time to pursue other interests.

Invest some time to organize yourself. You will find that invest-ment worthwhile. You will develop skills that will help you create a more satisfying, healthier life for yourself.

9

Keeping the Family Together and Healthy

I'll never forget his voice breaking with emotion, his tears choked back, as he eulogized his forty-two-year-old brother, prematurely dead:

> My brother need not be idealized or enlarged in death beyond what he was in life. To be remembered simply as a good and decent man who saw wrong and tried to right it, who saw suffering and tried to heal it, who saw war and tried to stop it. Those of us who loved him and who take him to his rest today, pray that what he was to us, and what he wished for others, will someday come to pass for all the world. As he said many times in many parts of this nation, to those he touched and who sought to touch him: Some men see things as they are and say "Why?" I dream things that never were and say, "Why not?"[1]

These words were spoken in New York City's St. Patrick's Cathedral in early June of 1968 as the nation joined Edward Kennedy in mourning the death of his brother Robert. As I listened to the eulogy and participated in the funeral from afar, I could not help thinking of *my* two brothers, Stephen and Mark. Stephen, a businessman bent on making a million dollars, and Mark, a musician and artist, are as different from me as they are from each other. And yet we are family. We grew up sharing a bedroom, fought with each other regularly, and shared the sorrows and joys of life in our twenty-some-odd years under one roof.

This chapter is about such bonds—family bonds—and how

---

1. "The Incredible Year," CBS-News, 1969.

those bonds can be maintained and strengthened in spite of the extreme stress of caregiving.

The Family

Someone once described *family* as a place where you are always welcome for Thanksgiving dinner. That probably sums it up better than any high-brow definition we might devise. We're reminded of a recent newspaper story about an automobile accident involving a family of five. The car crash killed the father, mother, and two young children, but the two-year-old youngest daughter, who wore a seat belt, survived. As we read the story, our heart went out to that child, and we felt her loss. That does not mean that we were concerned about who would care for her, feed her, or shelter her. Rather, we were empathizing with her *irreplaceable loss*—the loss of her blood relatives, whose connection with her could never be totally compensated. Something about the family bond makes it unique.

We all know, though, that some families function better than others. This is not a matter of chance, but the result of specific roles played by family members and of procedures adopted by the family. One observer of families, author Jane Howard, designated some characteristics of effective families:

1. They have a *chief*—someone around whom other family members cluster.
2. They have a *switchboard operator*—someone who keeps track of what all the others are up to.
3. They are *much to all their members but everything to none*—that is, family members are encouraged to be involved with and have some of their needs met by people outside the family.
4. They are *hospitable*—that is, they recognize that hosts need guests as much as guests need hosts, and they maintain a circle of honorary family members who become additional support systems.
5. They *deal squarely with direness*—that is, they deal quickly and openly with the occasional unavoidable trouble and do not allow it to threaten family bonds.
6. They *prize their rituals*—that is, they observe holidays together, grieve at funerals together, and in other ways encourage a sense of continuity and connectedness.
7. They are *affectionate*—that is, family members hug, kiss, and

warmly shake hands. They are quick to demonstrate love and caring for one another.

8. They have a *sense of place*—that is, there is a house or a town or some other place to which they feel connected. Even families who have moved often feel connected to the place in which they find themselves at present.

9. They *connect with posterity*—that is, family members feel linked to something that came before them and to something which will continue when they die.

10. They *honor their elders*—that is, grandparents and other elderly relatives are respected and cared for. Their experience and wisdom, and they themselves, are valued.[2]

We may be tempted to measure our families against these characteristics of effective families and to assign blame if we come up short. We would be better advised, however, to *analyze* our families as objectively as possible and to identify areas for and means of improvement. Assigning blame is dysfunctional and will interfere with improving the family's effectiveness. Below, we help you analyze your family and use that analysis to become a better caregiver.

Understanding and Using Your Family System

There was a time when extended families lived in the same town and visited frequently. When I was growing up, my "family circle" met one Sunday a month. Grandma Mary, Grandpa Barney, and the aunts, uncles, and cousins gathered to talk, play cards, play ball, argue, and eat. Sometimes we piled in the back of my grandfather's pickup truck, sat on empty wooden milk crates, and took off for a day at the beach. We all felt close to one another and were caught up in one another's lives. I knew the boys my cousin Marcia was dating, and she knew what sports I liked.

How times have changed! My children were born in Buffalo and now live near Washington, D.C. We have no relatives in either of these places. We make a point of renewing family ties once a year at a Passover seder, rather than once a month as when I was young. My children rarely play with their cousins and don't know much about their relatives' lives. Their grandmother doesn't come over

2. Jane Howard, *Families* (New York: Simon & Schuster, 1978).

every Friday night for dinner as mine did. She lives three hundred miles away. When they have a babysitter, it isn't their cousin Larry from next door, as it was for me. Instead, it is a nonrelative, someone from a list of sitters we maintain ("support" might be a more accurate term).

Because your family is probably similar to ours, it is imperative that you analyze your family structure to obtain the caregiving support you will need to maintain your own health, provide effective care, and maintain the health of your immediate and extended family. Add to the reality of family dispersement the large number of dual-career families and single-parent families, and you can see how huge a burden caregiving can be. You may not be surprised to learn that caregivers report less stress when more family members cooperate in the caregiving chores. One way to organize such cooperation is to understand each member's role in the family.

Your family probably has various members who, knowingly or unknowingly, perform specific family roles. In most instances, the role a person plays has a historical component—that is, he or she has functioned in that role for many years. The following list of family roles was developed by caregiving experts from the Pennsylvania Department on Aging:

1. *The Caregiver.* That's you! Some experts have called this person the "kinkeeper;" it is a role commonly assumed by someone with a long history of responsible involvement with the family. The Caregiver works harder than others at keeping the family in touch, perhaps through telephoning, writing, visiting, or organizing and hosting get-togethers, reunions, birthday parties, and other such events.
2. *The Ambassador.* In most families there is someone who represents the family to the outside world. This person ensures family representation at such events as funerals of friends, family, and distant relatives.
3. *The Comforter.* This individual serves as a listening ear to whom other family members go to discuss troubles and to seek advice and comfort.
4. *The Fence-Sitter.* Not especially active or involved with the family, this person usually has no opinion about caregiving matters but—in a worst-case scenario—may change opinions depending on who last had his or her ear.
5. *The Financial Adviser.* This member provides advice about financial matters to the other family members.

139

6. *The Consultant.* Considered influential or powerful, this individual is outside the mainstream of family matters but is seen as someone to reckon with. The Consultant rarely provides hands-on care and often spends little time with either the caregiver or the care-receiver. However, the little time that is spent is disproportionately noticed and appreciated. For example, the Consultant may come into town, take the care-receiver to lunch, and buy a few presents. For the next few weeks, the care-receiver refers to the Consultant in a highly positive way, setting up the caregiver in an unrealistic and unusually unfavorable comparison. The care-receiver may say, "Why aren't you like your brother? He takes me to lunch and buys me presents," even though these occasions are few and far between.[3]

Using these and any other roles you can identify in your family, write in the names of family members next to the roles they typically play:

1. *The Caregiver* _____
2. *The Ambassador* _____
3. *The Comforter* _____
4. *The Fence-Sitter* _____
5. *The Financial Adviser* _____
6. *The Consultant* _____
7. *Other*
    a. _____
    b. _____

Next, assess whether that person or role is a positive or a negative force. Then, develop strategies to maximize the positive forces and to minimize the negative ones.

For example, if financial matters are of particular concern, seek to meet regularly with the Financial Adviser in your family. Or, if the Consultant's visits are especially disruptive, ask another family member, perhaps the Comforter, to speak with the care-receiver and alert that person to your feelings, explaining the disruption these infrequent visits can create. How else could you use this knowledge of family roles? Make a chart that lists ways to use

---

3. Pennsylvania Department on Aging, *Caregivers: Practical Help* (Harrisburg: Pennsylvania Department on Aging, 1988).

family roles to increase support for your caregiving responsibilities.

Dividing the Responsibilities

In addition to the above suggestions, you can free up some time for yourself by having others assume certain regular caregiving responsibilities. Every Tuesday evening might be your free night; your son or daughter stays with Mom. Maybe your spouse or sister takes Dad out for lunch and some other activity (perhaps a visit to the library) every Monday afternoon. A close friend or relative (the Ambassador?) can drive the sick person to the doctor or run some other errands. You can't help others *all* the time; that will put *you* out of commission and create another problem.

In addition to freeing you to maintain your own health, other family members who share caregiving responsibilities will develop greater understanding of the enormity of those tasks. Rather than whining, "You don't spend enough time with me," a teenager may begin to say, "It's amazing how much you do for Grandma/Grandpa." Rather than being jealous and feeling neglected, your spouse may develop a greater appreciation for your willingness to sacrifice for your family and, thereby, grow in respect for you. Your children and your spouse will probably still feel deprived of your attention, and it's likely that your caregiving responsibilities will never be fully understood or appreciated. However, given the opportunity to participate, members of your family will respond more positively to your caregiving, and your family will be healthier.

Further—and we speak here from experience—the honor of being able to care for a loved one is a memory that should not be withheld from *anyone* in the family. When loved ones become ill, many family members feel at a loss. The opportunity to do something—and even very young children can do *something*—can alleviate feelings of helplessness.

Not to be overlooked in this discussion is the fact that the person who is being cared for can also provide some assistance. For example, elderly men and women may need to participate in housework—light dusting or cleaning—in order to fill their need to contribute. Many can be asked to change lightbulbs, help pick up certain foods in the supermarket, or make phone calls to find out whether items on order have been received. The care-receiver's feeling of usefulness and the help provided to the caregiver will be appreciated by both.

Contracts and IOU Cards

To ensure that you get the kind of support you need from family members, friends, and the care-receiver, you can formalize the process with a contract. Contracts can take many forms (see figure 9.1) but should include the following components:

1. The specific assistance to be provided
2. The person who agrees to provide that assistance
3. The time or date by when that assistance will be provided
4. The reward for providing that assistance
5. The signatures of the person agreeing to provide the assistance, the caregiver, and, when appropriate, the care-receiver

Describe the assistance to be provided as *specifically* as possible to prevent later disagreements or disappointments. Specify the date by which the activity should occur so that both the person agreeing to assist and the caregiver know when to expect the assistance. This will also let the care-receiver know who will do what and when. Identify the reward to reinforce the person's offer of assistance and to encourage subsequent help. Rewards need not be tangible nor costly. For example, the caregiver might agree to watch the children of the person offering assistance or to lend that person an article of clothing. You might even ask what that person would like, and then negotiate the reward.

One expert on caregiving suggests creating IOU cards to distribute to people who want to help but aren't immediately available, or who offer help when it is not needed. The IOU card specifies the assistance being offered and is signed by the person making the offer. At some future time when the assistance is needed, the caregiver (or the care-receiver, for that matter) can mail or deliver the IOU card to request the assistance. A supply of IOU cards can go a long way toward securing help when it is needed and relieving the burden and stress of caregiving.[4]

Family Meetings

Regular family meetings are a vital component of effective caregiving. Scheduling meetings at which family members can air their concerns serves several purposes: It identifies problem situations, it initiates a dialogue about matters that might otherwise fester

4. Joan Ellen Foyder, *Family Caregiver's Guide* (Cincinnati: Futuro, 1986).

Figure 9.1: Contract

I, _____,
                    (assistant's name)

agree to _____
                    (the specific activity)

for _____
                    (the care-receiver's name)

by _____. If I perform this assistance, I will be rewarded
        (date)

by _____ .
                    (the reward)

_____ *(Assistant's Signature)*	_____ *(Today's Date)*
_____ *(Caregiver's Signature)*	_____ *(Today's Date)*
_____ *(Care-Receiver's Signature)*	_____ *(Today's Date)*

and interfere with relationships among members of the family, and it allows time for the venting of frustration. When possible, all members of the family should be present at a family meeting. This includes the care-receiver, unless the topics to be discussed would bother him or her. Each person present should make a conscious effort to listen *carefully* to what is being said and to understand it. Use reflective (active) listening, which you learned in chapter 5, to resolve any conflicts that arise.

To help focus on listening rather than on planning how to organize your own message, try this: Every time you want to say something, paraphrase what was said by the person who spoke last. If you cannot paraphrase what was just said, ask the person to repeat his or her communication, and then paraphrase it to that person's satisfaction. In this way, you guarantee that you will listen before you speak. Imagine how effective your discussions would be if everyone really did listen to what was being said!

Be sure to draw out any participants who remain silent. It may be that they have little to say and are perfectly happy to listen. On the other hand, they may harbor feelings they are hesitant to share, or may just be too unassertive to speak up. If you notice that someone has remained silent, you might ask one of the following questions:

1. What do you think of that idea, Bill?
2. I wonder what your feelings are on this issue, Mary.
3. Gail, you have experience with this situation. What do you suggest?
4. Harry, you've been pretty quiet so far. Maybe we'll be quiet now and give you a chance to speak.
5. Sally, have you had a chance to express your thoughts or feelings about this?

Each participant in a family meeting should arrive with a list of concerns—clearly-identified issues. At the meeting, write down the steps needed to respond to each concern, who will be responsible for what, and by what date various activities should occur. If the issues cannot be solved, you might consider bringing in an outsider to mediate. A trusted clergy or health professional can serve in this role. Remember not to stifle expressions of feelings; they should actually be encouraged. Be cautious, however, about expressing in front of the care-receiver feelings that may be harmful to her or his self-esteem or emotional health.

Differential Resources

Although it is good for as many family members as possible to participate in caregiving, it should be recognized that different people bring different resources to the caregiving situation. Some family members may have more time, some may have more money, and some may live closer than others.

In addition, some may feel comfortable providing one form of service but uncomfortable providing another. For example, washing the care-receiver or cleaning up after him or her may be distasteful to some family members but not to others.

There may be a member of the family specifically trained in an area directly relevant to a caregiving need. Perhaps someone has been trained as a nurse or other health care provider, or as a social worker with exceptional counseling skills.

Recognizing these differences in the family allows maximum use of resources. Those who are more financially secure, for example, might be asked to contribute more than their share of funds, those with counseling skills might be called upon when sensitive matters need to be discussed with the care-receiver or other family members, and those with health care skills can be asked to take blood pressure readings or conduct other medical assessments.

Physical Arrangements

Once one recognizes that physical arrangements affect the family, one can make adjustments to improve relationships among family members. For example, sometimes an elderly person's room is in the main part of the house, so that frequent conflicts and disruptions are inevitable. For example, if the care-receiver wants to go to sleep early and the rest of the family wants to watch television, the family may feel resentful about turning off the television or keeping the sound barely audible. To prevent such resentments, the care-receiver may stay up past his or her preferred bedtime.

Whenever possible, house the care-receiver in the least disrupted part of the house. A furnished basement is ideal for this purpose. If you can afford to soundproof the care-receiver's room or build an addition to the house, these measures, too, will be beneficial.

When All Else Fails, Laugh

Humor can alleviate stress and keep people healthy. When frustrations pile up, when the situation appears hopelessly bleak, when there is nothing else to do, use the selective awareness skills described in chapter 7 to help you see the humor and laugh. We're reminded of a disabled person who tells the story of a gorgeous hunk of a man—a blond, blue-eyed, muscular Adonis—who complained to his psychiatrist that "people in wheelchairs keep staring at me." Confined to a wheelchair herself, the disabled woman relieved the discomfort she felt when people stared at her by reversing the roles and laughing.

Humor helps when two people are caring for each other. Consider the story of Betty and Morris. One afternoon Betty had a craving for ice cream. Morris, knowing that Betty was not feeling particularly well, offered to go to the ice cream parlor and pick up whatever she wanted. Betty thought for a moment and asked for an ice cream sundae. As Morris began to leave, she suggested, "Why don't you write it down so you won't forget?"

Offended, Morris replied, "I won't forget."

"Hold on a minute," Betty called out. "Make it a sundae with whipped cream." As Morris opened the door to leave, she again beseeched, "Why don't you write it down before you forget?"

Morris started becoming agitated and refused to write it down. "I won't forget," he insisted.

"Hold it," Betty called out, "Make it a sundae with whipped cream and a cherry on top, but write it down so you won't forget."

"Don't worry, I won't forget!" Morris called over his shoulder.

Half an hour later, Morris returned and handed Betty a bag containing a cheese sandwich. After inspecting it, she shook her head in disgust. "I knew you should have written it down! I told you no mustard on my sandwich!"

We realize that finding humor is easier said than done. There are many times when there just isn't anything funny about the situation. Yet often there is; we simply choose to ignore the funny part and focus on the distressing part. As you learned in our discussion of selective awareness, *you* choose what to focus on. If you choose to search for humor, you will usually find it. And you and your family will be healthier for it.

In Conclusion

Rest assured that you can maintain your family as a well-functioning group in spite of the stress of caregiving. Family well-being will not occur by happenstance, however. You must pay particular attention to your family's health in order to maintain positive relationships, relieve frustrations stemming from the demands of providing care for your loved one, and provide mechanisms for sharing concerns and resolving problems. Adopting the recommendations in this chapter will help you toward these goals.

It doesn't make any sense to allow such a meaningful responsibility (and honor) as caregiving to ruin your own immediate or extended family. That need not occur—and it will not occur if you recognize and incorporate the characteristics of effective families, if you identify roles played by family members and maximize their contributions, if you divide responsibilities by using contracts and IOU cards, if you conduct family meetings regularly, if you recognize and accept that family members have differential resources, if you arrange the physical environment in accordance with the family's needs, and if you use humor to alleviate feelings of distress.

10

How to Get Support: Emotional and Financial

I thought it would never work. How could I care for Mom in my home and still work and raise my own family? I had worked hard to get where I was in my field. I couldn't just give it up. Besides, we needed my income to make ends meet. We had bought our house, our car, and several other major items with my income as the deciding factor. And raising three children—including two teenagers with telephones and lots of clothing—required a serious financial commitment. So when we first started thinking about bringing Mom into our home, I didn't think it would be possible. That's when I contacted the staff at our local Center on Aging. They gave me some great suggestions for coping financially and emotionally.

Still, it wasn't particularly easy. Adjustments had to be made in our family schedule and in our expectations of how having Grandma live with us would affect our lives. The first two or three months were difficult, until everybody got used to a new person in the house and a new way of doing things. Each of us had to get used to taking responsibility for someone other than him- or herself. It was especially rough on the teenagers.

But we certainly are glad we made the changes. Mom is worth it. She has been with us now for three years. She is a cornerstone of our family life and gives it a perspective that no one else could. I can't say that it's always easy, or fun, or enjoyable. But making it all work out and getting through the tough times has made our family stronger, and we have all grown to appreciate each other more.

Working and Caregiving

The first issue you may face is how to continue working outside the home and still provide the care your loved one needs. Be comforted—others have faced, and managed to resolve, this same dilemma. It *is* possible to continue working and pursuing your career in spite of your caregiving responsibilities. However, it requires organization and planning.

First, find out what resources are available in your area to help you work and still be an effective caregiver. If your loved one is still quite active, you may only need to call home a couple of times a day to make sure everything is okay. If he or she is less mobile, you may need to plan meals, sitters, and transportation. Use local resources, friends, neighbors, and other family members. Try to set up a weekly routine. If possible, spread the responsibility around so that no one person feels unfairly overburdened.

Know Your Loved One's Capabilities

Before you bring your loved one home, use the assessment guides in chapter 2 to determine your home's safety and your loved one's capabilities. Depending on the care-receiver's capacity to care for her- or himself, you can organize home, neighborhood, and community resources to get you and your loved one through a successful day, week, and month. One way to organize your needs is presented in table 10.1. Following the format of table 10.1, list your loved one's needs (for example, meals, transportation to the doctor, socialization), your needs as they relate to care-giving (for example, someone to call while you're out of town), your primary resources for meeting your needs and those of your loved one, and back-up resources. Back-up resources can help distribute the caregiving workload and provide you with peace of mind if your primary resource falls through.

Be sure to delegate responsibility. For example, in spite of my teenagers' school and extracurricular activities, each of us was able to give a "Grandma afternoon." On that afternoon the designated person got home by 4:00 P.M., visited with Grandma, attended to her needs, and started dinner. That way no one person had to rush home every day. Those "off duty" could plan late meetings, travel home at a leisurely pace, and look forward to a home-cooked meal (or at least to pizza and a salad). We all came to enjoy our "Grandma afternoons" and the opportunity to contribute to the welfare of a very important person in our family.

If your loved one is quite dependent and needs assistance with

Table 10.1
Caregiving Schedule Worksheet

Date: 3 March 1993 Loved One's Needs	Solution	Primary Resource	Back-up
1. Meals	Fix ahead	Self	Son
2. Companionship	Telephone	Self	Neighbor
3. Safety	Stock room	Son	Husband
4. Doctor visit	Transportation	Husband	Neighbor

activities such as toileting and bathing, you will need to arrange for a sitter. Depending on the amount of assistance required, you might hire a licensed practical nurse, a trained nurse's aide, or an untrained sitter. You may be eligible for financial assistance to help defray these costs. (We will discuss sources of financial assistance below.) If your loved one is more independent—for example, can fix meals and use the telephone—a phone call a couple of times a day may be all that is needed.

Even if your loved one can get up and about, you will probably still want to organize your home and arrange the things the care-receiver uses. For example, you might put a bedside potty and washbasin in the elder's room. That room can also be furnished with a rocking chair and ottoman, a reading light, a bedside or cordless phone (with your number and emergency numbers written in large black lettering nearby), a pitcher of ice with a plastic glass, a wide-mouth thermos of hot fluid (broth, coffee, or tea) with an insulated cup, reading material, and a remote-control television set near enough for easy viewing. If your loved one can't safely use the stove, place a preplanned lunch on a cafeteria-style tray to be heated in a microwave. Alternatively, leave a nutritious cold lunch in the refrigerator. Set out utensils, a napkin, and anything else your loved one usually requires for a meal. He or she will not have to search in the cupboards, and the potential for injury will be diminished. You may be able to take advantage of a Meals-on-Wheels program in your area. In that case, someone will actually bring a meal to your home.

How to Keep Your Loved One Out of Your Workplace

No, we don't mean physically! We mean emotionally and psychologically. If you are not careful, your feelings and sense of responsibility for your loved one can spill over into your workplace. There are several reasons to avoid this. One, you need to concentrate on your work to succeed at what you do. Two, you need a break from thinking about and caring for your loved one. Three, although your coworkers want a periodic update on how Grandma or Grandpa is doing and how it is working out for your family, they probably do not want a lengthy daily report on the joys and tribulations of caring for a loved one in your home.

To leave your loved one at home and concentrate on your job may not be easy. At times you will be tired from your caregiving chores. You may be distressed because your plans for elder care and transportation have not gone as you planned. A sitter may call in sick at the last minute, and you may not be able to find a replacement. Should you stay at home, or should you go to work and worry all day? Plans for a vacation may be threatened because your loved one is ill or needs hospitalization. Perhaps everyone in the family understands, but they still feel disappointed and angry at Grandma for being sick and messing up the vacation. You're tired, frustrated, and having difficulty concentrating, and it may be hard not to complain. What can you do on days like these?

Unfortunately, we have no magic pill to offer you. Yet there are things you can do to manage your time and your stress. We suggest that you learn the skills of stress management (chapter 7) and time management (chapter 8). Also refer to chapter 9's discussion of the importance of maintaining your family's health in spite of the challenges accompanying your caregiving responsibilities.

Your employer may be able to help. Some businesses, for example, offer counseling and other services to help you work in spite of the rewarding but trying concerns of caring for a loved one in your home.

Getting Help from Your Employer

It is important to let your employer or immediate supervisor know that you will be caring for your loved one in your home. Assure your boss that you have mobilized available resources to minimize job interference as much as possible. However, should an emergency arise, you may need to leave work early, take a personal leave day or sick day, or make some other arrangements. Assure your supervisor that you will not abuse these privileges. Let your employer know that during the adjustment phase of moving your loved one into your home, you may seem preoccupied, but you will make every effort to minimize any effects on your job performance. To cushion the initial transition, you may want to consider taking a few days off when your loved one moves in.

You may find that you must modify your work schedule. If so, explore all available options. For example, some businesses have flex-time schedules allowing employees to work longer hours each day for fewer days per week (perhaps ten hours a day, four days a week). If you work part-time, perhaps you can work different hours or different days, reduce the number of hours, or job-share (divide your work hours with someone in a similar situation). If possible, explore job options *before* your loved one moves into your home.

Some employers provide more than understanding and flex-time support. There are companies that offer their facilities, secretarial services, and supplies for caregiving support groups. Some businesses actually organize caregiving support groups and pay professionals to serve as group leaders. Such support groups may meet during lunchtime or after work. Many larger companies such as IBM, Travelers Insurance, and American Express offer referral services to help their employees deal with adult home-care issues. Usually these corporations contract with private firms to offer such services. Larger companies may reimburse caregivers for the costs of adult day care. Perhaps one of the most responsive companies in meeting the needs of its employees for adult day care is Stride Rite Shoes. Its headquarters has an on-site facility for adult day care, as well as a child care center.

It is encouraging that at the time of the writing of this book, legislation has been introduced in the U.S. Congress to provide tax credit for adult day care. As more families begin to provide home care for the elderly, more employers will be forced to address the special needs of these employees. Likewise, state and federal legislation will be needed to ease the financial burden of caregiving.

Support Groups

Why did I join a support group when Mom moved in? At first I didn't think I needed one. I hardly had time to get everything done. How was I supposed to squeeze in another hour or two a week for a group meeting? Besides, I figured that all the members did was sit around and complain to each other about how hard it is to make it all work. I had enough of my own problems; I certainly didn't want to hear about anyone else's. But as the weeks went by after Grandma moved in, I began to realize that I needed to talk to someone outside our family, someone who understood what I was going through. I also realized that although I prided myself on planning and orchestrating this whole operation, I was not a professional. I often did things the hard way and learned by trial and error. Hearing how someone else approached the same situation might help me cut some corners. So I thought I'd give a support group a try. After all, I didn't need to sign up for a lifetime membership—right?

The group I eventually joined has been an invaluable asset as I've struggled to keep Grandma with us, continue working, raise a family, preserve a healthy marriage, and stay healthy myself. We don't sit around and complain—well, maybe sometimes—but usually we share concerns, information, caregiving tips, and resources. Our group members have become members of each other's extended families. We have also become friends. Joining the group was probably the single most important thing I did to help myself as a caregiver.

What They Are/What They Do

Support groups vary considerably, but there are four primary types. The first is a *therapy group*. A therapy group is usually sponsored by a hospital or agency. The group is usually small—ten to fifteen members—and is led by a trained therapist. Generally such a group tries to help its members solve and reach resolution of individual problems. A second type of group is the *information support group*. The information group's primary goal is to provide a variety of information to help group members better care for their loved ones, for themselves, and for their families. Usually these groups are led by a trained professional. The meetings consist of a lecture or some other informative program followed by a question-and-answer period. A third type of support group is the *sharing* or *peer support group*. Such a group is usually led by a layperson. Members get together to offer support, to listen, and to share information. A fourth type of support group is an *advocacy group*. Advocacy groups' primary goal is to effect political change regarding the care of elderly. Meetings are usually highly structured and focus on influencing political figures and lobbying for change.

Deciding to Join

When deciding whether to join a support group, you need to investigate several things. For example, what type of groups are available? Who makes up the group? Is it primarily made up of caregivers, or are various professionals also involved? What are the goals or objectives of the group? Is the primary goal to share experiences with each other? Or is the goal to help individual members solve specific problems? Does information come only from group experience, or do professionals provide guidance? Does the group have a program format, or are meetings unstructured? Is leadership provided by a professional such as a social worker, or is it rotated among members? When and where are the meetings? Are meetings scheduled too often for your schedule, or not often enough to meet your needs? Are meeting times convenient for you? Where are the group meetings held? Distance and travel time can be deciding factors, given your already hectic schedule.

In addition to finding out about various groups, you must determine your particular needs. Do you need information to help you care for your loved one? Do you want to learn how others have handled the same situation? Do you need to share your feelings about being a caregiver with someone going through the same experience? If you are not sure what type of group you need, visit two or more groups before deciding which one is right for you.

Although support groups offer a variety of services, there are some things they cannot do. For example, support groups cannot replace health professionals as primary sources for medical caregiving advice. Although home remedies can be helpful, they can also cause problems, delay healing, or aggravate a disease or condition. Likewise, support groups cannot meet your need for individual therapy. Support groups cannot take the place of caregiving services such as those provided by trained sitters or Meals-on-Wheels. Although a support group may be able to combine its resources and provide services, it is a waste of resources to duplicate existing services to caregivers.

Should you join a support group? Only if you think you can benefit from one, and only if you can find one that meets your needs. Remember, too, that your needs will change as you move through this experience of caring for your loved one. If you don't think you can benefit from a support group now, you can always reconsider that decision later.

How to Pay for It All: Sources of Financial Assistance

At one of our support group meetings, Annie told us how she went about uncovering funding sources to help her meet the financial demands of caring for her father. Initially, she thought all her savings would be drained within a few months. Never having cared for a loved one in her home, she was unsure where to turn. She was, however, determined to keep her father in her home, around people he loved, and in a place that was familiar.

Armed with a notebook, pen, and phone book, she began to ferret out sources of financial assistance. Because her father had social security coverage, she started by calling the Social Security Administration. Her father was an army veteran, so she called the nearest Veterans Administration hospital. Because her father had suffered for years from debilitating osteoarthritis, Annie called the local chapter of the Arthritis Foundation. She also inquired about financial assistance to make her home barrier-free and to employ home health aides. Next, she talked to her father's doctor to see whether her father was eligible for inclusion in any of the medical research studies being conducted on arthritis. She learned that a new drug investigation would be starting in a few months and, if he met the study requirements, he could receive free medication and medical care related to his arthritis for the duration of the study. Annie also contacted the local Chamber of Commerce and the United Way to determine what community services were available for her and her father.

After several days of adept detective work, Annie had a notebook full of leads and information to help her with the costs of caring for her father at home. With a little time and effort set aside for exploring sources of financial assistance, you can be as successful as Annie.

Several federal programs assist with the delivery of home care services. These include Medicare, Medicaid, Social Services Block Grants, and grants from the Administration on Aging and the Public Health Service. Additionally, in-home services for those with mental disabilities may be provided on a limited basis through mental health programs and mental retardation and developmental disabilities programs. Medicare and Medicaid provide funding for home health services that are directly relevant to a medical condition. The types of services covered include home nursing and occupational, physical, audio, or speech therapy.

Unfortunately, those who have saved and planned for financial security in their retirement years may not be eligible for some of these programs; they have too much money. As the regulations are currently written, they must spend their resources until they reach the poverty level before they can qualify for assistance. With the costs of health care and of accommodating elderly lifestyles, reaching the poverty level does not usually take very long.

Medicare

Medicare is a program of federal health insurance for Americans over the age of 65. Application for coverage and additional information about Medicare are available through Social Security Administration offices. As discussed earlier in chapter 2, DRGs have significantly decreased the length of time patients are permitted to stay in the hospital. This reduction in length of stay has added twenty-one million days of care per year to alternative home and community programs. While home care is a reasonable alternative to hospital recovery, Medicare is very strict about the types and levels of care it will fund in the home, and it insists that these services be terminated in a reasonable period of time. Medicare reimbursement for home case is generally allotted for services that are short-term and oriented toward acute rather than chronic conditions.

If a person is confined to home by injury or illness that requires medical treatment or therapy and the person is entitled to receive Medicare, she or he may qualify for part-time, skilled health care services. Medicare reimburses costs of home health aides who perform functions similar to those of hospital aides, but it does not reimburse the costs of services furnished primarily to meet personal, family, or domestic needs. Generally, you must pay for these services, unless you can find other financing.

Skilled services required in the home are reimbursable through Medicare and sometimes through Medicaid and a small but growing number of private insurance plans. Medicare provides payment to home care agencies if the following four conditions are met:

1. The level of care requires skilled nursing, physical therapy, and/or speech therapy.
2. The patient is under the care of a physician with an established plan of treatment.
3. The patient is homebound.
4. The care agency is certified by Medicare to provide home care services.

Medicare will cover one hundred days of care in a skilled nursing facility during a spell of illness, but only after the patient has been hospitalized for a minimum of three days in the thirty-day period prior to entering the skilled nursing facility.

To review, Medicare does not reimburse for: twenty-four-hour (full-time) home nursing services, medications, meals delivered to the home, general housekeeping services unrelated to direct patient care, and custodial or personal care services.

The Medicare Catastrophic Act passed in 1988 was repealed by Congress on 21 November 1989. Consequently, catastrophic, expensive health care remains nonreimbursable. For example, hospice care for terminally ill patients is covered for only 210 days. Medicare coverage of respite care for persons providing caregiving services in their home has been eliminated. The spousal impoverishment protection and the buy-in for low-income beneficiaries were the only benefits of the Catastrophic Coverage Act that were retained.

It is important to remember, should your loved one need to be hospitalized, that Medicare reimburses only for certain in-hospital expenses. Common expenses *not* covered by Medicare are charges for television, radio, or phone usage, fees for private duty nurses, and additional charges for a private room unless it is a medical necessity. Likewise, Medicare covers most, but not all, of a physician's services. These include cosmetic surgery (unless needed because of a disfiguring accident or to improve the use of a body part), immunizations (unless required because of injury or immediate risk of infection), vision and hearing examinations for fitting prescription lenses or hearing aids, and routine foot care.

Even if your loved one is eligible for Medicare benefits, he or she will still incur some medical costs. For example, Medicare has a yearly deductible. That means the patient must pay a specific amount (e.g., one hundred dollars) before Medicare will pay the remainder of your medical bills. Likewise, Medicare will pay only 80 percent of what it deems reasonable costs for your loved one's care. As you probably already know, what a hospital or a physician considers reasonable may not accord with Medicare's guidelines. You will be expected to pay the difference between your loved one's hospital or doctor bill and what Medicare deems reasonable, *plus* 20 percent of the approved changes. This is reason enough to seek supplemental insurance. One such insurance is provided by the American Association of Retired Persons (AARP) and similar policies are available through a variety of insurance carriers.

A free copy of a handbook on Medicare is available to those who send a request to "Your Medicare Handbook," U.S. Government Printing Office, Washington, D.C. 20402.

Medicaid

Medicaid is a federal program administered by individual states. Federal, state, and local funds finance the program, which is run by state governments according to federal guidelines issued under Title XIX of the Social Security Act. Administration, eligibility, coverage, and the laws that cover available assistance vary from state to state. The administering agency may be the department of welfare, the department of social services, or the state health department.

In general, Medicaid is designed to assist those who have exhausted their own funds in paying for health care. It is *not* designed to preserve the patient's savings. Therefore, it is limited by low income-eligibility criteria, such as monthly income limits and poverty requirements (limits on savings accounts, property value, and other assets). Some states have obtained a waiver from the federal government under Section 2176 of the Omnibus Reconciliation Act of 1981, which allows them to offer home- and community-based services to individuals who would otherwise be institutionalized.

Programs for the Disabled

The Social Security Administration also administers the Social Security Disability Program and the Supplemental Security Income Program. These programs are intended to aid disabled workers who have contributed to the Social Security Trust Fund through income tax deductions. The Supplemental Security Income Program guarantees a minimum income for aged, blind, and disabled persons who qualify because of financial need. Disability is defined as "an inability to engage in any substantial gainful activity by reason of a medically determinable physical or mental impairment which can be expected to end in death or has lasted or can be expected to last for a continuous period of not less than twelve months." Each state has its own special disability determination.

Veterans Administration System/CHAMPVA

The Civilian Health and Medical Program of the Veterans Administration (CHAMPVA) shares the medical bills for military-service-connected illnesses and disabilities of families and survivors of certain veterans. Several veterans' hospitals across the country have established pilot home health care programs for those who need them because of a service-connected disability. For more information, contact your nearest Veterans Administration office, or write to the Veterans Administration, Washington, D.C. 20402.

For more information on CHAMPVA contact the Central CHAMPVA Registry Center, 1055 Clermont Street, Denver, CO 80220; (800) 331–9935 (outside Colorado), or (800) 843–5710.

CHAMPUS

The Civilian Health and Medical Program of the Uniformed Services (CHAMPUS) provides some skilled home nursing care coverage for military dependents. If you think your loved one may qualify for CHAMPUS benefits, contact the health benefits adviser at the closest military or public health service facility. To get more information, you can write to CHAMPUS Benefit Services, Aurora, CO 80045–6900.

Other Sources of Home Care Assistance

Some agencies that provide supportive services for caregivers and care-receivers acquire funding under Title III of the Older Americans' Act or though Social Services Block Grants. These funds support homemaker or home health aide services not covered by Medicare or Medicaid for individuals who meet state-specified eligibility requirements. For further information and to determine your eligibility, contact the provider agency. Information on these agencies is located in appendix 1A.

The Federal Child and Dependent Care Credit Bill allows families to claim a federal tax credit for expenses incurred for home nursing services and special health-related equipment. Only a small number of caregivers are eligible, because the requirements are very restrictive. For more information, refer to IRS publication 502, "Medical and Dental Expenses."

Private insurance is another source of funding for home health care. Coverage varies greatly from carrier to carrier and from policy to policy. In the past, private insurance plans have not included coverage for home health services. Currently, though, many major insurance companies are incorporating partial coverage for home health care services into their policies.

Health maintenance organizations (HMOs) may also cover some home health care. If you belong to an HMO, contact the service representative and inquire about allowable coverage.

If your loved one suffers from a specific disease, it would be wise to contact the national or local association of that disease to determine whether financial assistance or equipment is available, as well as to discuss the possibility of participating in research or pilot projects that may include free medications, doctors' visits, and laboratory and X-ray services. The American Diabetes Association is one example of such an organization. These organizations are listed in alphabetical order in appendix 1A.

Home Remodeling or Reconstructive Costs

Home remodeling or structural changes required to care for your loved one may be reimbursable from public or private sources. Many of these sources were discussed in chapter 2. You should also contact your local homebuilders' association and Chamber of Commerce to see whether any voluntary organizations or professional agencies provide no-cost or low-cost assistance.

Information regarding private funding sources can be obtained by contacting the Foundation Center, which has offices in San Francisco, New York City, and Washington, D.C. A book titled *Stalking the Elusive Buck* is available for $5.00 plus postage from The Adaptive Environments Center, Massachusetts College of Art, 621 Huntington Avenue, Boston, MA 02114.

THE FINANCIAL COSTS OF caring for your loved one may be easily managed if she or he is in good health and requires few special services. As your elder ages, however, his or her health may deteriorate, and more services may be required. To receive financial support, you must be aware of potential funding sources and spend time and effort to track down knowledgeable persons in various agencies who can help determine whether your loved one meets eligibility requirements. A good starting point in this search may be a hospital social worker, your state Commission on Aging or your local Social Security Administration.

Sexuality: A Matter of Intimacy

One of our grandmothers recently celebrated her one hundredth birthday and is still going strong! She married her first husband in 1910; he died in 1945. She remarried in 1950; her second husband died in 1972. In 1977 she married her third husband; he was 77 and she was 87 on their wedding day. During the wedding reception Grandma whispered to my brother, "I picked a young one this time. I sure hope he outlives me!" Unfortunately, he died in 1984. After the death of her third husband, Grandma decided to move into the nursing home three blocks from where she had lived all her life. Within several months of Grandma's arrival, we learned that she had a boyfriend. She never discussed her new sex life with us, so we don't really know about that aspect of her relationship, but clearly Grandma has always liked the closeness and intimacy afforded by companions of the opposite sex. The nursing-home staff supported and even encouraged their relationship, which brought great pleasure to staff and residents alike. It was a sad time when Thurman's health deteriorated and he died. Grandma was 99 years old at the time.

Most older people want, and can lead, an active, satisfying sex life. Society, however, has been slow to recognize that older persons have sexual needs and often denies the existence of sexual activity among the elderly. In fact, sexual needs constitute very normal and very real needs for many elders.

This chapter discusses how you can get support for your caregiving responsibilities. We end with the need to *give* support: support for the sexual and intimacy needs of your elderly loved one. Meeting these needs is one of the principal antidotes to the loneliness that too often accompanies aging.

Sexual needs can be manifested in a variety of ways and do not necessarily require satisfaction through sexual intercourse or relating to others in stereotypical "sexy" ways. Sex for the elderly has as much to do with intimacy as it does with the act of sex. Often these needs can be met through expression of admiration, loyalty, and affection for one another, as well as actual physical touching, warmth, and companionship. For many women, dressing up, adorning themselves with jewelry, and having their hair or nails done are very important to their sexuality. Some expend much effort to remain attractive even when they rarely get to interact with other people. It makes them feel good—that is, sexual.

Physiologically Speaking

Sigmund Freud was the psychiatrist who pointed out the enormously strong influence of sexuality on a person's overall health and psyche. Physiologically, the peak of sexual performance is age 18 for both males and females. With age comes a gradual decline in frequency and duration of erection in males. Females gradually experience less frequent and less intense orgasms. The slowing of bodily functions, however, does not mean that sexual desire, sexual activity, and sexual satisfaction stop. Sexual enjoyment usually does not change and in fact may increase with age. While the old adage, "If you don't use it, you lose it," is essentially true, "resexualization" is possible for those who have totally abstained for prolonged periods of time. After menopause females typically notice a drying and shrinking of the vagina due to decreased estrogen levels or lack of sexual stimulation. Use of a surgical lubricant (for example, KY Jelly—not petroleum jelly) can help lubricate the vagina, and an estrogen vaginal cream can often restore some of its elasticity and moisture.

There are some medical conditions—for example, strokes, prostate enlargement—and some drugs (especially those for high blood pressure) that can affect sexual functioning. If this is a problem, the care-receiver can be encouraged to ask his or her physician to evaluate whether a different course of treatment or medication is an option. Problems with sexual functioning should not be ignored.

Establishing New Relationships

Too often children, friends, and caregivers are the biggest deterrents to the development of sexual relationships between the elderly. Children of all ages have trouble imagining their parents actually engaging in sexual activity. It is often difficult for them to understand why a widowed parent wants to establish a relationship after the death of a spouse. Some children devise numerous rationales for their parent not to begin a new relationship. When considered objectively, however, most of these rationales are invalid. Seeking new friendships speaks well for the recovery of the grieving spouse. Likewise, opposite-sex friendships and sexual activity help ensure that an important aspect of your loved one's health is being maintained.

Elders may choose to develop an intimate relationship but not to remarry. This can trouble their children. For elders, however, this decision seems perfectly rational. Sometimes the decision is based on economics. Elders may lose some benefits it they remarry. Others may chose not to remarry to ensure passage of their entire estate to their children. In any case, friends and family need to encourage elders to develop intimate relationships: relationships that take the form *they* desire and meet the needs *they* identify.

Intimacy and Home Care

Recognizing that your loved one is a sexual being, how can you address his or her sexual and intimacy needs? Becoming aware that your loved one has the right to meet such needs is a good first step. Beyond that, you can facilitate opportunities to meet persons of the opposite sex through home visits, time at the senior citizens' center, and attendance at church, synagogue, and other social gatherings. Provide privacy in the home. Always knock before going into your loved one's room or before entering a sitting area.

Bolster your loved one's feelings of attractiveness by complimenting his or her hair, clothing, accessories, and general appearance. Comment positively on his or her grooming, stature, and carriage. Remind your loved one that he or she is still attractive. If your loved one enjoys it, tease him or her about the interest of the opposite sex or how attractive he or she may be to the widow(er) down the street or at the senior citizens' center. Encourage him or her to wear cologne or perfume. Buy your loved one attractive underclothes and nightwear. Should he or she enjoy reading romance novels as an outlet for sexual feelings, do not discourage entry into this fantasy world.

In summary, sexuality isn't a stage of a person's life, it is a part of it. Your loved one needs the freedom to express his or her sexuality, free from disapproval and interference.

In Conclusion

Be comforted in the knowledge that other people and organizations are available to help you meet your emotional and financial commitments to caregiving. There are governmental agencies, private health insurers, support groups, and family and friends whose assistance you should seek out. Do not wait until you are in dire straits, either emotionally or financially. Plan well in advance to take advantage of the assistance that awaits your expression of need.

Know that you have a responsibility to give support as well as to receive it. Your elder, regardless of age, is still a sexual being. Although the form of sexual expression may change with age, the need for a sexual or intimate relationship does not disappear. Your support is an important first step in helping your loved one satisfy this need. Beyond that, set up your home to meet the privacy needs of your loved one, compliment her or his appearance and thereby enhance her or his sexual self-esteem, and facilitate meetings between your loved one and members of the opposite sex.

Receiving and giving support, then, is a caregiver's duty. In no small part, this responsibility has significant impact on the welfare of your care-receiver, your family, and yourself. Do it, as the once-popular beer commercial said, with *gusto!*

11

Keeping Yourself Healthy

Before we begin to discuss the importance of keeping yourself healthy and how to go about doing that, let's assess your current health habits. (see figure 11.1).

Figure 11.1: Health Habits

For each of the following items, write on the scale below the letter which represents how often you engage in the behavior described.

Scale: A = Almost always; S = Sometimes; N = Never

_____ 1. I avoid smoking cigarettes.

_____ 2. I smoke only low-tar and low-nicotine cigarettes, or I smoke only a pipe or cigar.

_____ 3. I avoid drinking alcoholic beverages, or I drink no more than one or two drinks a day.

_____ 4. I avoid using alcohol or other drugs (especially illegal drugs) as a way of handling stressful situations or the problems in my life.

_____ 5. I am careful not to drink alcohol when taking certain medicines (for example, medicine for sleeping, pain, colds, and allergies).

_____ 6. I read and follow the label directions when using prescribed and over-the-counter drugs.

_____ 7. I eat a variety of foods each day, such as fruits and vegetables, whole-grain breads and cereals, lean meats, dairy products, dry peas and beans, and nuts and seeds.

_____ 8. I limit the amount of fat and cholesterol I eat (including fat on meat, eggs, butter, cream, shortening, and organ meats such as liver).

_____ 9. I limit the amount of salt I eat by cooking with only small amounts, not adding salt at the table, and avoiding salty snacks.

_____10. I avoid eating too much sugar (especially frequent snacks or sticky candy or soft drinks).

(Continued next page)

Figure 11.1: *(Continued)*

_____11. I maintain a desired weight, avoiding overweight or underweight.
_____12. I do vigorous exercise for fifteen to thirty minutes at least three times a week (examples include running, swimming, brisk walking).
_____13. I do exercises that enhance my muscle tone for fifteen to thirty minutes at least three times a week (examples include yoga and calisthenics).
_____14. I use part of my leisure time participating in individual, family, or team activities that increase my level of fitness (such as gardening, bowling, golf, or baseball).
_____15. I get approximately seven to eight hours of sleep a night.
_____16. I find it easy to relax.
_____17. I have plenty of time for relaxation.
_____18. I engage in structured relaxation activities such as meditation, autogenics, progressive relaxation, or yoga.

Score this test by adding up the numbers assigned to each of your responses.

Item	Scoring	Item	Scoring
1.	A = 2; S = 1; N = 0	10.	A = 2; S = 1; N = 0
2.	A = 2; S = 1; N = 0	11.	A = 3; S = 1; N = 0
3.	A = 4; S = 1; N = 0	12.	A = 3; S = 1; N = 0
4.	A = 2; S = 1; N = 0	13.	A = 2; S = 1; N = 0
5.	A = 2; S = 1; N = 0	14.	A = 2; S = 1; N = 0
6.	A = 2; S = 1; N = 0	15.	A = 2; S = 1; N = 0
7.	A = 4; S = 1; N = 0	16.	A = 2; S = 1; N = 0
8.	A = 2; S = 1; N = 0	17.	A = 2; S = 1; N = 0
9.	A = 2; S = 1; N = 0	18.	A = 3; S = 1; N = 0

If you scored higher than 21, you generally behave in a healthy manner. If you scored less than 21, you generally behave in an unhealthy manner. The higher your score, the more healthy are your habits. However, you may do well in many areas but poorly in others. For example, you may eat well, refrain from abusing drugs, and not smoke cigarettes, but get only four hours of sleep each night. So even if your overall score reflects a healthy lifestyle, you may still need to read certain sections of this chapter.

Here we present ways to improve your health through exercise, nutrition, quitting smoking, and sleep (strategies to relax and manage stress are included in chapter 7). You may want to read only those sections that discuss behaviors you need to improve. On the other hand, reading all sections might reinforce healthy behaviors that are already a part of your lifestyle.

In any case, read this chapter carefully. It may be the most important chapter in this book. If you don't maintain your own health, how can you maintain someone else's? If you become ill, you may have to go from being a caregiver to being the recipient of care, which will benefit no one. With attention to the material presented in this chapter, you can prevent or postpone many illnesses and diseases. You cannot avoid illness forever, but you needn't be stricken at age 45 by a heart attack that would normally occur much later. Follow the advice presented in this chapter, and you will increase the likelihood of staying healthy.

Exercise

In chapter 7, I described how, in a moment of frustration and stress, I kicked my son. That was not appropriate, and, as I mentioned, I was ashamed of my behavior. To reduce stress, too many people seek similar inappropriate outlets. We know, for instance, that during times of high unemployment, incidents of child abuse, spousal abuse, and other violent acts increase. Unfortunately, caregivers have been known to abuse the elderly under their care. You can relieve stress by using stress products in a *positive* manner—a manner that will make you feel better and will not violate anyone else's rights. Exercise can help you do that.

Let me tell you about Dick. Dick and I played tennis together, and Dick never won. Our talents were not dissimilar, but Dick invariably hit the ball harder than necessary and, consequently, could not control it as I did. One day I suggested to him that he hit easier but try to exercise more control.

Dick's response taught me an important lesson. He said that the ball represented his boss, his wife, or anyone else he was upset with at the moment. No way was he going to hit that "sucker" with less force! I was concerned about winning; Dick was concerned about his health. I was frustrated when I hit a poor shot; as long as Dick got "good wood" on that ball, he was satisfied. Dick used physical exercise to alleviate stress.

Exercise and Health

Not only can exercise relieve stress, it is also good for your physical and psychological health. It strengthens your heart, makes your circulatory system and lungs work more efficiently, helps control your blood pressure and your weight, and even slows down the degenerative changes related to aging. In addition to these physical benefits, regular exercise can improve your self-esteem, make you more confident and poised, and decrease anxiety and depression.

How to Exercise

Assuming that you have determined that you need exercise, how do you begin? *Slowly!* If you have been sedentary, walking is a good way to start. Walking can be very enjoyable when you focus on your surroundings—the foliage, the sounds, the buildings, the people, the sky, the colors. Walking briskly is good exercise. After years of trying, I finally convinced my father to make it a practice to get off the bus one stop sooner on his way home from work and walk the rest of the way. Later, he told me he never felt better. His body felt limber, he had a sense of accomplishment, and he felt less stressed.

Swimming and bicycle riding are also good ways to begin an exercise program. If your body is like mine, you probably don't qualify to play Tarzan anyhow, so take it easy. Since your body is supported by water when swimming and by the seat when biking, these are excellent beginning activities. You can exert yourself more strenuously in these activities when you get in better shape.

Figure 11.2 depicts the benefits of several sports and exercises. Pay particular attention to the individual fitness component score for each of these sports. If you have a specific need, certain sports will be better than others. For example, if you need to lose weight, you would be well advised to jog (it gives you a twenty-one score). On the other hand, if flexibility is your concern, you would be better off doing calisthenics or playing handball or squash (they give you scores of nineteen and sixteen, respectively).

Remember these points when exercising:

1. Warm-up and Cool-down

Research has indicated that beginning exercise too abruptly can cause problems in cardiac rhythm. Since these problems can result in heart attacks (even in an otherwise healthy heart), a ten- or fifteen-minute warm-up is recommended before any strenuous exercise. The warm-up also helps stretch the muscles and decrease the chance of muscle strains during the exercise itself.

After vigorous exercise, blood can pool in the veins, leading to fainting. Though this possibility is somewhat remote, you should take a five- or ten-minute cool-down period after strenuous exercise. The cool-down will also help rid the muscles of lactate—a waste product of exercise—and thus decrease residual soreness in the muscles. Walking and stretching exercises are good for cool-down.

Figure 11.2: Physical Fitness Scorecard for Selected Sports and Exercises

	Jogging	Bicycling	Swimming	Skating (ice or roller)	Handball/Squash	Skiing—Nordic	Skiing—Alpine	Basketball	Tennis	Calisthenics	Walking	Golf*	Softball	Bowling
Physical Fitness														
Cardiorespiratory endurance (stamina)	21	19	21	18	19	19	16	19	16	10	13	8	6	5
Muscular endurance	20	18	20	17	18	19	18	17	16	13	14	8	8	5
Muscular strength	17	16	14	15	15	15	15	15	14	16	11	9	7	5
Flexibility	9	9	15	13	16	14	14	13	14	19	7	8	9	7
Balance	17	18	12	20	17	16	21	16	16	15	8	8	7	6
General Well-Being														
Weight control	21	20	15	17	19	17	15	19	16	12	13	6	7	5
Muscle definition	14	15	14	14	11	12	14	13	13	18	11	6	5	5
Digestion	13	12	13	11	13	12	9	10	12	11	11	7	8	7
Sleep	16	15	16	15	12	15	12	12	11	12	14	6	7	6
Total	148	142	140	140	140	139	134	134	128	126	102	66	64	51

Note: A rating of 21 indicates maximum benefit. Ratings were made on the basis of regular (minimum of four times per week) vigorous (duration of thirty minutes to one hour per session) participation in each activity.

*Ratings for golf are based on the fact that many Americans use a golf cart and/or caddy. If you walk the links, the physical fitness value moves up appreciably.

2. Intensity, Frequency, and Duration

For strenuous exercise to have a beneficial cardiovascular effect, it should raise the heart rate to 60–80 percent of its maximum. To indirectly determine your *maximal heart rate*, subtract your age in years from 220. Take 60–80 percent of that number; that is how fast your heart should be beating during strenuous exercise. For example, if you are thirty, your maximal heart rate is 190 beats per minute. You should, therefore, exercise so that your heart is beating between 60 and 80 percent of 190 (114–152 beats per minute). This is called your *target heart rate*. Aim for the 60 percent level when you are beginning an exercise program and gradually increase to the 80 percent level as your physical fitness improves. A good rule to follow is to take your pulse—every five minutes if you are just beginning to exercise, every fifteen minutes if you are more experienced—during exercise to determine whether you are working too hard or not hard enough. The pulse rate should be taken for six seconds and multiplied by 10 to get the one-minute rate.

You should exercise for twenty to thirty minutes three or four days a week. You might want to schedule your exercise as you do other events in your life. In this way you will view it as a commitment and be more likely to do the exercise. Otherwise, you may assume that you will exercise when you have the time and find yourself continually postponing it.

Nutrition

You've probably heard the expression, "You are what you eat." It's true. No, you won't turn into a hot dog, but your health is largely a function of the food substances you ingest. Among myriad other purposes foods serve, they allow you to move by fueling your muscles, give your heart and lungs the energy they need to function, and provide the building blocks your cells need to repair themselves and to recover from illness or injury. It is vital that you eat well—that is, take in enough of the right kinds of nutrients and limit the wrong kinds.

To help you organize your diet, remember the food groups:

Group 1: Milk and Milk Products
Group 2: Meat, Fish, Poultry, and Eggs
Group 3: Fruits and Vegetables
Group 4: Breads, Cereals, and Whole-Grain Products

You should eat servings from each of these food groups every day. In that way you will ingest the right amount of protein, carbo-

Table 11.1
Percentage of U.S. RDA for Some Common Foods[a]

Food	Amount or Description	Metric Weight (Grams)	Calories	Percentage U.S. RDA						
				Protein	Vitamin A	Vitamin C	Thiamine	Riboflavin	Calcium	Iron
Milk and milk products										
Milk, whole; yogurt	1 cup	(240)	160	20	6	2	6	25	30	—
Skim, unfortified; buttermilk	1 cup	(240)	90	20	—	2	6	25	30	—
Modified skim (99% fat free), fortified	1 cup	(240)	120	25	10	2	6	25	30	—
Evaporated, undiluted	½ cup	(120)	160	20	8	2	4	25	30	—
Nonfat dry solids, fortified	3 tbsp; 1 cup reconstituted	(23; 24)	90	20	10	2	6	25	30	—
Milkshake, chocolate	10 ounces (1 cup whole milk)	(345)	400	25	15	2	6	35	40	4
Cheeses: cheddar; American; Swiss; processed	1 ounce (1¼" cube)	(30)	115	15	6	—	2	8	20	—
Cheese, cottage creamed	½ cup	(115)	120	30	4	—	2	15	10	—
Ice cream (10% fat)	½ cup	(115)	130	6	6	—	2	8	10	—
Milk pudding, vanilla	½ cup	(130)	140	10	4	—	2	12	15	—
Cream, half & half	¼ cup	(60)	80	4	6	—	—	6	6	—
Vegetables										
Important Sources of Vitamins A and/or C[b]										
Broccoli	½ cup cooked	(75)	20	4	40	120	6	10	8	4
Brussels sprouts; green pepper	½ cup cooked; 1 medium pepper	(75; 90)	25	4	10	110	4	4	2	6

(Continued next page)

Table 11.1
(Continued)

Food	Amount or Description	Metric Weight (Grams)	Calories	Protein	Vitamin A	Vitamin C	Thiamine	Riboflavin	Calcium	Iron
							Percentage U.S. RDA			
Cabbage; cauliflower	⅔ cup raw; ½ cooked	(90)	15	2	2	50	2	2	4	2
Carrots	½ cup cooked or raw	(80)	30	2	150	10	4	2	2	2
Greens; beet; chard; collards; kale; mustard; spinach; turnip	½ cup cooked	(100)	20	2	100	50	6	10	10c	8
Plantain, green or ripe	½ cup cooked	(100)	140	2	25	10	4	2	—	2
Squash, winter; pumpkin; calabaza	½ cup cooked	(100)	60	2	90	20	4	6	2	4
Sweet Potato; yam, yellow	½ cup cooked	(100)	120	2	120	20	4	2	2	4
Tomatoes, raw; canned; juice	1 small; ½ cup	(100)	20	2	15	35	4	2	—	4
Other Vegetables										
Asparagus	½ cup cut pieces	(80)	15	2	15	30	8	8	2	4
Beans, lima	½ cup cooked	(80)	95	10	4	20	10	4	4	10
Beans, snap	½ cup cooked	(60)	15	2	8	15	4	4	4	4
Beets; onions	½ cup cooked	(80)	30	2	—	8	2	2	—	2
Celery; cucumber; radishes	½ cup sliced	(50)	10	—	—	8	—	—	—	—
Corn	½ cup cooked; 1 5-inch ear	(80; 140)	85	4	6	8	2	4	—	4
Lettuce, crisp head; loose leaf	1 cup shredded	(55)	8	—	8	8	2	4	—	4
Peas, green	½ cup cooked	(80)	65	8	10	25	15	6	2	8
Turnips; rutabaga	½ cup cooked	(80)	20	2	6	25	2	2	2	2
Mushrooms	½ cup cooked	(120)	20	4	—	2	—	15	—	2

Food	Measure	(grams)	Calories							
Potatoes, white	One: 4 per lb	(100)	85	2	—	25	6	2	—	4
Potatoes, white, mashed	½ cup, milk and butter added	(100)	90	4	—	20	6	4	2	2
Squash, summer; zuccini; crookneck	½ cup cooked	(100)	15	2	8	15	4	4	2	2
Viandas[d]	½ cup cooked	(100)	90–130	2	4	4	4	2	—	4
Fruits										
Important Sources of Vitamins A and/or C[b]										
Apricots, canned in syrup	½ cup	(130)	110	—	35	6	—	2	—	2
Cantaloupe	¼ (5 inch diameter)	(230)	40	—	90	70	2	2	—	2
Grapefruit, white (edible portion); juice	½ (4 inch diameter); ½ cup	(120)	50	—	—	70	4	2	2	2
Mangos, raw	½ cup sliced	(80)	55	—	80	45	2	2	—	2
Orange (edible portion); juice	1 (2½ inch diameter); ½ cup	(120)	65	—	4	100	6	2	4	2
Peaches, raw	One: 4 per lb	(100)	40	—	25	15	2	4	—	2
Strawberries; raw; frozen; sweetened	1 cup	(150; 250)	60; 250	—	2	150	2	6	4	8
Watermelon	1 cup diced	(160)	40	2	20	20	4	2	2	4
Other Fruits										
Apples; applesauce, sweetened	One: 3 per lb; 1 cup	(150; 240)	85; 200	—	2	10	2	2	—	4
Bananas	1 medium; 1 cup sliced	(175)	100	2	4	20	4	4	—	4
Blueberries; raspberries	½ cup unsweetened	(65)	40	—	—	25	—	2	—	2
Canned fruit in syrup: cocktail; pears	½ cup	(120)	80	—	2	2	—	—	—	2
Grapes	½ cup	(75)	60	—	—	6	2	—	—	2
Pears	One: 2½ per lb	(180)	100	—	—	10	2	4	—	2
Pineapple, raw	½ cup diced	(75)	40	—	—	20	4	—	—	2

(Continued next page)

Table 11.1
(Continued)

Food	Amount or Description	Metric Weight (Grams)	Calories	Protein	Vitamin A	Vitamin C	Thiamine	Riboflavin	Calcium	Iron
Prunes, dried; juice	5 medium, ½ cup	(30; 120)	80; 120	—	10	2	2	2	2	10
Raisins, seedless	⅓ cup; 1½ oz package	(45)	120	2	—	—	2	2	2	8
Meat, fish, poultry, eggs, legumes										
Beef; veal; lamb	3 ounces cooked, lean only	(90)	180–225	50	—	—	6	10	—	15
Chicken, fried	1 drumstick and thigh	(125)	250	50	—	—	4	10	—	8
Chicken; turkey	3 ounces, no skin	(90)	180	50	—	—	4	10	—	8
Fish: clams; shrimp	3 ounces meat, no fat/breading	(90)	100	50	—	—	4	6	8	15ᵉ
haddock; perch; cod	3 ounces, no fat added	(90)	100	50	—	—	4	6	2	6
tuna, canned	3 ounces in water, in oil	(90)	100; 170	50	—	—	4	6	2	6
Hamburger	3 ounces cooked	(90)	250	45	—	—	4	10	—	15
Hot dogs; bologna; cold cuts	1 hot dog; 2 ounces	(60)	160	15	—	—	6	6	—	6
Liver	2 ounces, no fat added	(60)	135	35	500	15	10	120	—	25
Pork; ham	3 ounces cooked, lean only	(90)	300	45	—	—	40	10	—	15
Pork sausage, cooked	1 link: 16 per lb	(20)	95	6	—	—	4	2	2	2
Eggs	1 large	(50)	80	15	10	—	4	8	2	6

Percentage U.S. RDA

Legumes: dried beans; peas	1 ounce dried; ½ cup cooked	(30; 90)	125	15	—	—	10	4	4	15
Peanut butter; nuts	2 tbsp peanut butter; ¼ cup	(30)	190	15	—	—	4	4	—	4
Cereal products, whole grain/enriched[f]										
Bread; toast, bagel	1 slice; ½ bagel	(25)	70	4	—	—	6	4	2	8
Cereals: oatmeal; wheat	1 cup cooked	(240)	110	4	—	—	10	4	—	6
ready-to-eat	1 ounce	(30)	100	refer to label on package						
Corn grits; corn meal	1 cup cooked	(240)	125	4	2	—	8	4	—	6
Hamburger roll	1 medium	(40)	120	6	—	—	10	6	2	10
Spaghetti: macaroni; noodles; rice	1 cup cooked	(150–200)	200	8	—	—	15	6	2	8

a. References: *Composition of Foods*, Agriculture Handbook No. 8, USDA, 1963; *Nutritive Value of American Foods in Common Units*, Agriculture Handbook No. 456, USDA, 1975; *Food Values of Portions Commonly Used*, Bowes and Church, Lippincott, 1970; *Tabla de Composición de alimentos de use corriente en Puerto Rico*, Reguero and Santiago, University of Puerto Rico, 1974; California Prune Advisory Board, 1973.

b. Highest vitamin A content is found in darker yellow-orange and green vegetables and fruits.

c. Some calcium in spinach, Swiss chard, or beet greens may combine with a plant acid and may not be absorbed.

d. Yautia (white tanier), name (white yam), malanga (taro, dasheen), yuca (cassava). Yuca has somewhat more vitamin C than listed.

e. Clams provide 30 percent iron.

f. Values for thiamine, riboflavin, and iron are based on enrichment levels specified by FDA, October 1973.

Note: Some figures represent judgments made to help the user identify the most dependable sources of individual nutrients.

hydrates, fats, vitamins, and minerals. Table 11.1 will help you select the right amounts for each food group.

If you take in too many calories, you are probably eating too many fatty foods, which can cause heart disease or cancer. Table 11.2 presents the recommended daily intake of calories.

In addition, the foods you eat can be related to the levels of stress you experience. Certain food substances produce a stresslike response, other nutrients can be depleted by stress, and certain stress-related illnesses can be made even worse by dietary habits.

Food substances that produce a stresslike response are called *pseudostressors*. That is, they mimic the stress response. Colas, coffee, tea, and chocolate (all containing caffeine) are examples of pseudostressors. Tea also contains theobromine and theophylline, which are pseudostressors. Nicotine (found in tobacco) is another pseudostressor. These substances increase your metabolism, make you highly alert, and release stress hormones which elevate your heart rate and blood pressure. Stress can also create a need for additional *vitamins*, in particular, the B-complex vitamins (thiamine, riboflavin, niacin, pantothenic acid, and pyridoxine hydrochloride) and vitamin C. A deficiency in these vitamins can result in anxiety, depression, insomnia, muscular weakness, and stomach upset.

Salt is another significant food substance. Some people are genetically susceptible to sodium and will develop high blood pressure if they ingest too much of it. The federal government recom-

Table 11.2
Recommended Calorie Allowances

	Ages	Calorie Allowance
Children	4–6	1,800
	7–10	2,400
Women[a]	11–14	2,400
	15–22	2,100
	23–50	2,000
	51+	1,800
Men	11–14	2,800
	15–22	3,000
	23–50	2,700
	51+	2,400

a. Add 300 calories for pregnancy, 500 for lactation.

Source: Adapted from *Nutrition Labeling: Tools for Its Use*, USDA, Agriculture Information Bulletin 382, 1975.

mends no more than five thousand milligrams of salt (sodium chloride), which translates to two thousand milligrams of sodium, daily. On a short-term basis, sodium ingestion can raise blood pressure by causing the retention of body fluids. When a person whose blood pressure is elevated encounters stress—such as that associated with caregiving—his or her blood pressure may rise to a dangerous level.

Your diet can and should be under your control. Take charge of what you eat, to maintain good health.

Smoking

Nicotine—contained in cigarettes, cigars, and pipe and chewing tobacco—has been associated with cancer at a number of different sites (for example, mouth, lip, lung), heart disease, hypertension, stroke, and circulatory problems. Obviously, smoking or chewing tobacco is not a healthy behavior! If you do use tobacco, think seriously about giving it up. If you don't, good for you; you can proceed to the next section of this chapter.

Why Do You Smoke?

For those who do smoke, help is available. To begin, assess your reasons for smoking by completing table 11.3. Do this now, before reading any further.

Let's analyze your responses to table 11.3A: a *stimulation* score of 11 or above suggests that you are stimulated by the cigarette to get going and keep going. Try a brisk walk or exercise, if possible, when the smoking urge arises.

If your score for *handling* was 11 or above, you get satisfaction from handling the cigarette. Substituting a pencil, a paper clip, or doodling may help you break the habit.

If your score for *pleasurable relaxation* was 11 or above, you get pleasure from smoking. Substitute other pleasurable habits (such as eating, drinking, social activities, or exercise) for smoking.

If your score for *crutch* was 11 or above, you probably use cigarettes to handle moments of stress or discomfort. The stress management strategies introduced in chapter 7 should be used as a substitute for the cigarette.

If your score for *craving* was 11 or above, you have an almost continual psychological craving for cigarettes. Going "cold turkey" (stopping all at once) may be your best shot at quitting smoking.

Table 11.3
Why Do You Smoke?

Here are some statements made by people to describe what they get out of smoking cigarettes. How *often* do you feel this way when smoking them? Circle one number for each statement.

Important: Answer every question.

	Always	Frequently	Occasionally	Seldom	Never
A. I smoke cigarettes in order to keep myself from slowing down.	5	4	3	2	1
B. Handling a cigarette is part of the enjoyment of smoking it.	5	4	3	2	1
C. Smoking cigarettes is pleasant and relaxing.	5	4	3	2	1
D. I light a cigarette when I feel angry about something.	5	4	3	2	1
E. When I have run out of cigarettes, I find it almost unbearable until I can get them.	5	4	3	2	1
F. I smoke cigarettes automatically without even being aware of it.	5	4	3	2	1
G. I smoke cigarettes to stimulate me, to perk myself up.	5	4	3	2	1
H. Part of the enjoyment of smoking a cigarette comes from the steps I take to light up.	5	4	3	2	1
I. I find cigarettes pleasurable.	5	4	3	2	1
J. When I feel uncomfortable or upset about something, I light a cigarette.	5	4	3	2	1
K. I am very much aware of the fact when I am not smoking a cigarette.	5	4	3	2	1
L. I light a cigarette without realizing I still have one burning in the ashtray.	5	4	3	2	1
M. I smoke cigarettes to give me a "lift."	5	4	3	2	1
N. When I smoke a cigarette, part of the enjoyment is watching the smoke as I exhale it.	5	4	3	2	1

(Continued next page)

Table 11.3
(Continued)

O. I want a cigarette most when I am comfortable and relaxed.	5	4	3	2	1
P. When I feel "blue" or want to take my mind off cares and worries, I smoke cigarettes.	5	4	3	2	1
Q. I get a real gnawing hunger for a cigarette when I haven't smoked for a while.	5	4	3	2	1
R. I've found a cigarette in my mouth and didn't remember putting it there.	5	4	3	2	1

National Clearinghouse for Smoking and Health (USPHS). Bethesda, MD, 1974).

If your score for *habit* was 11 or above, it is likely that you smoke purely out of habit and derive very little pleasure from cigarettes. Gradually reducing the number of cigarettes smoked may be the best method for you to quit smoking.

Reasons for Not Quitting

Stopping smoking is not easy, and many people have all sorts of reasons for not quitting. Some of these reasons appear in table 11.4. Check your reasons for not quitting before you read further.

For many smokers, smoking has become so deeply ingrained and has worked itself so thoroughly into their daily behavior patterns that they have developed many excuses for continuing to smoke. Some of these excuses are in the smoker's conscious mind, some may be unconscious, but none has any basis in fact. Did you check any of the following excuses?

"If I Quit Smoking, I'll Gain Weight."
This is a common fear: According to the U.S. Public Health Service, 60 percent of women and 47 percent of men say they continue to smoke because they are afraid of gaining weight. Studies have indicated, however, that most smokers do not gain weight when they quit. On the average, only about one-third of ex-smokers gain weight, one-third remain about the same, and one-third actually lose weight because they incorporate their quitting into a total self-improvement program.

"But I Really Enjoy Smoking. I Like the Taste."
The question here is, how many moments are truly enjoyable—and how many are just so-so? Is it real enjoyment you get, or just satisfaction for a physical craving? Almost every smoker can remember that after a day of particularly heavy smoking, cigarettes tasted terrible the next morning.

"If I Quit Smoking, I'd Be Too Nervous.
Smoking Helps Me Relax."
The truth is that nicotine is actually a stimulant, not a depressant—it is not a substance that helps people relax. After the first few days of trying to quit (when you may find yourself nervous because you have nothing to do with your hands), you'll discover that you have better self-control and are actually *less* nervous than you were when you smoked.

"I Have to Smoke in Order to Perform/Produce/Create/Study."
Here we're looking at habit again. For a long time, you may have associated smoking with caregiving, writing, studying, dealing with coworkers, or some other performance behavior. Actually, once you quit, you may find that you spend time more productively. As a plus, your body will function more efficiently once the excess carbon monoxide from inhaled smoke no longer displaces oxygen in your blood stream.

"I'll Quit When I Have To—When My Health Is Threatened."
The symptoms of many smoking-related diseases don't show up

Table 11.3A

Enter the numbers you circled in the spaces below, putting the number you circled for question A over line A, for question B over line B, and so on. Next, add the three scores on each line to get your total for that variable.

$$\overline{}_A + \overline{}_G + \overline{}_M = \text{———— (Stimulation Score)}$$

$$\overline{}_B + \overline{}_H + \overline{}_N = \text{———— (Handling Score)}$$

$$\overline{}_C + \overline{}_I + \overline{}_O = \text{———— (Pleasure Relaxation Score)}$$

$$\overline{}_D + \overline{}_J + \overline{}_P = \text{———— (Crutch: Tension Reduction Score)}$$

$$\overline{}_E + \overline{}_K + \overline{}_Q = \text{———— (Craving: Psychological Addiction Score)}$$

$$\overline{}_F + \overline{}_L + \overline{}_R = \text{———— (Habit Score)}$$

Table 11.4
Reasons for Not Quitting

Smokers who want to quit smoking cite many reasons that they haven't. Place a check alongside any of the following reasons that explain why you haven't quit smoking. Also, check any statements you believe to be true.

_____ 1. If I quit, I'll gain weight.

_____ 2. I really enjoy smoking; I like the taste.

_____ 3. If I quit smoking, I'd be too nervous; smoking helps me relax.

_____ 4. I have to smoke in order to perform/produce/create/study.

_____ 5. I'll quit when I have to—when my health is threatened.

_____ 6. It's too late to quit; I've been smoking too long.

_____ 7. The air is polluted anyway; I might as well smoke.

_____ 8. I can't afford to join a stop-smoking program.

until after the disease is well established. Moreover, many such diseases lead to a long, painful death. If you smoke, your health is already in danger!

"It's Too Late to Quit. I've Been Smoking Too Long."
It's never too late, as long as you quit before a serious disease has developed. After you quit, your chances of dying from smoking-related diseases gradually decrease till they're close to those of people who have never smoked.

"The Air Is Polluted Anyway: I Might as Well Smoke."
In fact, even in a heavily polluted urban area, the concentrations of pollutants in the air are tiny in comparison with the concentrations in the cigarette smoke you inhale.

"I Can't Afford to Join a Stop-Smoking Program."
Most approaches to quitting cost nothing. But if you think paying to join a formal program is the only way to succeed, you should take into account the money you'll be saving by not buying cigarettes.

Quitting

Many different programs have been established to help people give up cigarette smoking. The American Lung Association has a self-care program that allows you to quit by yourself rather than by joining a program. Other people have "just quit" cold turkey. Still others have found help by joining the Seventh Day Adventist Church's Five-Day Plan. You can contact the local chapter of these organizations if you are interested in their programs, or you can consult your physician, who can prescribe a nicotine gum that has helped some people quit smoking.

Unfortunately, it seems that regardless of the program, the smoker quits only when she or he is ready. If you're ready to quit, here are some tips from the American Cancer Society to increase your likelihood of success:

1. Set an exact date, one to four weeks ahead, when you will stop smoking completely.
2. As Quit Day approaches, gradually reduce your daily or weekly number of cigarettes.
3. Use whatever suggestions below work for you:
   a. Smoke only one cigarette an hour.
   b. Avoid smoking between 9:00 and 10:00 A.M., 11:00 and 12:00 P.M., or 3:00 and 4:00 P.M., and gradually extend the nonsmoking time by a half-hour, an hour, two hours.
   c. Smoke exactly half as many cigarettes the first week and half this amount again the second week until Quit Day arrives.
   d. Inhale less and with less vigor.
   e. Smoke each cigarette only halfway.
   f. Remove the cigarette from your mouth between puffs.
   g. Smoke slowly.
   h. Smoke brands with low nicotine and tar content.
   i. Make it difficult to find a cigarette by leaving yours at home, not carrying pocket change, and so forth.
   j. Place unlighted cigarettes in your mouth when you have the urge to smoke.
   k. Switch to a brand you dislike.

You can quit if you really want to! Do it—*now*!

Sleeping

No one really knows how much sleep you should get each night. Eight hours is usually recommended, but some people need less and others need more. If you are tired throughout the day, you probably need more sleep.

Beyond simply not going to sleep early enough, there are several conditions that affect people's ability to sleep. For example, some people have difficulty getting to sleep in the first place. This is called *insomnia*. Other people experience a condition in which they stop breathing for a period ranging from a few seconds to two minutes. This is called *sleep apnea.*

This section recommends ways to get to sleep if you have difficulty doing so. We will not consider sleep apnea, other than to caution that researchers believe that people who suffer from sleep apnea and take sleeping pills are risking heat attacks and sudden death during the night. As you will see, sleeping pills are not generally recommended. If you suspect that you suffer from sleep apnea, consult your physician.

If you experience difficulty falling asleep, the following steps are recommended:

1. *Refrain from taking sleeping pills.* You can develop a tolerance to the medication in these pills, so that they eventually interfere with your getting to sleep.
2. *Get up at the same time every day.* This will stabilize your "biological clock." Going to sleep at the same time each day may be beyond your control, because you may not be tired at the same time each night.
3. *Keep a sleep log.* Document any situations associated with difficulty in getting to sleep. Try to eliminate these interferences as much as possible.
4. *Establish presleep routines.* Examples are drinking a warm glass of milk and setting out your clothes for the next day. A routine helps you settle down and get ready to sleep.
5. *Exercise regularly, preferably in the late afternoon.* This will make your body just tired enough to relish sleep when the time comes. Exercising too late in the day (after 6:00 P.M.), however, may energize you and interfere with your getting to sleep.
6. *Engage in sex before sleep, if possible.* Sex has been shown to be an excellent sleep inducer.
7. *Keep the room in which you sleep as quiet and as dark as possible.* Soundproofing and lightproofing your bedroom will eliminate stimulation that can interfere with your sleep.
8. *Be sure the temperature in your bedroom is comfortable.* If it is either too warm or too cool, you may have difficulty getting to sleep.
9. *Avoid ingesting stimulants after 6:00 p.m.* Caffeine in coffee, tea, and some soft drinks, and nicotine in cigarettes, are stimulants that increase your alertness and readiness for physical activity—not exactly what you want when trying to get to sleep.

Table 11.5
Sleep Checklist

Before going to sleep each night, place a check alongside those sleep-inducing activities that you did during the day.

_____ 1. I refrained from taking sleeping pills today.

_____ 2. I awoke at the same time today as all other days.

_____ 3. I have made the appropriate entries in my Sleep Log today.

_____ 4. I used all my established sleep routines today prior to going to bed.

_____ 5. I exercised today, before 6:00 P.M.

_____ 6. I made my bedroom quiet tonight.

_____ 7. I made my bedroom dark tonight.

_____ 8. I made the temperature in my bedroom comfortable tonight.

_____ 9. I refrained from ingesting any stimulants after 6:00 P.M.

_____ 10. I refrained from taking a nap today.

10. *Don't take naps during the day.* Especially if you know they interfere with getting to sleep later at night. Irregular sleep patterns such as occasional naps can lead to your not being tired at night.

You can use the checklist in table 11.5 above to help prepare yourself for a good night's sleep. As with other aspects of your health behavior, you *can* do something about getting enough sleep. Whether because of difficulty getting to sleep or because of your busy schedule, if you need more sleep, use these suggestions. The control is in your hands! Exercise it.

In Conclusion

You have no more important responsibility than maintaining your own health. Not only will you and your family suffer if you needlessly become ill, but the person for whom you provide care will be deprived of your services. By adopting healthy habits of exercise, nutrition, and sleep, and by quitting smoking—as well as using the stress management strategies presented in chapter 7—you will increase your likelihood of staying healthy.

Get to it—and keep at it! You owe it to yourself and to those around you.

Appendix 1

Resources

This section is divided into two parts. Part A lists organizations that may be of assistance, and part B lists publications that may be of interest to you. We have gathered this list of organizations and publications from many sources. Listing them does not necessarily imply endorsement, merely that each is a possible resource to consider when seeking additional assistance or information. Telephone numbers with an 800 area code are toll-free to the caller.

A. Organizations That Can Help

There are many federal and local organizations that may help you care for yourself, your family member, or your friend. First, we give examples of the sorts of local organizations that can be found in your own telephone book. Next we list some national organizations, and finally we list organizations by topic in case you want to know what's available in a specific area.

Resources Available from Local Telephone Books

You can use the *county* or *city listings* in the telephone book for information on resources such as:

- area agency on aging
- Catholic Charities
- Family Services of America
- health department
- home care services
- human services
- information and referral services
- Jewish Family Services
- library

• local city or county office on aging
• mayor's office on aging
• Protestant welfare agencies
• senior centers
• Social Security Administration

From the *local/federal government section* of the telephone book
• State Governor's Committee or Council for the Handicapped
• Veterans Administration

From the *white pages,* or under "Associations"
• Alzheimer's Disease and Related Disorders Association
• American Cancer Society
• American Diabetes Association
• American Heart Association
• American Red Cross
• Cerebral Palsy Society
• Knights of Columbus
• Meals-on-Wheels
• Multiple Sclerosis Society
• National Association for Home Care

From the *yellow pages*
• aging services
• home health organizations
• homemaker services
• senior citizen services
• social services
• social workers

If you or another member of your family belongs to specific organizations, you can contact them for assistance. For example:

• B'nai B'rith
• Chamber of Commerce
• church, synagogue, or other religious organization
• 4-H Clubs
• Knights of Columbus
• Masons
• Serotoma
• Shriners Club

General Organizations

Many of the addresses listed below are the national headquarters of the organization. Contact the national headquarters for information about and assistance through their local chapters and affiliates. If no 800 number is listed, call 1–800–555–1212 to find out if the orgaization has an 800 listing.

Administration on Aging
Department of Health and Human Development, DHHS
330 Independence Avenue S.W.
Washington, DC 20201
(202) 619–0556 general information
(202) 619–0441 publications
This federal agency provides information about social services, nutrition, education, senior centers, and other programs for older Americans. The AoA develops federal government programs and coordinates community services for older people. It also offers *A Directory of State and Regional Agencies on Aging*. These area agencies can help find local services to answer a specific need.

Aging Network Services
4400 East-West Highway, Suite 907
Bethesda, MD 20814
(301) 657–4329
This organization is a nationwide, for-profit network of private-practice geriatric social workers who serve as care managers for older parents who live apart from their adult children. Their purpose is to bridge the physical distance between family members. Licensed clinical social workers across the country act as a substitute family network. They help maintain the independence of older family members by arranging for personal assistance with daily living activities, such as shopping, housekeeping, transportation, and other needed services. They counsel family members and serve as a liaison with out-of-town family.

American Association of Homes for the Aging
1129 20th Street N.W., Suite 400
Washington, DC 20036–3489
(202) 296–5960
The AAHA is a professional organization of nonprofit nursing homes, independent housing facilities, continuing-care communities, and community service agencies. Free information on long-term care and housing for older people is available to the public.

American Association of Retired Persons (AARP)
601 E Street, N.W.
Washington, DC 20004
(202) 434-2277
The AARP is a consumer organization that seeks to improve the quality of life for older people.

American Geriatrics Society
770 Lexington Avenue
New York, NY 10021
(212) 308–1414
This is a professional organization of physicians and other health care providers who specialize in caring for older people. Individuals can contact

the society for help in locating a geriatrician (a doctor with special training in the diagnosis, treatment, and prevention of disabilities in older persons).

American Health Care Association
1201 L Street N.W.
Washington, DC 20005
(202) 824–4444
The AHCA is a professional organization that represents the interests of licensed nursing homes and long-term care facilities to Congress, federal regulatory agencies, and other professional groups. Consumers can contact the association for educational materials on long-term care.

American Society on Aging
833 Market Street, Suite 512
San Francisco, CA 94103
(415) 543–2617
This nonprofit membership organization informs the public and health professionals about issues that affect the quality of life for older persons and promotes innovative approaches to meeting the needs of these individuals. Printed and audiovisual materials dealing with subjects of interest to older people are available through its information clearinghouse. Topics include long-term care, health care needs of older women, employment, and retirement planning.

B'nai B'rith International
1640 Rhode Island Avenue N.W.
Washington, DC 20036
(202) 857–6600
This voluntary service organization helps people of Jewish faith. It supports community action programs and works to improve living conditions for those who are disadvantaged. Members of local chapters visit and care for the sick and offer programs to help the poor, older people, and widowed persons. They build and maintain apartment houses for older adults throughout the United States. Additionally, they provide printed material and consultation to other organizations in the areas of community development, housing programs, and volunteer services for older people.

Catholic Charities
1319 F Street N.W.
Washington, DC 20004
(202) 639–8400
This social service organization offers assistance to individuals with a broad range of social problems and needs. Extensive services are provided to older people, including counseling, homemaker services, foster family programs, group homes and institutional care, public-access programs, home health care, health clinics, emergency assistance, and shelter.

Catholic Golden Age
400 Lackawanna Avenue
Scranton, PA 18503
(717) 342–3294
Catholic Golden Age sponsors charitable work and offers religious worship opportunities for older individuals. It helps older people meet their social, physical, economic, intellectual, and spiritual needs. It also offers various group insurance plans, as well as discounts on eyeglasses, prescription drugs, and travel. Local chapters plan a wide range of activities for members, including disease prevention and health promotion programs. Future plans include involvement in providing hospice care.

Children of Aging Parents
2761 Trenton Road
Levittown, PA 19056
(215) 945–6900
This nonprofit, self-help organization provides a variety of services, including starter packages for those interested in becoming caregivers, a "matching" service for people starting a support group, workshops for the general community, and printed material. It also distributes a monthly newsletter. Caregivers nationwide can contact the information and referral service to learn about local resources.

Disabled American Veterans
P.O. Box 14301
Cincinnati, OH 45250
(606) 441–7300
This private, nonprofit organization represents veterans with service-connected disabilities and their families. Services available to veterans include employment programs, counseling, and assistance in obtaining free health care. The DAV helps veterans and family members file claims for VA benefits, including disability compensation, pensions, and death benefits. The Older Veterans Assistance Program works to supplement existing community programs for older veterans and their families, to help them meet their daily needs.

Episcopal Society for Ministry on Aging
317 Wyandotte Street
Bethlehem, PA 18015
(215) 868–5400
An agency of the Episcopal Church, this organization is responsible for developing and supporting programs with and for older adults, to meet their physical, mental, and spiritual needs. The Ministry with the Homebound Program strives to involve housebound persons in the activities of their community.

187

Foundation for Hospice and Home Care
519 C Street N.E.
Washington, DC 20002
(202) 547–7424
This foundation is made up of community agencies that provide home-maker–home health services. Professional homemaker–home health aides care for individuals in their own homes in times of illness and stress. Individuals can contact the foundation for assistance in locating approved homemaker–home health services in their area.

Gray Panthers
311 S. Juniper Street, #601
Philadelphia, PA 19107
(215) 545–6555
The Gray Panthers is an advocacy group that works to eliminate ageism, discrimination against older people on the basis of chronological age. It provides an information and referral service listing resources for older people.

National Association for Home Care
519 C Street N.E.
Washington, DC 20002
(202) 547–7424
The NAHC monitors federal and state activities affecting home care and focuses on issues relating to home health care. It publishes *Caring* magazine on a bimonthly basis. Free publications on home care are distributed by the association. A list of these materials is available on request.

National Association of Area Agencies on Aging
600 Maryland Avenue S.W., Suite 208, West Wing
Washington, DC 20024
(202) 484–7520
The NAAAA represents the interests of approximately 650 area agencies on aging across the country. It acts as an advocate for older persons and for local agencies that provide supportive services to older individuals. The area agencies on aging offer services such as transportation, legal aid, nutrition programs, housekeeping, senior center activities, shopping assistance, employment counseling, preretirement advising, and information and referral programs.

National Association of State Units on Aging
2033 K Street N.W.
Washington, DC 20006
(202) 785–0707
The NASUA is a public interest group that provides information, technical assistance, and professional development support to state units on aging. The addresses for the state units are listed at the end of appendix 1A.

National Coalition on Older Women's Issues
2401 Virginia Avenue N.W.
Washington, DC 20037
(202) 466–7837
The NCOWI is a nationwide network made up of member organizations and individuals concerned with improving the status of older women. Its focus is on areas of employment, retirement income, and health and well-being of women. The organization offers a list of organizations called "Midlife and Older Women: A Resource Directory."

National Council on the Aging
600 Maryland Avenue S.W., Suite 100, West Wing
Washington, DC 20024
(202) 479–1200
In conjunction with other organizations, the NCOA promotes concerns of interest to older persons. The council conducts seminars on wellness, offers a range of publications (public policy/advocacy, education, and training), and functions as a resource for public education.

National Hispanic Council on Aging
2713 Ontario Road N.W.
Washington, DC 20009
(202) 265–1288
This private, nonprofit organization works to promote the well-being of older Hispanic individuals. It supports demonstration projects to evaluate innovative programs that provide health care and social services to older Hispanics.

National Hospice Organization
1901 N. Fort Myer Drive, Suite 307
Arlington, VA 22209
(703) 243–5900
This organization promotes quality care for terminally ill patients and provides information about hospice services available in the United States. Individuals can contact the NHO to learn about hospice services in their area. Some hospices help families care for patients at home; some offer services in a hospice center or hospital.

National Institute on Aging
Public Information Office
Federal Building, Room 6C12
9000 Rockville Pike
Bethesda, MD 20892
(301) 496–1752
The NIA, part of the National Institutes of Health, is the federal government's principal agency for conducting and supporting biomedical, social, and behavioral research related to the aging process and the diseases and

special problems of older individuals. The Public Information Office prepares and distributes information about issues of interest to older people.

National Shut-in Society
225 W. 99th Street
New York, NY 10025
(212) 222–7699
This society is a private, nonprofit organization whose members work to bring comfort and support to housebound individuals. Members of the society offer written correspondence and telephone communication to those who are chronically disabled and housebound. Some local chapters have wheelchairs, walkers, hospital beds, and other medical equipment to lend to members.

Older Women's League
730 11th Street N.W., Suite 300
Washington, DC 20001
(202) 783–6686
OWL's national membership is committed to helping meet various special needs of middle-aged and older women, especially in areas such as social security, pension rights, health insurance, and caregiver support services. OWL uses volunteers to help with mailings, to maintain a referral resource file, and to respond to women who write in from across the country with questions. Local chapters offer mutual aid and supportive services, especially to women who are alone.

U.S. Office of Disease Prevention and Health Promotion
Healthy Older Americans Program
2132 Switzer Building
330 C Street S.W.
Washington, DC 20201
(202) 472–5660
(800) 336–4797 (toll-free outside Maryland)
(301) 565–4167 (for Maryland residents)
This organization, part of the U.S. Public Health Service, supports and coordinates federal programs in health promotion and disease prevention. It offers information that can reduce older people's risk of developing disabling illness and increase their chances of leading healthy, active lives.

United Way of America
701 N. Fairfax Street
Alexandria, VA 22314–2045
(703) 836–7100
This organization is an association of local, independent United Way agencies in over two thousand cities and towns across the United States and Canada. Local United Way agencies support social service and public assistance programs, including a variety of community programs for older persons. Local agencies are listed in the telephone directory.

Veterans Administration
Office of Public Affairs
810 Vermont Avenue N.W.
Washington, DC 20420
(202) 233–2843
The VA is the federal agency that provides benefits to veterans of military service and their dependents.

Volunteers of America
3813 N. Causeway Boulevard
Metairie, LA 70002
(504) 837–2652
This nonprofit organization offers programs and services to meet the specific needs of a local community. Social services are provided to young people, older persons, families, persons with disabilities, alcoholics, and others. The services include child care centers, adolescent group homes, senior centers, rehabilitation centers, and community-based support groups for individuals with disabilities. Programs specifically for older people include home repair services, homemaker assistance, Meals-on-Wheels, and transportation programs. It sponsors foster grandparent and senior volunteer programs and offers adult day care, group homes for older people, and nursing home care.

Organizations Listed by Topic

Alzheimer's Disease

Alzheimer's Association (also known as the Alzheimer's Disease and Related Disorders Association)
70 E. Lake Street
Chicago, IL 60601
(312) 853–3060
(800) 621–0379
(800) 572–6037 (Illinois residents)
This voluntary organization sponsors public education programs and offers supportive services to patients and families who are coping with Alzheimer's disease. Its twenty-four-hour toll-free hotline provides information about Alzheimer's disease and links families with nearby chapters, which are familiar with community resources and can offer practical suggestions for daily living.

John Douglas French Foundation for Alzheimer's Disease
11620 Wilshire Boulevard
Los Angeles, CA 90025
(310) 470–5462
(800) 537–3624
This organization funds research to find a cure for Alzheimer's disease and works with hospitals and other institutions to create facilities to care for individuals with Alzheimer's disease and related disorders. Its center in

Los Alamitos, California, offers long-term care exclusively to individuals with Alzheimer's disease and related disorders. The center also provides day care and respite care programs. Additional centers are planned in Massachusetts, Michigan, Minnesota, Ohio, Oregon, Pennsylvania, and Texas.

Arthritis

Arthritis Foundation
1314 Spring Street N.W.
Atlanta, GA 30309
(404) 872–7100
(800) 283–7800
This foundation is a voluntary organization with a nationwide program committed to examining the cause and cure for arthritis and to improving treatments for arthritic patients. Services offered include public information and education about arthritis (through a variety of publications and referrals to specialists) and community activities, such as arthritis clinics and rehabilitation and home care programs.

National Institute of Arthritis and Musculoskeletal and Skin Diseases
Public Information Office
Building 31, Room B2B15
National Institutes of Health
9000 Rockville Pike
Bethesda, MD 20892
(301) 496–8188
NIAMS, one of the National Institutes of Health, supports clinical research on such chronic disabling diseases as osteoporosis, arthritis, and other musculoskeletal and skin diseases. A variety of printed materials on arthritis and skin diseases is available to the general public upon request.

Blindness: see Vision

Cancer

American Cancer Society
1599 Clifton Road
Atlanta, GA 30329
(404) 320–3333
(800) 227–2345 Information Service
The ACS, a voluntary organization, funds research to find a cure for cancer and carries out programs to educate the public and health professionals about cancer prevention, detection, treatment, and research. Local ACS chapters sponsor a wide range of services for cancer patients and their families, including self-help groups, transportation programs, and limited financial aid. Cancer patients and family members who participate in the I Can Cope and CanSurmount support groups learn about cancer, how to cope with their feelings, and where to find local resources.

National Cancer Institute
Office of Cancer Communications
Building 31, Room 10A24
9000 Rockville Pike
Bethesda, MD 20892
(301) 496–5583
(800)-4-CANCER/(800) 422–6237 Cancer Information Service (CIS)
The NCI, part of the National Institutes of Health, is the federal government's principal agency for funding cancer research and for distributing information about cancer to health professionals and the public. The Cancer Information Service staff can answer your questions, refer you to the nearest cancer center, provide resources for answers to your cancer questions, and mail you free booklets about your cancer concerns.

Caregiving

Children of Aging Parents
2761 Trenton Road
Levittown, PA 19056
(215) 945–6900
This nonprofit, self-help organization provides a variety of services, including starter packages for those interested in becoming caregivers, a "matching" service for people starting a support group, workshops for the general community, and printed material. It also distributes a monthly newsletter. Caregivers nationwide can contact the information and referral service to learn about local resources.

National Shut-in Society
225 W. 99th Street
New York, NY 10025
(212) 222–7699
This society is a private, nonprofit organization whose members work to bring comfort and support to housebound individuals. Members of the society offer written correspondence and telephone communication to those who are chronically disabled and housebound. Some local chapters have wheelchairs, walkers, hospital beds, and other medical equipment to lend to members.

Dental Health

American Dental Association
Division of Communications
211 E. Chicago Avenue
Chicago, IL 60611–2678
(312) 440–2500
The American Dental Association is a professional organization that works to improve the dental health of the public and to promote the art and

science of dentistry. Some state dental associations offer a number of free or low-cost services for older people.

Diabetes
American Diabetes Association
1660 Duke Street
Alexandria, VA 22314
(703) 549–1500
The ADA, a voluntary organization, supports research to find a cure for diabetes and seeks to improve the well-being of people with diabetes and their families. The toll-free telephone service provides information about the diagnosis and treatment of diabetes and about resources available to individuals with this disease. The ADA will send you information on diabetes and a list of its publications. A $20.00 annual membership fee includes national and regional publications. Local affiliates have free brochures and materials for newly diagnosed diabetics and others seeking information about the disease.

American Dietetic Association
216 W. Jackson Boulevard, Suite 800
Chicago, IL 60606–6995
(312) 899–0040
This organization is a professional society of dietitians who work in health care settings, schools, day care centers, business, and industry. It offers Spanish and English programs for nutrition professionals to teach the basics of nutrition, weight loss, and diabetic meal planning. Members provide direct nutrition counseling to older persons or indirect assistance through state and local meal programs such as area agencies on aging, Meals-on-Wheels programs, home health agencies, and other health care facilities focusing on the special nutritional needs of older people.

National Diabetes Information Clearinghouse
Box NDIC
9000 Rockville Pike
Bethesda, MD 20892
(301) 468–2162
This organization, part of the National Institutes of Health, offers pamphlets on all aspects of diabetes to health professionals, patients, and the general public. It also distributes materials created by other organizations as well as a publications list.

Foot Care
American Podiatric Medical Association
9312 Old Georgetown Road
Bethesda, MD 20814
(301) 571–9200
This organization is a professional society of doctors who specialize in diagnosing and treating foot injury and disease. Podiatrists make special

devices to correct foot problems, provide care for nails, prescribe certain medications, and perform foot surgery.

Health

National Health Information Clearinghouse
P.O. Box 1133
Washington, DC 20013
(703) 522–2590
(800) 336–4797
The clearinghouse will help locate resources pertaining to health information; specific questions about health are referred to appropriate experts or federal agencies.

Hearing Impairment

Some of the telephone numbers listed below are identified as "Voice" and/ or "TTY." "TTY" indicates that teletypewriters can be used to send and receive typed messages through the telephone. "Voice" or no identification next to the number means that it is a traditional voice telephone system.

Alexander Graham Bell Association for the Deaf
3417 Volta Place N.W.
Washington, DC 20007–2778
(202) 337–5220 (Voice/TTY)
This organization offers a variety of educational brochures, books, and videos.

American Speech-Language-Hearing Association
10801 Rockville Pike
Rockville, MD 20852
(301) 897–5700 (Voice/TTY)
(800) 638-TALK (Voice/TTY)
This is a consumer-oriented, nonprofit organization for hearing-impaired persons. It distributes literature and referral lists to provide assistance with hearing, speech, and language problems. It can provide a list of centers for demonstrating assistive listening devices and a list of public places that are equipped with such devices.

American Tinnitus Association
P.O. Box 5
Portland, OR 97207
(503) 248–9985
This voluntary organization supports research to find a cure for tinnitus (constant ringing or buzzing in the ears or inside the head) and distributes information to the public about this disorder, which is found most often in people 55 years of age and older. It sponsors self-help groups nationwide

to offer individuals with tinnitus and their families information, support, and referrals to community services and resources.

Better Hearing Institute
5021B Backlick Road
Annandale, VA 22003
(703) 642–0580
(800) 424–8576
This is a nonprofit educational organization. Its Hearing HelpLine will provide lists of health care professionals in your area who specialize in treating hearing problems.

Food and Drug Administration
Office of Consumer Affairs
HFE-88
5600 Fishers Lane
Rockville, MD 20857
(301) 443–3170
This is a federal agency that publishes some consumer-oriented materials about hearing impairment and hearing aids.

Hearing Industries Association
1800 M Street N.W.
Washington, DC 20036
(202) 833–1411
This organization represents firms that manufacture or distribute hearing aids, components, and health care products. It produces and disseminates publications on hearing aids and their proper use.

National Association for the Deaf
814 Thayer Avenue
Silver Spring, MD 20910
(301) 587–1788 (Voice/TTY)
This private, nonprofit membership association serves as an advocate for all deaf and hearing-impaired individuals. It can supply brochures, catalogs, and referral lists of organizations around the country that provide services to individuals who are deaf and their families.

National Captioning Institute
5203 Leesburg Pike, Suite 1500
Falls Church, VA 22041
(703) 998–2462 (Voice/TTY)
This is a nonprofit organization that provides captions for commercial, cable, and public television and home video manufacturers. It manufactures and distributes closed caption decoders for televisions. Information and publications are available upon request.

National Hearing Aid Society
20361 Middlebelt Street
Livonia, MI 48152
(313) 478–2610
(800) 521–5274 Hearing Aid Helpline
This is a professional organization of hearing-aid specialists. The toll-free Hearing Aid Helpline offers information to the public on hearing loss, hearing aids, and how to locate a qualified hearing-aid specialist. The organization also handles consumer complaints about hearing aids.

National Information Center on Deafness
Gallaudet University
800 Florida Avenue N.E.
Washington, DC 20002
(202) 651–5051 (Voice/TTY)
(800) 672–6720 (Voice/TTY) Ask for the National Information Center on
    Deafness
This organization provides a clearinghouse for information on hearing impairment and deafness. Fact sheets are available on hearing loss and aging, sign language, education of people who are deaf, and assistive devices, as well as organizations that provide services to deaf and hard of hearing individuals.

Self Help for Hard of Hearing People (Shhh)
7800 Wisconsin Avenue
Bethesda, MD 20814
(301) 657–2248 (Voice)
(301) 657–2249 (TTY)
This is a national advocacy group for the hearing impaired, with membership chapters throughout the country. The national office publishes a bimonthly journal reporting the experiences of those with hearing impairments as well as new developments in the field of hearing loss. Publications and reprints are available for the hard of hearing. Special programs for older people offer information about coping with hearing problems, hearing aids, and ways to communicate effectively.

High Blood Pressure

National High Blood Pressure Information Center
4733 Bethesda Avenue #530
Bethesda, MD 20814
or
120/80 National Institutes of Health
Bethesda, MD 20892
(301) 951–3260
The center is operated by the National Heart, Lung, and Blood Institute of the National Institutes of Health and provides information relating to

research on the causes, prevention, methods of diagnosis, and treatment of high blood pressure and information about programs on hypertension.

Home Modifications and Remodeling
ABLE-DATA
National Rehabilitation Center
4407 8th Street N.E.
Washington, DC 20017
(202) 635–6090
This is a federally funded database available by phone to people searching for rehabilitation equipment, adaptive devices, and furniture for home accessibility.

National Center for a Barrier-Free Environment
Paralyzed Veterans of America
801 18th Street N.W.
Washington, DC 20006
(202) 872–1300
The Paralyzed Veterans of America—Architecture and Barrier Free Design Program—took over the National Center for a Barrier Free Environment in 1983. This program offers information bulletins, design guides, as well as pamphlets and books on accessible design, many of which are free of charge.

Housing/Long-Term Care
American Association of Homes for the Aging
1129 20th Street N.W., Suite 400
Washington, DC 20036
(202) 296–5960
The AAHA is a national organization whose members include nonprofit nursing homes, independent housing facilities, continuing care facilities, and homes for the aging. It offers a brochure called "The Continuing Care Retirement Community: A Guidebook for Consumers, 1984."

National Citizens' Coalition for Nursing Home Reform
1424 16th Street N.W., Room L2
Washington, DC 20036
(202) 797–0657
The coalition serves as a voice enabling consumers to be heard on issues concerning the development of long-term care systems.

Nursing Home Information Service
National Council of Senior Citizens
National Senior Citizens Education and Research Center
925 15th Street N.W.
Washington, DC 20005
(202) 347–8800

This information service is a referral center for consumers of long-term care services. It offers information on nursing homes, alternative community and health services, and how to select a nursing home.

Incontinence

HIP (Help for Incontinent People)
P.O. Box 544
Union, SC 29379
(803) 585–8789
HIP is a self-help and patient advocacy group that offers encouragement, information, and resource listings about the prevalence, diagnosis, and treatment of urinary incontinence for the public, health professionals, and incontinent individuals. It also publishes "Resource Guide for Continence Aids and Services" and the quarterly newsletter *The HIP Report.*

Simon Foundation
Box 815
Wilmette, IL 60091
(708) 864–3913
(800) 237–4666 Information Service
This foundation, a nonprofit educational group, serves as a clearinghouse for information on incontinence to professionals and the general public. It publishes the newsletter *The Informer.* The foundation distributes up-to-date information about urinary incontinence and offers assistance and support to individuals who suffer from incontinence and to their families.

Legal

American Bar Association Commission on the Legal Problems of the Elderly
1800 M Street N.W., 2d Floor, South Lobby
Washington, DC 20036
(202) 331–2297
The Commission on the Legal Problems of the Elderly analyzes and responds to the legal needs of older people in the United States. It works to improve the quality and quantity of legal services for older citizens and refers requests for services to appropriate agencies or groups.

National Senior Citizens Law Center
2025 M Street N.W., Suite 400
Washington, DC 20036
(202) 887–5280
This organization is a public interest law firm with attorneys who specialize in areas of federal law having impact on older people. It serves as a clearinghouse of information about legal problems that affect the elderly, including problems with social security, age discrimination, pension plans, Medicaid, Medicare, nursing homes, and consumer products. Other

services include consulting services, data compilations, and referrals to other sources of information.

Medications

AARP Pharmacy Service

P.O. Box NIA
1 Prince Street
Alexandria, VA 22314

This organization will provide information on common prescription drugs, side effects, and cost differences between brand name and generic drugs. It has published a series of leaflets called Medication Information Leaflets for Seniors, which discuss 350 prescription drugs. For copies, write to the Pharmacy Service, specifying the drugs in which you are interested.

Food and Drug Administration

Legislative, Professional, and Consumer Affairs Branch (HFN-365)
Division of Regulatory Affairs
Center for Drugs and Biologics
5600 Fishers Lane
Rockville, MD 20857
(301) 295–8012

This federal office can answer questions about drug approval, drug reactions, and other issues concerning new or approved medications.

Nutrition

American Dietetic Association

216 W. Jackson Boulevard, Suite 800
Chicago, IL 60606–6995
(312) 899–0040

This organization is a professional society of dietitians who work in health care settings, schools, day care centers, business, and industry. They are interested in improving the dietary habits of all people and work to advance the science of dietetics and nutrition, as well as to promote education in these areas. The association offers Spanish and English programs for nutrition professionals to teach the basics of nutrition, weight loss, and diabetic meal planning. A professional practice group, made up of dietitians who work in area agencies on aging, Meals-on-Wheels programs, home health agencies, and other health care facilities, focuses on the special nutritional needs of older people. Members provide direct nutrition counseling to older persons or indirect assistance through state and local meal programs.

Food and Drug Administration

Office of Consumer Affairs
5600 Fishers Lane #1663
Rockville, MD 20857
(301) 443–3170

This organization establishes federal regulations concerning the safety and effectiveness of food products and additives, human and veterinary drugs, cosmetics, products that emit radiation, and medical devices. It offers free consumer education materials on nutrition.

U.S. Department of Agriculture
Human Nutrition Information Service
6505 Belcrest Road #360
Hyattsville, MD 20782
(301) 436–8617
This organization offers free consumer education materials on nutrition.

Osteoporosis

Arthritis Foundation
1314 Spring Street N.W.
Atlanta, GA 30309
(800) 283–7800
This organization offers free publications on osteoporosis information and referrals.

Melpomene Institute for Women's Health Research
2125 E. Hennepin Avenue
Minneapolis, MN 55413
(612) 378–0545
This organization offers materials for consumers as well as a videotape for rental on osteoporosis.

National Osteoporosis Foundation
2100 M Street N.W., Suite 602
Washington, DC 20037
(202) 223–2226
This organization offers information and programs nationwide to educate professionals and the public about osteoporosis and related research.

Pets

Delta Society
P.O. Box 1080
Renton, WA 98057–1080
(206) 226–7357
This nonprofit organization sponsors animal companionship and pet-facilitated therapy programs. Chapters of the society provide pets to hospitals, nursing homes, hospices, older people, individuals with disabilities, and people who are homebound. Their chapters work with local humane societies to find animals to serve as companions to those in need. All veterinary care for the pets, including shots and any needed medical care, is provided by the society.

201

Safety

National Safety Council
444 N. Michigan Avenue
Chicago, IL 60611–3991
(312) 527–4800
This organization offers pamphlets and programs on many aspects of health and safety.

Stress/Support Groups

American Institute on Stress
124 Park Avenue
Yonkers, NY 10703
(914) 963–1200
This organization offers materials and information on stress.

National Institute on Mental Health
5600 Fishers Lane, #15C-05
Rockville, MD 20857
(301) 443–4517
This organization, a part of the National Institutes of Health, offers information on help groups, mutual help groups, and support groups.

Strokes

National Stroke Association
300 E. Hampden Avenue, Suite 240
Englewood, CO 80110
(303) 762–9922
This association provides information about strokes to the general public and health professionals and offers supportive services to stroke survivors and their families. It supports self-help services for those recovering from a stroke and their families and offers guidance to those interested in forming stroke clubs and support groups.

Vision

American Council of the Blind
1010 Vermont Avenue N.W., Suite 1100
Washington, DC 20005
(202) 393–3666
(800) 424–8666 information service (weekdays 3–5 P.M. EST)
This organization seeks to improve the living conditions of people who are blind and individuals with visual impairments.

American Foundation for the Blind
15 W. 16th Street
New York, NY 10011
(212) 620–2147
(800) 232–5463 information hotline (weekdays 8:30–4:30 EST)

This organization develops and provides programs and services to help people who are blind and those with visual impairments to achieve independence in all sectors of society. The foundation records Talking Books.

National Society to Prevent Blindness
500 E. Remington Road
Schaumburg, IL 60173–4557
(708) 843–2020
(800) 221–3004
This organization offers a variety of brochures on eye problems. Its National Center for Sight toll-free information line provides information on a broad range of eye health and safety topics.

State Offices/Units on Aging

State units on aging are required by law to offer information and referral services (called I&R) at no cost. States are divided into smaller areas called area agencies on aging (AAA). There are 662 AAAs. The state units on aging can refer you to the AAA that covers the area where you live. Your local AAA can provide you with information on local community resources.

A list of the state units follows:

Alabama
Commission on Aging
State Capitol
Montgomery, AL 36130
(205) 261–5743

Alaska
State Agency on Aging
Older Alaskans Commission
Pouch C, Mail Stop 0209
Juneau, AK 99811
(907) 465–3250

Arizona
Aging and Adult Administration
P.O. Box 6123
1400 W. Washington Street
Phoenix, AZ 85005
(602) 255–4448

Arkansas
Arkansas State Office on Aging
Donaghey Building, Suite 1428
7th and Main Streets
Little Rock, AR 72201
(501) 682–2441

California
Department on Aging
Health and Welfare Agency
1600 K Street
Sacramento, CA 95814
(916) 322–5290

Colorado
Aging and Adult Services
    Division
Department of Social Services
1575 Sherman Street, 10th Floor
Denver, CO 80203
(303) 866–5913

Connecticut
Department on Aging
175 Main Street
Hartford, CT 06106
(203) 566–7725

Delaware
Division on Aging
Department of Health and Social
    Services
1901 N. Dupont Highway
New Castle, DE 19720
(302) 421–6791

District of Columbia
District of Columbia Office on
    Aging
1424 K Street N.W., 2d Floor
Washington, DC 20005
(202) 724–5622

Florida
Program Office of Aging
Department of Health and
    Rehabilitation Services
1317 Winewood Boulevard
Tallahassee, FL 32301
(904) 488–8922

Georgia
Office of Aging
Department of Human Resources
878 Peachtree Street, N.E., Room
    632
Atlanta, GA 30309
(404) 894–5333

Hawaii
Executive Office on Aging
Office of the Governor
State of Hawaii
335 Merchant Street, Room 241
Honolulu, HI 96813
(808) 548–2593

Idaho
Idaho Office on Aging
Statehouse, Room 114
Boise, ID 83720
(208) 334–3833

Illinois
Department on Aging
421 E. Capitol Avenue
Springfield, IL 62706
(217) 785–2870

Indiana
Department on Aging and
    Community Services
251 N. Illinois Street
Indianapolis, IN 46207
(317) 232–7020

Iowa
Commission on Aging
914 Grand Avenue
Jewett Building
Des Moines, IA 50319
(515) 281–5187

Kansas
Department on Aging
610 W. 10th Street
Topeka, KS 66612
(913) 296–4986

Kentucky
Division for Aging Services
Bureau of Social Services
275 E. Main Street
Frankfort, KY 40601
(502) 564–6930

Louisiana
Office of Elderly Affairs
P.O. Box 80374
Capitol Station
Baton Rouge, LA 70898
(504) 925–1700

Maine
Bureau of Maine's Elderly
Department of Human Services
State House, Station 11
Augusta, ME 04333
(207) 289–2561

Maryland
Office on Aging
State Office Building
301 W. Preston Street
Baltimore, MD 21201
(301) 225–1100

Massachusetts
Department of Elder Affairs
38 Chauncy Street
Boston, MA 02111
(617) 727–7751

Michigan
Office of Services to the Aging
300 E. Michigan
P.O. Box 30026
Lansing, MI 48909
(517) 373–8230

Minnesota
Board on Aging
204 Metro Square Building
7th and Robert Streets
St. Paul, MN 55101
(612) 296–2770

Mississippi
Council on Aging
301 W. Pearl Street
Jackson, MS 39201
(601) 949–2070

Missouri
Office of Aging
Department of Social Services
P.O. Box 1337
2701 W. Main Street
Jefferson City, MO 65101
(314) 751–3082

Montana
Department of Family Services
P.O. Box 8005
Helena, MT 59604
(406) 449–5900

Nebraska
Department on Aging
P.O. Box 95044
301 Centennial Mall South
Lincoln, NE 68509
(402) 471–2306

Nevada
Division of Aging Services
Department of Human Resources
505 E. King Street, Room 600
KinKead Building
Carson City, NV 89710
(702) 885–4210

New Hampshire
Division of Elderly and Adult
    Services
6 Hazen Drive
Concord, NH 03301
(603) 271–4680

New Jersey
Department of Community
    Affairs
CN 807
South Broad and Front Streets
Trenton, NJ 08625
(609) 292–4833

New Mexico
State Agency on Aging
LaVilla Rivera Building
224 E. Palace Avenue
Santa Fe, NM 87501
(505) 827–7640

New York
Office for the Aging
Agency Building 2
Empire State Plaza
Albany, NY 12223
(518) 474–4425

North Carolina
Division on Aging
Department of Human Resources
1985 Umstead Drive
Raleigh, NC 27603
(919) 733–3983

North Dakota
State Agency on Aging
Department of Human Services
State Capitol Building
Bismarck, ND 58505
(701) 224–2577

Ohio
Commission on Aging
50 W. Broad Street
Columbus, OH 43266
(614) 466–5500

Oklahoma
Special Unit on Aging
Department of Human Services
P.O. Box 25352
Oklahoma City, OK 73125
(405) 521–2281

Oregon
Senior Services Division
Human Resources Department
Public Services Building, Room
    313
Salem, OR 97301
(503) 378–4728

Pennsylvania
Department of Aging
231 State Street
Harrisburg, PA 17101
(717) 783–1550

Rhode Island
Department of Elderly Affairs
79 Washington Street
Providence, RI 02903
(401) 277–2858

South Carolina
Commission on Aging
400 Arbor Lake Drive, Suite
    B-500
Columbia, SC 29223
(803) 758–0210

South Dakota
Office of Adult Services and
    Aging
Division of Human Development
Richard F. Dreip Building
700 N. Illinois Street
Pierre, SD 57501
(605) 773–3656

Tennessee
Commission on Aging
706 Church Street, Suite 201
Nashville, TN 37219
(615) 741–2056

Texas
Department of Aging
P.O. Box 12786
Capitol Station
Austin, TX 78741
(512) 444–2727

Utah
Division of Aging Services
120 North–200 West
Box 45500
Salt Lake City, UT 84145
(801) 538–3910

Vermont
Office on the Aging
103 Main Street
Waterbury, VT 05676
(802) 241–2400

Virginia
Office on Aging
700 E. Franklin Street, 10th Floor
Richmond, VA 23219
(804) 225–2271

Washington
Bureau of Aging and Adult
    Services
Department of Social and Health
    Services, OB-44A
Olympia, WA 98504
(206) 753–2502

West Virginia
Commission on Aging
State Capitol
Charleston, WV 25305
(304) 348–3317

Wisconsin
Department of Health and Social
    Services
1 W. Wilson Street, Room 686
Madison, WI 53702
(608) 266–2536

Wyoming
Commission on Aging
Hathaway Building, Room 139
Cheyenne, WY 82002
(307) 777–7986

B. Written Material

The following publications are organized by topic. The name of the publication is given first, followed, when possible, by a description of the information it contains, the publication number, the date of publication, and the cost. Because several publications can be obtained from the same source, sources are listed first and numbered. After each publication's title you will find a bold face number in parentheses. This refers to the source of that publication. When no source is indicated, contact your local bookstore for information.

If you wish to obtain a book we've listed, you may want to contact your local library first, to see whether the book is on the shelf or can be requested through an interlibrary loan. If you wish to purchase the book, write to the publisher.

1. AARP Books
American Association of Retired Persons
601 E Street, N.W.
Washington, DC 20004
(202) 434-2277

2. Alzheimer's Disease and Related Disorders Association
70 E. Lake Street #600
Chicago, IL 60601
(800) 621-0379

3. American Association of Retired Persons
AARP Fulfillment Section
601 E Street, N.W.
Washington, DC 20004
(202) 434-2277

4. American Association of Retired Persons
Program Scheduling Office
601 E Street, N.W.
Washington, DC 20004
(202) 434-2277

5. American Association of Homes for the Aging
1129 20th Street, N.W., #400
Washington, DC 20036
(202) 783–2242

6. American Dental Hygienists Association
444 N. Michigan Avenue, #3400
Chicago, IL 60611
(312) 440-8920

7. American Planning Association
1776 Massachusetts Avenue N.W.
Washington, D.S. 20036
(202) 872-0611

8. Center for the Study of Pharmacy and Therapeutics for the Elderly
University of Maryland School of Pharmacy
20 N. Pine Street
Baltimore, MD 21201
(301) 328-8433

9. Consumer Reports
Reprints
P.O. Box 1949
Marion, OH 43305

10. Council of Better Business Bureaus
1515 Wilson Boulevard
Arlington, VA 22209
(703) 276-0100

11. Food and Drug Administration
5600 Fishers Lane
Rockville, MD 20852
(301) 443-3170

12. Foundation for Hospice and Home Care
519 C Street, N.E.
Washington, DC 20002
(202) 547-7424

13. Government Printing Office
Superintendent of Documents
710 N. Capitol, N.W.
Washington, DC 20402
(202) 783-3238

14. Health Insurance Association of America
P.O. Box 41455
Washington, DC 20018
(202) 223-7780

15. High Blood Pressure Information Center
120/80, National Institutes of Health
Box AP
Bethesda, MD 20892
(301) 496-4000

16. LCE
P.O. Box 19269-K
Washington, DC 20036

17. MTPS/A-V Sales Library
5000 Park Street North
St. Petersburg, FL 33709

18. National Center for a Barrier-Free Environment
Paralyzed Veterans of America
801 18th Street, N.W.
Washington, DC 20006
(202) 223-0039

19. National Home Caring Council
235 Park Avenue
New York, NY 10003

20. National Institute on Aging
Public Information Office
National Institutes of Health
9000 Rockville Pike
Bethesda, MD 20892
(301) 496-4000

21. NIH Office of Medical Applications of Research
Building 1, Room 216
National Institutes of Health
Bethesda, MD 20892
(301) 496-4000

22. National Osteoporosis Foundation
1625 Eye Street, N.W. #822
Washington, DC 20006
(202) 223-2226

23. National Hospital for Orthopedics and Rehabilitation
2455 Army–Navy Drive
Arlington, VA 22206
(202) 877-1000

24. ODPHP Health Information Center
P.O. Box 1133
Washington, DC 20018–1133

25. Pennsylvania Department on Aging
Publications
231 State Street
Harrisburg, PA 17120
(717) 783-3126

26. Public Citizen's Health Research Group
2000 P Street, N.W. #708
Washington, DC 20036
(202) 833-3000

27. R. Wood
Consumer Information Center
Pueblo, CO 81009
(719) 948-3334

28. United Seniors' Health Cooperative
1334 G Street, N.W. #500
Washington, DC 20005
(202) 393-6222

29. U.S. Consumer Product Safety Commission
Washington, DC 20207
(800) 638-2772

30. U.S. Government Printing Office
710 N. Capitol St., N.W.
Washington, DC 20402

31. U.S. Pharmacopoeial Convention
Drug Information Division
12601 Twinbrook Parkway
Rockville, MD 20852
(800) 227-8772 (Publications ordering service)

Alzheimer's Disease

Choosing a Nursing Home for the Person with Intellectual Loss (**4**), edited by F. McDowell, 1980. $1.25. The purpose of this pamphlet is to help those who must select a nursing home for someone with dementia, so that the result is good and provides twenty-four-hour care and protection for the patient. It examines when, where, and how to select and includes sections on meeting the costs, conservatorship, day of admission, and subsequent visits. It includes additional sources of information and references.

"Coping and Caring: Living with Alzheimer's Disease" (**3**) [D12441] provides information on Alzheimer's disease and suggestions for care of both the patient and family.

Loss of Self: A Family Resource for the Care of Alzheimer's Disease and Related Disorders, by D. Cohen and C. Eisendorfer. New York: W. W. Norton, 1986. This sensitive, well-written book by two highly experienced professionals contains a wealth of case histories and accurate medical and research information. The book is an excellent resource on Alzheimer's disease for caregivers, family, and friends of Alzheimer's disease victims, and is valuable for professionals as well.

Managing the person with Intellectual Loss at Home (**4**), edited by F. McDowell, 1980. $1.75. The editor says this is "an encyclopedia of information" for the caregivers of adults with progressive memory loss. It specifically addresses the problems created by Alzheimer's disease. It includes suggestions for aids to memory, bathing and grooming, incontinence, dressing, exercise, legal matters, nighttime supervision, and respite for the family. It lists additional sources of help.

Q & A: Alzheimer's Disease (**20**), 1981. This pamphlet describes the disease, symptoms, diagnosis, research, possible causes, and treatments.

The 36-Hour Day: A Family Guide to Caring for Persons with Alzheimer's Disease, Related Dementing Illnesses, and Memory Loss in Later Life (**4**), by N. Mace and P. Rabins. Baltimore: Johns Hopkins University Press, 1981. $8.45. This book contains practical suggestions for learning to live with and care for a victim of dementia. It explains dementia, the management of a dementia victim, and the changes to expect in lifestyle and in everyday life, including hazards to watch for and changes in family relationships. It outlines legal and financial factors to consider and offers a guide to selecting a nursing home or other living arrangements. Extensive references and additional sources of information are included.

Arthritis

"Arthritis Advice" *Age Page* (**20**), is prepared by the National Institute on Aging.

"Total Hip Joint Replacement" (**21**) is an NIH Consensus Development Conference Summary, vol. 4, no. 4, 1982. Single copies are available from the NIH.

Assistive Devices for Independent Living/Self Care

A Catalog of Products and Services to Enhance the Indepencence of the Elderly (**25**). This catalog outlines many specialized products and services currently available to older persons. It is quite thorough and includes prices and where to write to place the order. Your area agency on aging should have a copy. It is suggested that before you make any purchases, you obtain professional assessment of the appropriateness of the item or product for your care-receiver.

The Gadget Book: Ingenious Devices for Easier Living (**1**), by D. R. LaBuda, 1985. $10.75 ($7.95 for AARP members) + $1.75 for postage and handling.

Caregiving

All about Home Care: A Consumer's Guide (**19**), by the Council of Better Business Bureaus and the National Homecaring Council. $2.00. This consumer guide answers basic questions about home care. It is designed to help in the selection of home care services.

All about Homecare: Family Caregiver's Guide (**12**) is available from the Foundation for Hospice and Home Care.

Caregivers: Practical Help (**25**).

Caregiving: Helping an Aging Loved One (**1**), by J. Horne [order #819]. $13.95 ($9.85 for AARP members + $1.75 for postage and handling). The author writes from experience. Her insights are valuable in making appropriate choices that recognize the emotional burdens such as guilt, frustration, exhastion, and depression common to caregivers and receivers alike.

Caring for Your Aging Parents: A Practical Guide to the Challenges, the Choices, by J. Kenny and S. Spicer. Cincinnati: St. Anthony Messenger Press, 1984.

"Checklist of Concerns, Resources for Caregivers" (**2**) [D12895] helps caregivers identify issues of concern and lists available resources to meet needs. It identifies the problems inherent in long-distance caregiving and lists resources for support. It shows how to create a network of assistance that includes family, friends, neighbors, and social service workers.

Family Caregiver's Guide (**2**), by Joan Ellen Foyder (Cincinnati, Ohio: Futuro, 1986).

Family Caregiving and Dependent Elderly, by D. Springer and T. Brubaker. Beverly Hills, Calif.: Sage Publications, 1984.

A Handbook about Care in the Home (**2**) [D955] describes the range of home health care and homemaker services available and how to assess home care agencies.

Home Is Where the Care Is (**17**), $16.00, AARP's new home care program for informal caregivers, includes five audio cassettes and three work booklets, all in a handy three-ring binder.

Miles Away and Still Caring (**2**) [D12748] is for persons concerned about elderly relatives living at a distance.

Understanding Aging Parents (**29**), by A. and J. Lester. Philadelphia: Westminister Press, 1980.

"Where to Turn for Help for Older Persons: A Guide for Action on Behalf of an Older Person" (**29**) is prepared by the Administration on Aging [stock # 01706200139–1]. $1.75.

You and Your Aging Parent: The Modern Family's Guide to Emotional, Physical, and Financial Problems, by B. Silverstone and H. Kandel. New York: Pantheon Press, 1982.

Dental Health

A Beautiful Smile Is Ageless (**6**) provides information on nutrition and oral hygiene.

An Ounce of Prevention (**6**) discusses brushing and flossing for older adults.

Exercise/Fitness

Pep Up Your Life: A Fitness Book for Seniors (**2**) [D549] provides various exercise options for getting and staying physically fit.

Finances/Financial Planning

A Guide to Understanding Your Pension Plan: A Pension Handbook (**2**) [D13533] presents information to help you understand your pension plan.

Managing Your Personal Finances (**26**) is a three-part series that includes "The Principles of Managing Your Finances" ($3.25), "Financial Tools Used in Money Management" ($1.50), and "Coping with Change" ($1.75). The series is written by the Department of Agriculture.

Modern Maturity Special Personal Finances Issue (**2**) [D13098] discusses how to thrive and survive in taxation, financial planning, investing, banking, and housing.

Money Matters: How to Talk to and Select Lawyers, Financial Planners, Tax Preparers, and Real Estate Brokers (**2**) [D12380] presents information on when and where to go for help.

"Planning Your Retirement" (**2**) [D12322] presents ways to develop your retirement lifestyle, improve health and fitness, and plan for financial security.

Relocation Tax Guide (**2**) [D13400] is a fifty-state guide to the state and local taxes that should be evaluated by an older person considering moving to another state.

"Social Security: Crucial Questions and Straight Answers" (**2**) [D13645] provides answers to the questions most often asked about social security.

"The Time to Fix the Roof Is When the Sun Is Shining" (**2**) [D13073] lists AARP publications about long-range financial planning, where to live, protecting your rights and receiving public benefits, managing assets, and planning ahead for disability and death.

"A Woman's Guide to Social Security" (**26**) is prepared by the Social Security Administration.

Health Care Providers

Healthy Questions (**2**) [D12094] provides tips on selecting and using the services of health professionals—physicians, dentists, vision care specialists, and pharmacists.

The Prudent Patient (**2**) [D12031].

Strategies for Good Health (**2**) [D12261] provides an overview of good health practices and tips on finding and communicating with physicians.

Hearing Impairment

Facts About Hearing Aids (**10**) [#03-250,G100883], 1981. Single copies are free. This 15-page brochure discusses hearing aids, types of hearing loss, evaluations by a doctor or an audiologist, types of hearing aids, and the adjustment period. It also mentions contracts and warranties.

Facts About Hearing and Hearing Aids (**29**) [SN 003-003-02024-9], 1978. $1.75. This 31-page booklet examines hearing impairments and hearing aids. It explains how hearing aids work, how to select them, and how to care for them.

Have You Heard? (**2**) [D12219] is a booklet that describes various hearing impairments that often accompany aging. It provides information on how to cope with hearing loss, including when and where to go for hearing aids.

"How to Buy a Hearing Aid" (**9**) [#R-013], 1976. $1.00. This 10-page article provides information for the consumer and professional about hearing aids and their costs.

Tuning in on Hearing Aids (**11**) [HHS(FDA)80-4024EV], 1981. Single copy free. This booklet generally explains hearing loss and types of hearing aids. It also discusses the role of the hearing aid dispenser and provides sources for further information.

High Blood Pressure

"Questions about Weight, Salt, and High Blood Pressure" (**15**).

Housing Alternatives, Home Modifications, and Remodeling

ABLE-DATA (**23**). This federally funded database is available by phone to people searching for rehabilitation equipment, adaptive devices, and furniture for home accessibility.

Access Information Bulletins (**18**) are published by the National Center for a Barrier-Free Environment.

Accessory Apartments: Using Surplus Space in Single Family Houses (**7**), by P. Hare, 1981. $10.00. This report focuses on the issues raised by the addition of an accessory apartment to a single-family home and the relevant zoning restrictions. Included is sample language for a zoning amendment to permit accessory apartments.

The Continuing Care Retirement Community: A Guidebook for Consumers, 1984 (**5**).

"The DoAble, Renewable Home" (**2**) [D12470] details instructions on minor adaptations needed to keep a home livable as you age.

ECHO Housing Slide/Tape Presentation and Fact Sheet (**2**) is a program designed to introduce to the concept of ECHO housing and to encourage the use of ECHO housing in communities across the country. No charge to borrow.

ECHO Housing: A Review of Zoning Issues and Other Considerations (**2**) [D1023] is a manual reviewing the technical zoning issues raised by ECHO housing.

ECHO Housing: Recommended Construction and Installation Standards (**2**) [D12212] is a technical guide to standards for constructing and installing ECHO housing units that can be attached to existing structures. It offers guidelines for size, energy efficiency, safety, maintenance, and utility hookup.

"ECHO Housing Fact Sheet" (**2**) [D1006] provides general information on small, self-contained ECHO cottages designed to be placed on available yard space of a single family home, usually as housing for older relatives.

Housing Interiors for the Disabled and Elderly, by B. Boetticher Raschko. New York: Van Nostrand Reinhold, 1982. $34.50. This is a thorough guide to the housing design requirements of older and handicapped individuals. It includes sections on the entry, doors, living room, kitchen, dining room, bathroom, bedroom, storage, mechanical systems, and design considerations for the blind.

Incontinence

Managing Incontinence: A Guide to Living with the Loss of Bladder Control, by C. B. Gartley. Ottawa, Ill.: Jameson Books, 1985.

"Urinary Incontinence," (**20**) *Age Page* is prepared by the National Institute on Aging.

Intimacy

Growing Older, Getting Better: A Handbook for the Second Half of Life, by J. Porcino. Reading, Mass.: Addison-Wesley, 1983.

Legal/Life Planning

AARP (**2**) provides booklets with state-specific information about issues, such as insurance, health care, estate taxes, and housing, which can affect the survivor when a spouse dies. Request by *state*.

"How to Choose and Use a Lawyer" (**26**) is prepared by the U.S. Office of Consumer Affairs.

The Rights of Older Persons: An ACLU Handbook (**16**), 1988. $9.45. This book provides lawyers, paralegals, and family members with answers to their questions on eleven different topics affecting the lives of older persons. It addresses problems relating to social security, Supplemental Security Income, Medicare, Medicaid, age discrimination, private pensions, guardianships, civil service, railroad retirement benefits, nursing homes, and the right to refuse medical treatment.

"Tomorrow's Choices: Preparing Now for Future Legal, Financial, and Health Care Decisions" (**2**) [D13479] is a guide to planning for critical personal choices we may face in the future.

Long-Term Care: Services and Financing

"A Consumer's Guide to Long-Term Care Insurance" (**14**) is a free publication including a list of companies offering long-term care policies.

Long-Term Care: A Dollars and Sense Guide (**27**) is available for $6.95.

"Making Wise Decisions for Long-Term Care" (**2**) [D12435] provides information on various long-term-care services, what Medicare and Medicaid cover, and where the gaps are.

"Nursing Home Life: A Guide for Residents and Families" (**2**) [D13063] provides information for evaluating individual needs when selecting a nursing home and how best to cope with nursing-home life.

When You Need a Nursing Home (**20**), *Age Page* is prepared by the National Institute on Aging.

Medicare and Medicaid

Knowing Your Rights (**2**) [D12330] is a booklet that describes how changes in Medicare's reimbursement policies are designed to reduce health care costs. It suggests steps that Medicare beneficiaries, their families, and friends can take to ensure that they continue to receive quality care under the Prospective Payment System.

"Medicaid Discrimination and Consumer Rights" (**2**) [D13715] is a fact sheet with information about Medicaid discrimination.

Medicare: What It Covers, What It Doesn't (**2**) [D13133] is a booklet covering Medicare benefits, including catastrophic coverage, appeals, and community resources.

Medications

"About Your Medicines" (**30**) is prepared by the U.S. Pharmacopeial Convention. It provides information on several hundred of the most common over-the-counter and prescription drugs (e.g., purpose of the drug, side effects, and precautions for drug use).

The Caregiver's Guide to Medication Management (**8**), $15.00. This is a large-print book that lists some home assessment tools, agencies that can assist, preventive measures to take, and specifics about medication and side effects for various medical problems.

"Daily Personal Medication Schedule and Personal Health Record" (**24**) Single copies are available from Healthy Older People.

"Using Your Medicines Wisely" (**2**) [D317] discusses what to know and what to watch for when taking prescription and over-the-counter medications.

Nutrition

"Diet and the Elderly" (**26**) was prepared by the Food and Drug Administration.

Eating for Your Health (**2**) [D12164] is a guide to special diets, including low-sodium and low-cholesterol. The booklet includes recipes and tips on how to shop.

Eating Smart is a video program that assesses one's diet risks, lists nutritional steps that can be taken to reduce the risk of getting various kinds of cancer, and provides tips on food preparation and meal planning for a healthier diet. Contact your local chapter of the American Cancer Society.

"How Does Your Nutrition Measure Up?" (**2**) [D12994]. This pamphlet assesses your nutritional health and ways to improve it.

"Nutrition and Your Health: Dietary Guidelines for Americans" (**26**) is prepared by the Department of Agriculture.

Osteoporosis

Boning Up on Osteoporosis (**22**) is an informative booklet on osteoporosis.

"Osteoporosis: Cause, Treatment, Prevention" (**26**) is prepared by the National Institute of Arthritis and Musculoskeletal and Skin Diseases. $.50.

Safety

"Home Safety Checklist for Older Consumers" (**28**).

"How-To Series" (**2**) consists of seven different pamphlets [D393, D394, D395, D396, D397, D12244, D12779] offering common-sense tips on how to protect yourself, your family and friends, and your possessions against crime.

"Personal Emergency Response Systems (PERS): Meeting the Need for Security and Independence" (**2**) [D12905].

"Personal Emergency Response Systems: A Product-Specific Study of PERS" (**2**), from "Consumer Affairs," Program Department.

"Safety Steps for Pedestrians" (**2**) [D12757] provides suggestions to improve community safety for pedestrians, especially older people.

Support Groups

Self-Help Groups for Coping with Crisis: Origins, Members, Processes, and Impact, by M. Liebermann. San Francisco: Jossey-Bass, 1979.

Support Groups for Caregivers of the Aged: A Training Manual for Facilitators, by H. Rzetelney and J. Mellor. New York: Community Services Society, 1981.

Visual Problems

Aging and Vision: Making the Most of Impaired Vision (**2**) [D12363] is a booklet that discusses the four leading causes of vision loss in older people: cataracts, galucoma, macular degeneration, and diabetes.

Cataracts: A Consumer's Guide to Choosing the Best Treatment (**25**) is a large-print book. $3.50.

The Eyes Have It (**2**) [D12460] is a booklet that examines general principles of eye care for older Americans and the symptoms and treatment of common eye-related diseases.

"Keeping an Eye on Glaucoma" (**11**) is a reprint from the June 1980 issue of the *FDA Consumer*. It is available free; send your request on a postcard.

Widows/Widowers

"On Being Alone: A Guide for Widowed Persons" (**2**) [D150] discusses coping with grief, financial and legal affairs, employment, and housing.

Women

"Action for a Healthier Life: A Guide for Mid-life and Older Women" (**2**) [D13474] provides an overview of health issues for mid-life and older women. It discusses simple steps every woman can take in areas of prevention, detection, and treatment, including recommendations for actions that every woman can take to ensure her own health.

"Divorce after 50: Challenges and Choices" (**2**) [D12909] discusses issues older women need to consider when faced with the prospect of divorce.

"Protect Yourself: A Woman's Guide to Pension Rights" (**2**) [D12258] provides information about pensions and lists questions individuals should ask about their own or their spouse's coverage; it includes names and addresses of several resource agencies.

"Women in Their Dynamic Years" (**2**) [D12344] is a collection of articles about work opportunities and lifestyle issues for middle-aged and older women.

Appendix 2

A Glossary: Caregiving and Medical Terminology

accommodation: adjustment of the eyes to focus at various distances.

active listening: reflecting or paraphrasing to another person his or her words and feelings.

activities of daily living: functions of daily living such as eating, bathing, going to the toilet, dressing, grooming, walking, and going to and from the house.

activity tolerance: the amount of energy expenditure an individual can manage without unpleasant signs and symptoms such as shortness of breath, pain, and rapid pulse.

acute care: usually short-term hospital care for an illness or injury from which the patient is expected to recover.

adult day care: a daytime community-based program for impaired adults that provides a variety of health, social, and related support services in a protective setting.

adverse drug reaction: an undesirable reaction to a drug.

advocate: a person or organization that maintains, advances, and defends particular individual or social rights of another.

aged: a relative term, usually used to mean having grown old or having attained a specified age; often refers to people specifically seventy-five years of age and older.

ageism: the tendency to draw conclusions about an individual solely on the basis of chronological age.

aggressive behavior: efforts to dominate or to get one's own way at the expense of others.

Alzheimer's disease: an incurable form of mental impairment usually occurring in old age, related to changes in the nerve cells of the outer layer of brain which result in the death of a large number of brain cells.

ambulatory: able to walk without assistance.

area agency on aging: a local (city or county) agency, funded under the federal Older Americans Act, which plans and coordinates various

221

social and health service programs for persons sixty years of age or more; the network of AAA offices consists of more than six hundred approved agencies.

assertive behavior: self-expression, satisfaction of one's own needs without hurting others in the process.

bedsore (pressure sore/decubitus ulcer): a sore or ulcer caused by lack of or decreased blood circulation to some area of the body; such an ulcer usually results from sitting or lying in one position or from putting pressure on an area long enough to impede circulation.

caregiver: a relative or friend who assists another person to attain and maintain optimum health and functional status; the services may include help with meals, shopping, and one or more daily functions such as eating, bathing, dressing, or using the bathroom.

chore services: minor household repairs, cleaning, and yard work.

chronic illness: an illness marked by long duration or frequent reoccurrence, such as arthritis, diabetes, heart disease, asthma, and hypertension.

cognitive: having to do with thinking ability or mental processes.

cognitive appraisal: the mental interpretation of a situation or event.

community-based services: services designed to help older people remain independent and in their own homes; these may include senior centers, transportation, delivered meals or congregate meal sites, visiting nurses or home health aides, adult day care, and homemaker services.

companion animal: any animal regarded as a significant other by a human being.

conflict resolution: the communication skill for settling conflicts effectively, thereby improving interpersonal relations and meeting the needs of all parties.

continent: able to control the passage of feces and urine.

control: the ability to determine a course of action.

coping mechanisms: nonpathologic measures utilized by an individual to reduce her or his level of anxiety.

day care: a collection of health- social-related services provided in a setting to which elderly people can be transported on a daily basis.

dementia: the medical term for senility, the symptoms of which include serious forgetfulness, confusion, and other changes in personality and behavior.

developmental tasks: responses to normal stressors encountered by all individuals throughout the aging process as they experience certain physiological, psychological, and sociological changes.

early discharge concept: a prospective payment plan, organized in 1983, designed to reduce length of stay and create a more aggressive discharge policy from hospitals for the purpose of containing health care costs.

ECHO housing (Elder Cottage Housing Opportunity): small, self-contained, portable home units that are barrier-free, energy efficient, portable, and can be placed in the yard of a single-family house.

elderly: past middle age, usually sixty-five years of age or older.

euthanasia: the putting to death, painlessly, of someone suffering from an incurable, life-taking condition. *Passive euthanasia* is the withholding of life-supporting treatment or measures that would prolong life. *Active euthanasia* is an action taken to cause a death.

exercise program: prescribed or planned physical activity involving a group or an individual.

extended-care facility: a long-term health care facility equipped to provide skilled nursing care twenty-four hours a day, seven days a week.

fight-or-flight response: an evolutionary response of the human body to life-threatening stressors which prepares one physically to fight back or to flee from the threat. Also known as stress reactivity, this response includes such physiological reactions as increased heart rate, increased rate of breathing, increased muscle tension, and increased perspiration.

frail elderly: old persons who have such social, economic, physical or mental limitations that they need help from family, friends, or social agencies to perform the ordinary tasks of daily living.

functional assessment: the systematic measurement of the level at which a person functions in terms of physical health, quality of self-maintenance, quality of role activity, intellectual status, emotional status, social activity, and attitudes toward the world and self.

geriatric: pertaining to the medical treatment of age-associated diseases in the elderly.

geriatrician: a medical doctor with special education and training in the diagnosis, treatment, and prevention of disabilities in older persons.

geriatric psychiatrist: a physician who specializes in psychological and mental problems of the elderly (for example, Alzheimer's disease).

gerontology: the study of all aspects of the aging process and their consequences in humans and animals.

glaucoma: abnormally increased intraocular pressure, which can cause irreversible damage to the optic nerve fibers.

grab bar: a railing placed on a wall, used to steady oneself, as a safety measure.

graying of America: the increasing percentage of elderly persons in the United States, many of whom will probably need health and social services and the assistance of a caregiver.

guardianship: a court-ordered arrangement in which one party is entrusted with the care of another person and/or that person's property. Some elderly people may require this protective arrangement when they are unable to manage their own affairs.

health assessment: a collection of data related to a person's level of wellness.

hearing aid: an instrument placed in or near the ear to amplify sound.

home care: health and/or personal care provided in the home setting.

home-delivered meal service: a program for delivering one or more meals to the homebound to enable people to remain in their homes.

home health-aide program: a service that provides workers trained to give nonskilled nursing care, personal care, and sometimes limited house-keeping services to elderly people in their own homes. Home health aides work under the supervision of a skilled nurse.

home health care: a wide variety of services that bring care to the home and that may include nursing, physical therapy, and personal care services.

homemaker service: a program that provides a trained housekeeper who can shop, cook, clean, and otherwise assist elderly people in their own homes.

hospice care: a flexible service provided in freestanding hospice facilities, a designated area of a hospital, a long-term care facility, or a home. The service emphasis is on palliative and supportive care to meet the special needs of dying clients and their families during the final stages of illness.

immobility: the limitation or absence of the ability to move.

incompetence: usually a state of being unable to manage one's money and/or social behavior (i.e., the inability to act with legal effectiveness) due to cognitive impairment, personality disorder, or motor impairment.

incontinence: the lack of ability to consistently control the passage of urine and/or feces.

informed consent: a patient's agreement (or the agreement of the patient's representative in the event of patient incompetence) to a proposed medical treatment. This requires that the physician inform the patient or caregiver of all risks and benefits of the suggested treatment and of alternative treatments available.

intergenerational day care program: a combined elder care and child care program in which the elders and children interact to the benefit of both.

intermediate care facility: an institution (or separate part of an institution) licensed under state law to provide regular health-related care and services to individuals who do not require the degree of care or treatment that a hospital or skilled nursing facility provides, but who because of their mental or physical condition require care and services above the level of room and board.

life care: a type of financing to secure lifetime housing and/or health care. The elder pays a fee or turns over personal assets to the owner of a residential facility in return for housing, meals, and health and personal care for as long as the person lives.

life lease: a type of financing to secure lifetime housing and/or health care. A specified sum is paid in return for lifetime occupancy of an apartment; upon death of the tenant, the dwelling unit reverts to the owner.

lifestyle: a person's usual pattern of behavior; a person's usual pattern of activities or interactions with the environment.

living will: a written, witnessed statement that instructs doctors not to use life-prolonging medical procedures when a person's condition is hopeless (i.e., there is no chance of regaining a meaningful life). Within the living will, the **proxy designation clause** identifies someone to make medical decisions in accordance with the wishes of the person signing the living will at a time when that person is unable to make those decisions for him- or herself.

long-term care: a comprehensive range of medical, personal, and social services delivered over time to chronically ill or disabled persons.

long-term care facility: any institution in which people reside for an extended time to receive health and social services.

long-term care ombudsman: an individual, who is part of a federally mandated program, who can provide information to the public about nursing homes in a particular area. This person can also help resolve complaints on behalf of nursing-home residents. (The telephone number of the ombudsman can be found in the local government section of the telephone book.)

macular degeneration: selective deterioration of the central portion of the retina at the back of the eye, causing a gradual loss of clear central vision.

Medicaid: a federal and state program intended to provide reasonably complete medical care services to the needy, regardless of age. The Medical Assistance Program is funded under Title XIX, 1965, and subsequent amendments to the Social Security Act.

Medicare: a federal health insurance program funded under Title XVIII, 1965, and subsequent amendments to the Social Security Act, which helps Americans sixty-five years of age and older (as well as severely disabled persons under sixty-five) with hospital [part A] and medical [part B] care. Medical coverage requires payment of a monthly premium.

mobility aid: any device used to enhance ease of movement; e.g., canes and walkers.

nonassertive behavior: denial of one's own wishes to satisfy someone else's; sacrifice of one's own needs to meet someone else's needs.

noncompliance: deviation from a prescribed or recommended therapeutic regimen.

nursing home: an institution that offers skilled health care provided by a range of health professionals (nurses, social workers, physical therapists, and physicians); a long-term or extended-care facility.

orientation: an individual's exhibited degree of awareness of appropriate time, person, and place.

osteoporosis: a thinning or loss of bone mass which can result in bone fragility and increased potential for fracture.

Patient Bill of Rights: a bill or list of policies and procedures to be followed to ensure that consumers of health care services will be treated with dignity and will participate fully in decisions relevant to their health.

pension: a periodic payment to a person (or her or his family), earned as a result of previous work or service.

perception: the process of evaluating information gathered by the senses and giving meaning to it.

personal care: assistance provided to individuals who need help with activities of daily living such as dressing, bathing, personal hygiene, grooming, and eating.

physiological arousal: bodily changes in reaction to stressful events.

postural hypotension: a temporary reduction in blood pressure occurring with sudden changes in posture, such as from the lying to the standing position. In susceptible people (those with normally low blood pressure or those primarily on bed rest), this can result in brief episodes of lightheadedness, dizziness, and confusion.

power of attorney: a written instrument of agreement authorizing a person to act as the agent or attorney for another person. The added words "This power of attorney shall not be affected by my subsequent disability or incapacity" create a **durable power of attorney,** which should be filed with the living will. A **durable power of attorney for health care decisions** limits a person's ability to make decisions for another person to matters related to health.

presbycusis: hearing loss caused by the aging process.

presbyopia: a loss of visual accommodation that accompanies the aging process.

primary care: basic or general health care provided at the person's first contact with the health care system. Usually this contact is for common illnesses. The primary health care provider assumes ongoing responsibility for health maintenance and therapy for illnesses, including consultation with specialists.

psychological arousal: mental changes in reaction to stressful events.

reality orientation: measures performed to increase awareness of time, person, and place.

reminisce: to recall and tell about past experiences and events.

remotivation techniques: measures designed to increase a person's activities and involvement with the environment.

resources: personal characteristics (ego strength, energy, time, money, material goods), social institutions (practices, relationships, or organizations), objects, services, and people that the elderly may utilize in the absence of their usual means or sources of supply.

respite care: a program of intermittent or periodic care for an older homebound person to provide relief to the primary caregiver. The care can be provided by volunteers, an institution, or an adult day care center and may be available for several hours, several days, or several weeks.

retirement community: a self-contained development that admits only older people as residents. Entry age may range from fifty-five to sixty-five; spouses may be of any age.

self-care: bathing, dressing, toileting, medicating, and feeding oneself. Basically, self-care is a person's ability to perform the activities of daily living without assistance.

self-concept, self-image: the way in which a person perceives him- or herself.

self-esteem: feelings of self-worth.

senescence: biological processes in which the organism becomes less viable and more vulnerable as chronological age increases; manifested as an increased probability of disease, injury, and death.

senior center: a voluntary organization that offers members a range of services (such as recreation, nutrition, education, transportation, and referral) and that has a specific meeting place for its purposes. Senior centers are primarily designed for mentally alert and physically active elderly persons.

sexuality: a person's feelings about herself or himself and the person's physiological, psychological, and sociological interactions with persons of the same or of the opposite sex.

significant others: humans or animals of particular importance to the well-being of an individual.

skilled nursing facility: an institution (or a section of an institution) which primarily provides posthospital, convalescent, rehabilitation care, usually on a short-term basis.

social security: the general public retirement pension administered by the federal government. Social security also provides benefits to survivors and disabled people, including the administration of Medicare. Benefits are paid from money contributed by workers, employers, and self-employed individuals.

stress: the nonspecific response of the body to any demand placed upon it to adapt, whether that demand produces pleasure or pain. Stress can also be defined by identifying its two major components: a stressor and stress reactivity.

stress incontinence: involuntary urination upon coughing, laughing, or sneezing.

stressor: a stimulus with the *potential* of triggering the fight-or-flight response.

stress reactivity: also known as the fight-or-flight response; a reaction that prepares one for swift action when such a response is warranted. It prepares the body to do something physical.

Supplemental Security Income (SSI): a federal and state program under the Social Security Administration which provides a minimum income for needy people sixty-five years of age or over, blind, or disabled.

telephone reassurance: a volunteer service which makes regular telephone contact with or receives calls from the homebound.

thanatologist: an expert on death and dying.

vertigo: a sensation that the external world is revolving or that the person is revolving in space.

walker: a lightweight frame with a four-point base and a broad-based handle, held and moved by an individual to provide stability in walking.

Index